BATTLESHI
BISMAI

1936–41

COVER CUTAWAY: KMS *Bismarck*. *(Roy Scorer)*

First published in February 2015

A catalogue record for this book is available from the British Library.

ISBN 978 0 85733 509 8

Library of Congress control no. 2014946455

Published by Haynes Publishing,
Sparkford, Yeovil,
Somerset BA22 7JJ, UK.
Tel: 01963 442030 Fax: 01963 440001
Int. tel: +44 1963 442030
Int. fax: +44 1963 440001
E-mail: sales@haynes.co.uk
Website: www.haynes.co.uk

Haynes North America Inc.,
861 Lawrence Drive, Newbury Park,
California 91320, USA.

Printed in the USA by Odcombe Press LP,
1299 Bridgestone Parkway, La Vergne,
TN 37086.

Acknowledgements

The author would like to thank the staff of the National Maritime Museum, Greenwich; the Royal Naval Museum, Portsmouth; The Imperial War Museum, London; the Deutsches Marinenmuseum, Wilhelmshaven; the Wrackmuseum, Cuxhaven; Museum für Hamburgische Geschichte, Hamburg; the Kieler Schifffahrtsmuseum, Kiel; and the Deutsches Schifffahrtsmuseum, Bremerhaven.

BATTLESHIP BISMARCK

1936–41

Owners' Workshop Manual

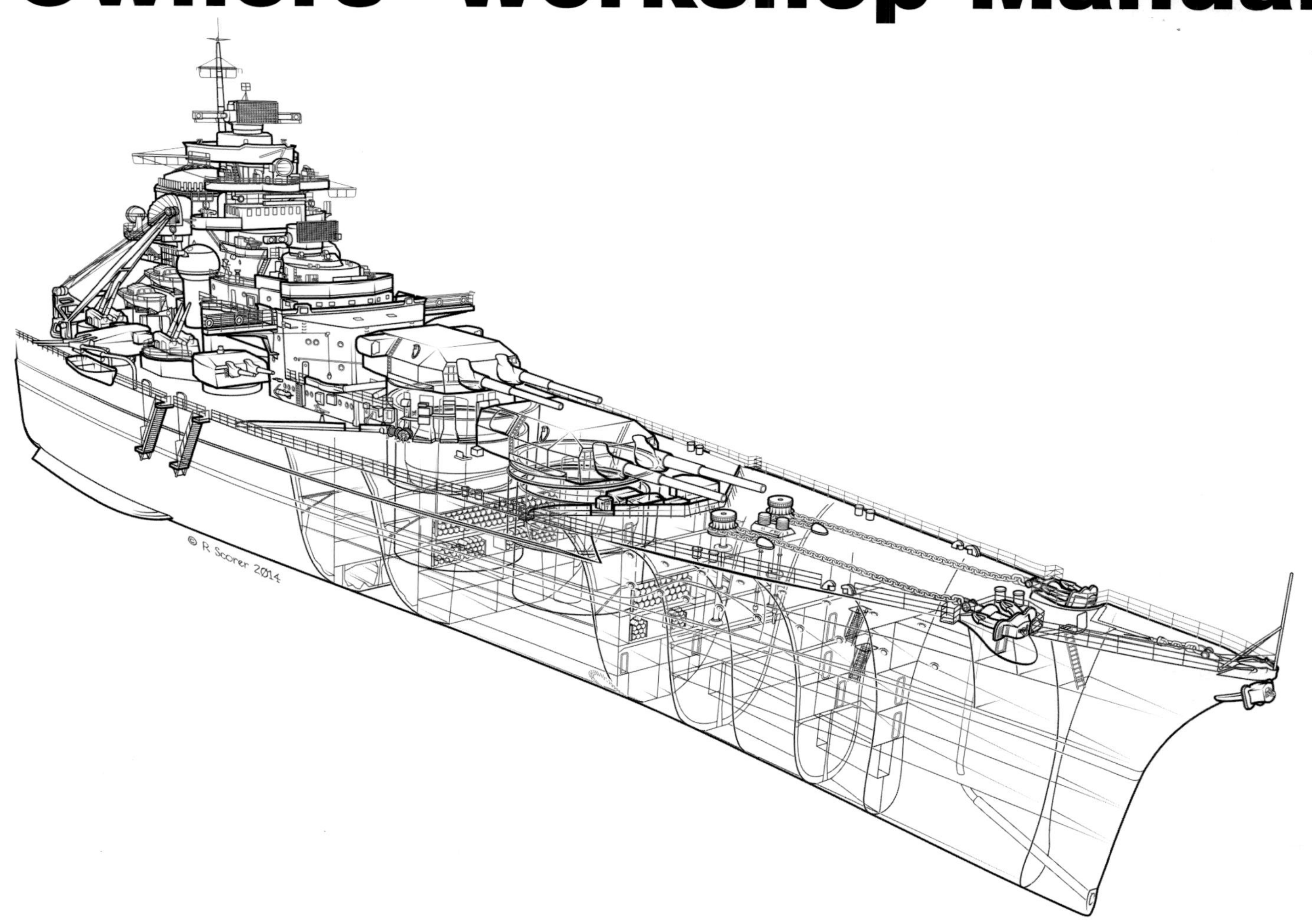

An insight into the design, construction and operation of Nazi Germany's most famous and feared battleship

Angus Konstam

Contents

OPPOSITE *Bismarck* in the Blohm & Voss floating dry dock at Hamburg, while still under construction in 1940. *(Bundesarchiv)*

Introduction

When KMS *Bismarck* was commissioned in August 1940 she was regarded as one of the most powerful warships in the world. A combination of her excellent design, powerful modern armament and excellent armoured protection made her a formidable warship. Arguably she became the largest single threat to British naval supremacy during the dark early years of the Second World War. The German propaganda machine dubbed her unsinkable – the latest word in modern battleship design. Critics have questioned this, citing her relatively weak armament and conventional layout, claiming she was greatly overrated. In this book we shall examine these opposing views and provide a balanced assessment of the fighting potential of Germany's greatest warship.

Whatever her strengths and weaknesses, when *Bismarck* was built there was nothing quite like her. Unlike many other large and powerful warships she was also a machine of great aesthetic beauty. The author and broadcaster Ludovic Kennedy, then a British sub-lieutenant who saw *Bismarck* just before her final battle, described her as: 'Black, massive, beautiful – the most marvellous-looking warship that I or any of us had ever seen.' In this respect *Bismarck* was the epitome of naval power – beautiful and at the same time utterly deadly. Therefore, although she fought only one brief naval campaign – a sortie into the North Atlantic that lasted just ten days – she ensured her place in history as Germany's most famous warship.

Bismarck joined the Kriegsmarine (German Navy) at a time when Great Britain was fighting for her life. The Battle of Britain was still raging, and German invasion barges filled the Channel ports. Britain's new battleships were still under construction, losses were mounting and Britain's naval defences were stretched very thinly indeed. Immediately she entered service *Bismarck* became a latent threat, and for nine months she would force the British to tie down powerful naval resources in the Home Fleet – vessels that were desperately needed in the Mediterranean. At the same time the Battle of the Atlantic was entering a new and more deadly phase, and Britain's vital maritime artery was in peril. It was inevitable that the Kriegsmarine would be tempted to use the *Bismarck* to attack these transatlantic convoys, particularly as the battleship was considered superior to any British capital ships

BELOW This dramatic bow view of *Bismarck* was taken on 9 December 1940, as the battleship was returning to Hamburg after conducting her sea trials in the Baltic. The black panel off her port side indicates that due to her size she has to remain in the centre of the channel – in this case the River Elbe – and serves as a warning for smaller ships to keep clear. Note that the extendable bridges have been deployed for the battleship's passage through the confined waters of the Kaiser Wilhelm Canal and the river beyond it.

she might encounter. The result would be Operation *Rheinübung*, the maiden sortie of the *Bismarck*, where she was pitted against the hastily assembled might of the British Home Fleet.

The dramatic story of that campaign is recounted here, while a detailed description of the great German battleship provides the reader with the chance to experience something of what life was like on board *Bismarck* during her brief career. However, after three-quarters of a century mere words and still images can only offer a shadowy glimpse of what it was like to face this naval leviathan in battle, or to form part of her crew as they began their last doomed battle against the warships of the Home Fleet. While historians might eulogise the fiery Wagnerian death of the *Bismarck*, we must also spare a thought for the hundreds of young sailors who were trapped inside her when she slipped beneath the oil-covered waves. Together with their counterparts from HMS *Hood*, sunk by *Bismarck* three days earlier, this book is dedicated to their memory.

ABOVE This colour view of *Bismarck* was taken as the battleship lay at her mooring in Kiel Roads in September 1940. By October she was in Gotenhafen, where rangefinders were fitted to her main turrets. The boom extending from the port side of her forecastle was rigged to attach the ship's boats to, within reach of the port side gangway.

BELOW In this dramatic reconstruction of *Bismarck*'s final battle, the German battleship is shown firing at *Rodney*, while 14in and 16in shells exploded against her forward superstructure – and have already silenced some of her guns. *Bismarck* fought back with her guns firing under local control, until one after the other they were all put out of action.

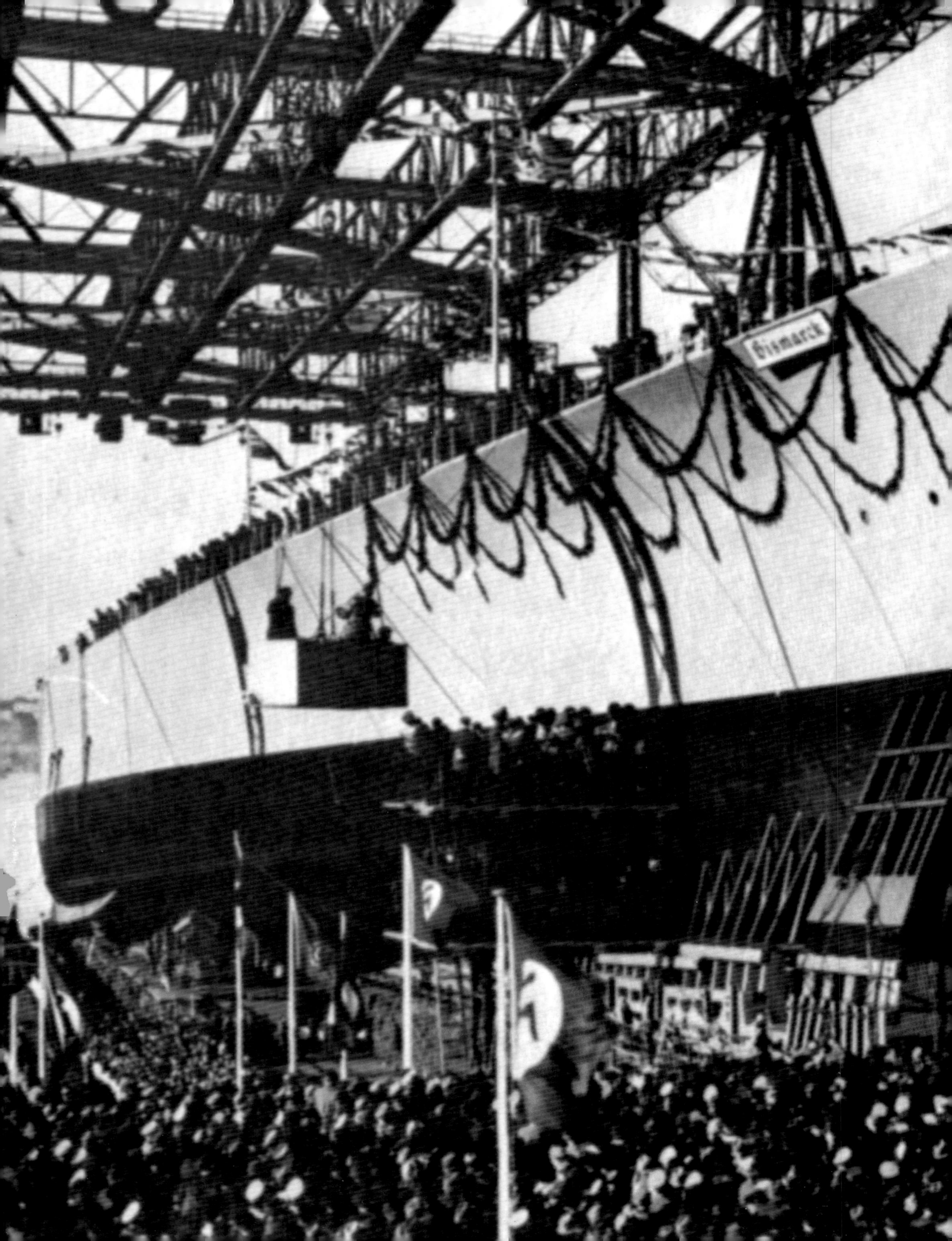
Bismarck

Chapter One

The *Bismarck* story

The design and building of the battleship *Bismarck* was set against the backdrop of the resurgence of the German Navy, and the flouting by Nazi Germany of the naval constraints imposed by international treaties. After the outbreak of war *Bismarck* would become a vital asset for the Kriegsmarine and a latent threat to the Royal Navy.

OPPOSITE On both sides of her forecastle a name plate was unveiled during the launch, bearing the name *Bismarck*. More than 60,000 people watched the ceremony.

ABOVE **The battleship *Bismarck* as she appeared during the summer of 1940, when she was conducting her sea trials and working-up exercises in the Baltic.**

BELOW **The battleship *Bismarck* pictured on the open sea. This photograph of her was almost certainly taken during her sea trials in the Baltic, most probably in late September 1940. Her suite of three radars had yet to be fitted when this photograph was taken.**

Background

While the Armistice of 11 November 1918 brought an end to the bloodshed of the First World War, it would be another seven months before the conflict officially came to an end. That happened on 28 June 1919, when representatives of Germany and the Allied powers signed the Treaty of Versailles. They did so five years to the day since the assassination of the Archduke Franz Ferdinand, the catalyst for the global conflict that would claim more than 17 million lives. It had taken six months to negotiate the treaty – the leading Allied powers had conflicting aims, and found it hard to agree on the level of punishment they should mete out on Germany. In its final form the terms were Draconian. While crippling war reparations and the loss of German territory in Europe and overseas were bad enough, the treaty also imposed severe restrictions on the size and offensive capability of the German armed forces, particularly the German Navy.

According to the terms, the navy could not exceed 6 battleships, 6 light cruisers, 12 destroyers and 12 torpedo boats. Even then, armoured ships – the battleships – couldn't displace more than 10,000 long tons. Given that even the oldest and smallest of the German wartime dreadnoughts displaced more than twice that when fully laden, this effectively meant the battleship force of the new Reichsmarine was restricted to a half-dozen obsolete pre-dreadnoughts. Consequently three Deutschland class and three Braunschweig class pre-dreadnoughts were retained to form the core of the new post-war navy. Four of them were still in service at the outbreak of the Second World War.

The Treaty of Versailles was followed by the Washington Naval Treaty of 1922, signed by the five wartime Allies: Great Britain, the United States, Japan, France and Italy. Its aim was to prevent a post-war arms race, and allowed these five navies to scale back the size of their fleets. In the process they limited the size of their capital ships to 35,000 long tons, and

LEFT **Moments after her launch on 14 February 1939, *Bismarck* is pictured floating on the waters of the River Elbe, with the waterfront of Hamburg forming a backdrop. Her launch was watched by thousands of the city's inhabitants.**

specified that the 16in gun would be the largest piece of ordnance carried on their warships. While Weimar Germany was excluded from this treaty, the limits imposed by it were adhered to by the larger naval powers when they began building new battleships. The Washington agreement was modified in 1930 when the London Naval Treaty was ratified by the same five powers.

Once again Weimar Germany was excluded from the talks, but German delegates were invited to participate in the Geneva Naval Conference, which began two years later in 1932. By then the Reichsmarine (Imperial Navy) had overcome strong political opposition to begin building a class of three *panzerschiffe* (armoured ships), designed to conform to the restrictions imposed by the Treaty of Versailles. The first of these powerful modern warships, the *Deutschland*, was launched in May 1931. Despite French opposition this led directly to German inclusion in the Geneva Conference, by which time German naval designers had begun drawing up plans for two more powerful warships, which exceeded the Versailles limitations, armed with nine 11in guns apiece. These were destined to become the *Scharnhorst* and the *Gneisenau*. While the British rated them as battlecruisers, the Germans always regarded them as battleships because their armoured protection was considerably more substantial than that of any comparable battlecruiser. The rebuilding of the German Navy had begun.

These international negotiations and the design of new warships were set against a background of political turmoil in Germany. In the 1928 German elections the Nazi party (NDSAP) won less than 3 per cent of the vote, but their paramilitary supporters became increasingly vocal – and violent. The Nazi share of the vote increased significantly in the 1930 elections, and in 1932 they became the largest single party in the German Reichstag. Amid a mood of growing anti-Semitism, attempts to ban the NDSAP's paramilitary supporters came to nothing and in January 1933 President von Hindenburg appointed the NDSAP leader Adolf Hitler the new German Chancellor in an attempt to calm the volatile political situation. Instead he let the Nazi genie out of the bottle.

Within a month civil liberties were being suspended and political opponents silenced. Hitler only gained full dictatorial powers after the death of von Hindenberg in 1934, but the move towards a one-party state had now become irrevocable. One of Hitler's first acts was to repudiate the signing of the Treaty of Versailles. However, despite his public rhetoric, he only officially abrogated the treaty in March 1935. In the meantime, Hitler ordered German delegates to walk out of the Geneva

BELOW ***Bismarck* pictured from the deck of *Prinz Eugen* during her working-up exercises in the Baltic, before the commencement of Operation *Rheinübung*.**

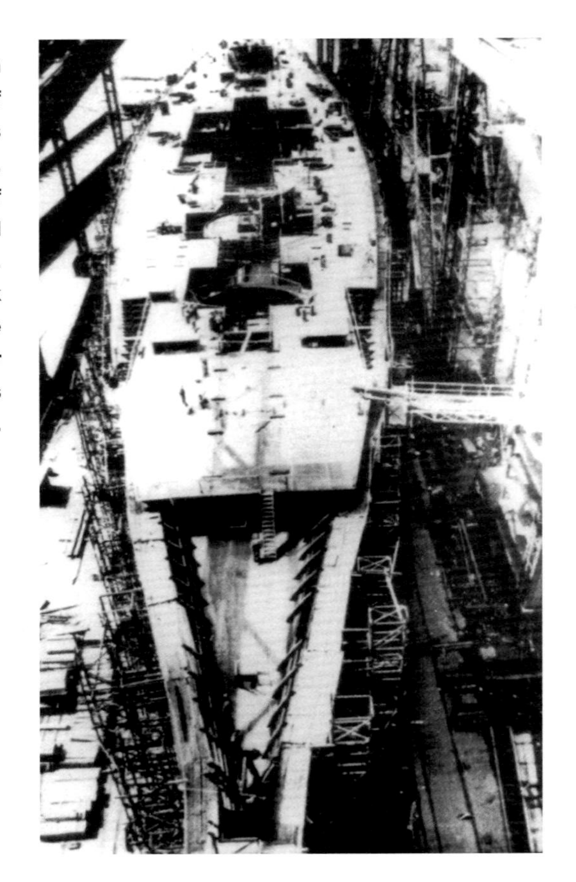

RIGHT By March 1937 the shape of *Bismarck*'s bows had been defined, and large portions of her upper deck had been put in place. Further aft this deck had not reached the areas that would later house the battleship's superstructure.

RIGHT The layout of *Bismarck*'s platform decks are revealed in this photograph, taken in August 1937. In between the various turret barbettes work has begun on the sides of the torpedo bulkhead and the central compartments housing the funnel ducting.

Conference, and to withdraw from the League of Nations. Unofficially then, the Reichsmarine was free to design and build whatever size of warships it wanted. However, Hitler had no desire to challenge the Royal Navy, and so he entered into a private treaty arrangement with Great Britain. The resulting Anglo-German Naval Treaty of June 1935 established the relative size of the British and German fleets. The Reichsmarine (renamed the Kriegsmarine in 1935) could now build battleships of up to 35,000 tons, and could expand to 35 per cent of the size of the Royal Navy's surface fleet. Nazi Germany now had carte blanche to build a new and even more powerful class of battleship – one that would greatly exceed the size of the Scharnhorst class. The result would be the creation of the battleship *Bismarck*.

Design

As early as 1932, the German Reichstag approved a *Schiffbauersatzplan* (Replacement Ship Construction Programme), which would last until 1936. It was designed to begin the rebuilding of the Reichsmarine by replacing some of its older vessels, and secure the funding for the building of the Deutschland and Scharnhorst classes of capital ships.
In early 1934 plans were formulated for the construction of a new German capital ship – a modern battleship that dramatically exceeded the limitations imposed on the Deutschland and Scharnhorst classes. Coden amed *Schlachtschiff* 'F' *Ersatz Hannover* (Battleship 'F', *Hannover* Replacement), this new vessel was officially meant to replace the ageing pre-dreadnought battleship *Hannover* – a veteran of the Battle of Jutland (1916) – that had been decommissioned in 1931.

This, though, would be no straightforward replacement. When the SMS *Hannover* was commissioned in 1907 she displaced a little under 14,000 tons, and had a maximum speed of 18 knots. *Ersatz Hannover* would displace 35,000 tons and was designed to steam at 30 knots. Even more dramatically, the pre-dreadnought carried two 280cm (11in) guns, while her replacement would boast eight 33cm (13in) main guns, making her a formidable modern warship. Like previous German capital

RIGHT The launch of *Bismarck* in Hamburg on 14 February 1939 was watched by a large crowd of dignitaries, as well as thousands of people who lined the banks of the River Elbe. The swastika flag draped over her bow obscures the ship's crest, which was unveiled before she made her way down the slipway.

ships, emphasis would be placed on substantial armoured protection, and so the new battleship would be much better armoured than any of her predecessors. This is the battleship that would eventually evolve into the *Bismarck*.

Battleship 'F' was soon joined by Battleship 'G' – a vessel that was destined to become *Tirpitz*, the sister ship of the *Bismarck*. The Chief of the Department of Ship Construction was Dr Hermann Burkhardt (1881–1969), and during 1934 and 1935 he supervised the formulation of design plans for these two new battleships. His initial brief was to limit their displacement to 35,000 tons, which was the maximum allowed under the terms of the Washington Naval Treaty of 1922. Although Germany wasn't a signatory, Hitler's later abrogation of the Treaty of Versailles meant that it was diplomatically expedient to abide by the restrictions of this earlier agreement. The ceiling of 35,000 tons was ratified in the Anglo-German Naval Treaty of 1935, but by that time Burkhardt and his team had already ignored the restrictions and were reconfiguring their plans to produce a much larger pair of battleships. In effect the designers were working with total disregard of international restrictions.

In early November 1934 a design meeting was held between senior Kriegsmarine officers and Burkhardt's team. Various design requirements for Battleships 'F' and 'G' were considered. It was finally decided that the vessels would have to be superior in protection and firepower to the latest French battleships of the Dunkerque class. They displaced 35,000 tons, carried eight 33cm (13in) guns, and had a top speed of more than 30 knots. Several designs were considered, all of which displaced over 37,000 tons and were therefore rejected by Admiral Raeder, Chief of the Kriegsmarine, who for diplomatic reasons wanted to retain the 35,000-ton ceiling.

ABOVE **The funnel of *Bismarck*, revealing the venting tubes which surround its outer surface. In the foreground a dockyard supervisor can be seen, wearing his bowler hat. To his left the starboard searchlight housing still remains uncovered by its retractable dome.**

On 21 December 1934 Raeder examined the latest designs submitted by Burkhardt and his team, and finally agreed that a larger displacement would be required. However, he stressed that this was only worthwhile if the vessels' firepower was increased as well. He ordered the preparation of several new plans, involving the mounting of 35cm as well as 33cm main guns, and turbo-electric propulsion – a system used by the US Navy. He also stressed the need to limit the size of the vessel so it could pass through the Kaiser Wilhelm Canal (now the Kiel Canal). Burkhardt and his team went back to the drawing board.

Raeder's move towards a larger calibre of main gun is significant. He was a great believer in the fighting potential of the battleship. For him, nothing other than a new fleet built around powerful, well-armed capital ships would expunge the shame of defeat in 1918 and the subsequent loss of the High Seas Fleet. Earlier in 1934, Raeder wrote: 'The scale of a nation's world power status is identical with its scale of seapower.' Indeed, Raeder was already formulating his 'Plan Z' – a dramatic expansion of the Kriegsmarine which involved a decade-long building programme that would create a fleet capable of challenging British and American naval supremacy. For Raeder, Battleship 'F' would be the next major step along that road.

The need for Battleship 'F' to pass through the Kaiser Wilhelm Canal was important, as it allowed the vessel to operate from German ports on the North Sea and Baltic coasts. The canal was a secure way of moving from one coast to the other. It had an average depth of 11m (36ft) and a width of 38m (124ft 7in). Also, the main dock in the Kriegsmarine Werft (naval dockyard) in Wilhelmshaven was 250m (820ft) long. Whatever the other design constraints might be, these size and draft restrictions were unavoidable. Burkhardt and his team wanted Battleship 'F' to be a stable gun platform, and so her final beam was just 1m (about 3ft) less than the narrowest part of the canal.

Another design meeting was held in mid-January 1935. This time it was agreed that the displacement ceiling had to be exceeded, and that both the 33cm and 35cm gun options should be considered. To compensate for the additional weight of the heavier armament, the maximum speed was reduced to 28 knots. Two days later on 19 January Raeder decided that the larger-calibre guns would be used,

RIGHT **With the scaffolding marking her birthplace behind her, *Bismarck* is pictured alongside the Equipping Pier at Blohm & Voss shipyard in Hamburg, during the final weeks of her fitting-out.**

RIGHT *Bismarck* on slipway 9 at Hamburg's Blohm & Voss shipyard, as final preparations are made for her launching ceremony. The launching podium has already been built and can be seen in the foreground, while behind it are the first of the many wooden and metal chocks designed to hold the ship in place until the moment of launch.

and that the 28 knots should be the vessel's continuous cruising speed, not her maximum speed. In order to maintain the speed and protection requirements envisaged by the Kriegsmarine, their displacement would have to be increased to at least 39,000 tons. As they displaced 32,100 tons, *Schlachtschiffe* 'D' and 'E' (*Scharnhorst* and *Gneisenau*) would fall within the limits of the Washington Treaty, and the forthcoming Anglo-German Naval Treaty. *Schlachtschiffe* 'F' and 'G' (*Bismarck* and *Tirpitz*) would not, and so their design had to be kept secret.

In March 1935, Hitler formally abrogated the Treaty of Versailles, and two months later negotiations began between Britain and Germany that led to the Anglo-German Naval Treaty, which was ratified on 18 June. By then, though, the design of the new German battleships had changed again. Admiral Raeder was considering the fitting of even larger guns, even though the Kriegsmarine's Department of Ship Construction had drawn up its plans based on the 35cm weapons agreed by Raeder two months earlier. The design was already nudging past the 40,000-ton mark, and any increase might jeopardise the ability of the vessel to fit through the Kaiser Wilhelm Canal. On 1 April, Raeder declared the displacement would be limited to 41,000 tons, but that the new warships should carry eight 35cm (15in) guns apiece, in four twin turrets. Once again Burkhardt and his team began revising their plans.

ABOVE *Bismarck* – or rather *Schlachtschiff* 'F' (Battleship 'F') – is shown here in early February 1939, just a few days before her launch. This photograph provides us with a good view of slipway 9 at the Blohm & Voss shipyard, with its towering gantry framework encompassing the hull of the new battleship. To the left and hidden from sight is the much smaller slipway 10, where U-boats were built. Beyond the sheds behind it was the Kuhwerder Basin, where the Equipping Pier lay, and where *Bismarck* would be towed for her fitting-out.

RIGHT This picture of *Bismarck*'s tapering forward hull being constructed was taken just a few days before the end of 1937. The photograph shows clearly how work on the amidships section – encompassing the armoured citadel – was carried out first, before the less well armoured bow and stern sections were built.

RIGHT This picture shows how *Bismarck* appeared in early September 1937. By then her upper and middle platform decks were almost complete, and were already pierced by the lower barbettes of her forward main turrets.

The designers warned Raeder that this reconfiguration would add 1,500 tons of displacement and add six months to the building time, but the admiral was not concerned. As an advocate of the big gun he would now get a battleship that could rival the British in terms of firepower, while being superior to them in protection and speed. This reconfiguration certainly caused the designers problems. As designed, the battleships would be unable to pass through the canal unless armour was removed. Burkhardt briefly considered a nine-gun design, carrying its 35cm guns in three triple turrets, but this was rejected. That configuration would have permitted a slightly shorter armoured citadel, but would have meant using an unproven turret configuration, and would actually have increased the displacement of the vessel.

Warship design was a balance between firepower, protection and speed. Raeder had already established that the sustained speed needed to be at least 28 knots. Therefore there was no option but to sacrifice armoured protection in order to benefit from increased firepower. On 9 May 1935 Raeder, in his capacity as head of the Kriegsmarine, approved the revised plans, which now featured 38cm guns on Battleships 'F' and 'G', in the four twin-turret configuration Raeder favoured.

The decision to use larger-calibre guns was one of many design questions that Burkhardt and his team were trying to solve that summer. Others included the propulsion system, with three different configurations of steam turbines and boilers being considered. A fourth option involved the use of a turbo-electric drive system similar to that employed on contemporary American battleships. This was the system favoured by Admiral Raeder. Burkhardt and his Ship Construction Office preferred a conventional steam turbine propulsion system, with three powerful turbines powered by twelve boilers, located in three large turbine rooms forward of the main turbine room. Other configurations involved six boiler rooms forward of the turbines, and one where the turbine room had a boiler room on either side of it, with six boilers in each.

Four propulsion room plans were drawn up, and these were laid before another design meeting held in early June 1935. Raeder insisted that the turbo-electric option remain the leading choice, despite the additional 600 tons this would add to the final displacement, and called for detailed plans to be drawn up. His insistence that displacement remain less than 41,000 tons meant that Burkhardt had to find a way to reduce the weight of the armour even further, to make provision for the extra weight of the propulsion system. On 23 August Raeder was presented with Drawing A13, designed around three turbines and a turbo-electric drive system. He approved them, although Burkhardt remained unconvinced that this was the best. So, he simultaneously drew up detailed plans for a more conventional propulsion system using geared turbines, just in case the weight problem reasserted itself.

The June design meeting was also used to examine plans for the secondary armament. It had already been decided that the new battleships would carry 12 15cm (6in) guns, and a tertiary battery of 16 10.5cm (4.1in) quick-fire weapons, which were primarily used for anti-aircraft defence. Four different layouts were considered, as was the use of casemates for the guns – a largely outdated configuration used

FAR LEFT In this overhead photograph of the slipway taken in early October 1937 we can see two of *Bismarck*'s internal watertight bulkheads, while work is advancing on the central portion of her armoured deck. This formed the top of *Bismarck*'s armoured citadel.

LEFT By early December 1937 the central portion of the battleship's armoured citadel was finished, and her torpedo bulkheads were in place.

in earlier German dreadnoughts. Additional light anti-aircraft guns were added – eight 3.7cm guns in twin mountings. By August these were increased to 16 guns.

The size and thickness of the armour was also discussed. Originally the thickness of the main armoured belt had been set at 350mm, but this was reduced to 320mm following the modifications to armament and speed demanded by Raeder. Forward and aft of the turrets this was 150mm thick, while a 100mm-thick armoured deck above it protected this area from plunging fire. This armoured deck curved diagonally towards the hull sides, and was thicker (at 120mm) there, to better protect the ships' vitals. The barbettes of the main gun turrets were 380mm thick, decreasing to 320mm below the upper deck, while the secondary gun barbettes were protected by 150mm of armour.

The hull would be divided into 22 watertight compartments, numbered sequentially (in Roman numerals) from forward to aft. All but five of these were within the all-important central portion of the hull, between the gun turrets and behind the armoured belt. This main armoured belt was 320mm thick, but tapered to 170mm below the waterline. It extended for just under 170m (about 550ft), before stepping down to the thinner 150mm sections designed to protect the less vital areas towards the bow and stern. This meant that over 70 per cent of the ship's waterline and hull were protected by an armoured belt that was deemed impervious to direct hits by 38cm (15in) armour-piercing shells. It is easy to see why German propagandists described *Bismarck* as 'unsinkable'.

The main armoured deck was below the upper deck, and between the two the Ship Design Office proposed creating an armoured citadel 150mm thick, protecting the secondary and tertiary batteries. The full extent of this armoured citadel had still not been established by September 1935, but the decision to place some living quarters outside the citadel allowed the designers to extend it to cover the area between all four turrets. While changes were still being made to just about every aspect of the design, on paper at least, Battleships 'F' and 'G' were finally taking shape.

By the autumn of 1935 Raeder decided

ABOVE This view of *Bismarck*, photographed from the southern end of the Equipping Pier, was taken during the early summer of 1940, when the fitting-out of *Bismarck* was nearing completion. Now naval staff mingle with shipyard workers, as the battleship's new crew struggle to acquaint themselves with their new ship.

that plans for Battleship 'F' had advanced far enough for the construction of the new vessel to be commissioned. The sheer scale of *Schlachtschiff* 'F' meant that the choice of shipyards capable of undertaking the work was limited. After all, the new ship would displace around 42,000 tons, with a beam of 36m (118ft) and an overall length of 250m (820ft). Other yards were already busy building smaller warships. That left the Kriegsmarine with two choices – Wilhelmshaven and Hamburg. The decision was made, and so on 16 November 1935, and with the approval of Hitler, the Kriegsmarine placed an order for New Construction 'F' at the Blohm & Voss shipyard in Hamburg. The shipyard assigned the construction project a yard number of BV-509, and a date was set for the laying of the keel the following July. Delivery to the Kriegsmarine was scheduled for October 1939.

During the intervening eight months secondary contracts were issued for a host of vital materials, parts, weapons and fittings. Back in the Ship Construction Office in Kiel, Burkhardt and his team worked feverishly to complete the final plans. As late as January 1936 the designers were still struggling to comply with Raeder's directive to limit displacement to 41,000 tons. Raeder remained immovable on his choice of propulsion system and armament, and so the only remaining area where weight could be saved was the ship's armoured protection. The thickness of the barbettes below the upper deck was reduced by 100mm, while the armoured deck above the propulsion system was reduced by 20mm. To compensate slightly, the armoured bulkheads at either end of the armoured belt were extended up to the upper deck, thereby enclosing the whole of the armoured citadel.

This, though, was still not enough. Finally, in early June 1936, just three weeks before the laying of the keel, Raeder agreed to abandon his demand to use a turbo-electric propulsive drive, and the designers spent a frantic few weeks modifying their final plans to accommodate Burkhardt's alternative plan for using more conventional geared steam turbines. This saved between 600 and 800 tons of additional weight, and the designers used the saving to increase several areas of armoured protection, including the depth of the main section of armoured belt.

In fact Raeder's desire to save weight meant little by 1936, as in the Second London Naval Treaty agreed in March 1936 an 'escalator clause' allowed signatories to build battleships displacing more than 35,000 tons if it was found that non-signatory maritime powers were doing so. In that case the limit was set at 45,000 tons of displacement. As both Japan

LEFT The winter of 1939/40 was a particularly harsh one, and work on *Bismarck* slowed down slightly. Still, by the time this photograph was taken in January 1940, all of *Bismarck*'s four main turrets were in place, positioned there by the large 250-ton crane in the background. By this stage the funnel was also built, as was most of the foretop superstructure.

and Italy were already in breach of the 35,000-ton limit, then the gloves were off. Effectively this removed any final diplomatic constraints on the design of Germany's latest battleship. While this meant *Bismarck* could have carried more armour, her design had been finely tuned, and this would inevitably lead to a decrease in speed. That was something Raeder refused to compromise on, and so the final specifications were approved just before the shipbuilders began work.

Building

The first keel plate was laid in slipway 9 of the Hamburg shipyard on schedule, on the morning of 1 July 1936. For the next two and a half years the great battleship would grow steadily, the scaffolding surrounding her towering over the dockyard. Slipway 9 no longer exists – it has been filled in and built over, but otherwise much of the Blohm & Voss shipyard looks much the same now as it did in the late 1930s. It is built on the island of Kuhwerder on the southern bank of the River Elbe, across the river from the heart of the city. The yard was founded in 1877 by Hermann Blohm and Ernst Voss, and it developed a reputation for excellence. Before the First World War the shipyard built several highly regarded battlecruisers, including the *Seydlitz* and the *Von der Tann*. This new contract proved to be a much-needed boost for a shipyard and an industry still recovering from the post-war recession.

The business of building the battleship continued steadily, with the centreline keel and centreline longitudinal bulkhead followed by the frames and transverse bulkheads – the ones that would divide the hull into 22 watertight compartments. A double bottom covered more than four-fifths of the lower portion of the hull, while above it nine longitudinal frames joined the frames and transverse bulkheads together. Heavier transverse bulkheads were also installed to support the weight of the four turrets and barbettes. A centreline bulkhead also divided the two turbine rooms to reduce the risk of torpedo damage. By early 1937 much of the lower hull below the armoured deck had been framed out, and work began on attaching the belt armour.

LEFT Taken in December 1937, this photograph shows how the armoured citadel was completed before work was begun on the upper portions of *Bismarck*'s turret barbettes. This is why they appear as rectangular spaces, set between her vertical watertight bulkheads.

LEFT A little after New Year 1938 *Bismarck*'s armoured citadel was almost complete, and work had begun on the less well armoured compartments that formed her bow.

RIGHT By the start of February 1938 the decks beneath *Bismarck*'s forecastle had almost been completed, and had nearly reached the height of the battery deck. This was the deck level below the battleship's upper deck.

FAR RIGHT By early March 1938 *Bismarck* had been raised a deck level, so that much of her battery deck was now in place. In this photograph the various turret barbettes rise up over the internal bulkheads, forming the battery deck compartments. Then, during the summer of 1938, *Bismarck*'s upper deck would gradually be put in place.

RIGHT By mid-September 1938 the upper deck was almost complete, pierced by the barbettes of her four main and six secondary turrets. Similarly, the armoured bridge structure can be seen rising from the deck, immediately behind 'Bruno' turret's upper barbette.

FAR RIGHT By September 1938 the stem of the *Bismarck* was in place, which effectively finished off work on the hull. This bow was a temporary one designed to be used during the launching ceremony. *Bismarck*'s more modern clipper bow would be incorporated during her fitting-out.

LEFT At 1.34pm on 14 February 1939 *Bismarck* was launched and ran down the slipway. Unfortunately she stuck fast halfway down, due to a problem with her launching chains. This was quickly dealt with, though, and 3 minutes later *Bismarck* continued her launch into the River Elbe.

Above the armoured deck were the 34 transverse bulkheads, and by the spring of 1937 work had begun on these. By October the upper deck above the armoured citadel had been added, with holes in it corresponding to the six secondary turret barbettes. As 1937 drew to a close, virtually the full length of the hull had been plated in, but forward and aft of the central citadel the deck remained unfinished, save for the shafts where the four main turret barbettes would eventually go. Two months later the superimposed barbettes of 'Bruno' and 'Caesar' turrets were being installed. The bow and stern were also finished, which effectively completed the main construction of the hull below the upper deck, with the exception of the remaining barbettes.

Work on these continued throughout the late spring and early summer of 1938. By late September the barbettes were in place and work began on the central superstructure. Photos from this period reveal just how impressive the battleship was becoming. The sheer scale of the armour plating was staggering, as throughout 1937 and 1938 regular shipments of armoured plate were transported to the slipway, hoisted into place one piece at a time, and then welded firmly in position. The main armoured belt alone weighed 4,293 metric tonnes – composed of hundreds of plates of 110mm-thick Wotan Hart high-tensile steel. The launch had been scheduled for mid-February, by which time the hull had to be complete and the battleship ready for fitting-out. It is a testimony to the skill of the Blohm & Voss workforce that this great ship was built on schedule.

Launching and fitting-out

The guest of honour at the launching ceremony on 14 February 1939 was Adolf Hitler, who had travelled from Berlin the day before, visited the Otto von Bismarck mausoleum at Friedrichsruh and spent the night in Hamburg's prestigious Hotel Atlantic, overlooking Alster Lake. Shortly after noon Hitler boarded a steam yacht and was ferried across the River Elbe to the shipyard. There he was welcomed by a 21-gun salute from

The battleship *Bismarck* was named in honour of Otto von Bismarck (1815–99), Germany's 'Iron Chancellor', the man responsible for unifying Germany into a single state. During the last decades of the 19th century Bismarck dominated the European diplomatic stage through a combination of successful wars and skilful negotiation. It was therefore entirely fitting that Germany would name its most powerful battleship after the man who personified national power and unity. Otto Eduard Leopold, Fürst von Bismarck was born into a noble Prussian family, but rather than following his father into military service he studied law instead, at the University of Göttingen. In 1847 he embarked on a political career when he joined the Prussian legislature. He developed a reputation as a monarchist and a conservative, and initially viewed German unification with suspicion.

Bismarck's experience as Prussia's representative at the Diet of the German Confederation in Frankfurt eventually convinced him that if Prussia wanted to counter the power and influence of its arch rival, the Austro-Hungarian Empire, then it needed to embrace the cause of unification. By 1862 he had become Prussia's Ministerpräsident (Prime Minister), and was free to embark on a policy of rapid military and political expansion, designed to unite Germany into one Prussian-dominated state. He began by giving what became known as his 'Blood and Iron' speech. He said:

'Prussia must concentrate and maintain its power for the favourable moment which has already slipped by several times. Prussia's boundaries according to the Vienna treaties are not favourable to a healthy state life. The great questions of the time will not be resolved by speeches and majority decisions – that was the great mistake of 1848 and 1849 – but by iron and blood.'

This policy was soon put into practice on the battlefield. The Prusso-Danish War of 1864 was ostensibly fought over the ownership of Schleswig-Holstein, on behalf of the German Confederation, but in reality it established Prussian military dominance over its smaller German neighbours. Next came the Austro-Prussian War of 1864, where a highly professional Prussian army humbled the Austrians in a campaign that culminated in Prussia's great military victory at Königgrätz. Bismarck's policies were bearing fruit. Not only was Prussia growing in international standing, but it was gaining political and military control of the majority of smaller German states.

In 1867, Bismarck was appointed the Chancellor of the North German Confederation. France was becoming alarmed by the rapid expansion of Prussian power, and in 1870 she declared war on Prussia. In the Franco-Prussian War (1870–71) that followed France was comprehensively defeated, and this success encouraged the South German Confederation to view Bismarck's diplomatic overtures more favourably. So, on 18 January 1871, Germany was formally united into one nation state. To rub salt into open French wounds, the unification treaty was signed in Versailles. Wilhelm of Prussia became the first

RIGHT The 'Iron Chancellor' Otto von Bismarck, in whose honour the battleship was named. The Prime Minister of Prussia, and in turn the Chancellor of the North German Federation and the German Empire, Bismarck was seen as the man who united Germany into a single, powerful country.

Kaiser (Emperor) of this new German Empire, and Bismarck became its first Reichsckanzler (Imperial Chancellor).

For the next two decades he used diplomacy to foster peace abroad, and political unity within Germany's borders. However, he was also an innate conservative, and devoted as much energy countering the influence of liberals and socialists as in building a unified German state. In 1879 he formed an alliance with his old enemy Austria-Hungary, to preserve Germany's southern borders, and also promoted strong diplomatic bonds with Russia, to discourage French diplomatic or military interference. By the time Bismarck retired in 1890 Germany was a powerful modern state, led by a new Kaiser, Wilhelm II. The Iron Chancellor was wary of this new ambitious young ruler, and his retirement came after a succession of clashes between the two men. Bismarck retired to his estates, and died there in the summer of 1898.

Bismarck was an advocate of German unity, but he used war to achieve limited political objectives, rather than to ensure German dominance over the rest of Europe. After unification he promoted peace, and to maintain it throughout his Imperial Chancellorship was a feat of considerable diplomatic skill. Unfortunately Kaiser Wilhelm II lacked Bismarck's abilities, and without the 'Iron Chancellor's' guiding hand he set Germany on a course that led to war in 1914. By the 1930s, Bismarck was generally viewed as one of Germany's great leaders – the father of the modern German state. By naming the new battleship after him, Hitler was linking his own regime and Chancellorship to the halcyon years of German strength and unity, before it was consumed by the horrors of modern war.

Incidentally, *Bismarck* wasn't the first German warship to be named after the 'Iron Chancellor'. In 1877 a steam-powered iron-hulled corvette was launched, and given the name *Bismarck*. She remained in service until 1891, when she became a floating barrack ship in Wilhelmshaven. Then, in 1897 the *Fürst Bismarck* (Prince Bismarck) was launched in Kiel, one of a new group of armoured cruisers designed to protect German trade routes and colonies. She spent nine years in the Far East, but on returning to Kiel in 1910 she was relegated to coastal defence duties. Effectively she had been rendered obsolete by the 'Dreadnought revolution', where older warships were no match for the new breed of dreadnought battleships and battlecruisers. The battleship *Bismarck* was therefore the third and last German warship to bear the name.

ABOVE The Reichschancellor and Führer Adolf Hitler was the principal guest at the launching ceremony, but the battleship was actually launched by Dorothea von Löwenfeld-Bismarck, granddaughter of the 'Iron Chancellor'.

ABOVE The installation of the battleship's main armament was completed as she lay alongside the Equipping Pier in Hamburg's Blohm & Voss shipyard, part of which can be seen on the right of the photograph. In the foreground the innards of the starboard anchor capstan are exposed.

ABOVE This photograph was taken during the fitting out of *Bismarck* in Hamburg. The scaffolding shows that work was still being done on the final installation of 'Anton' and 'Bruno' turrets.

the Panzerschiff *Admiral Scheer*, and mounted the rostrum. The ceremony began at 1.00pm, and was watched by a crowd of 60,000 people. At the launching rostrum Hitler gave a brief speech, revealed that *Schlachtschiff* 'F' was to be named after Germany's great statesman Otto von Bismarck. He was then joined by Dorothea von Löwenfeld-Bismarck, granddaughter of Germany's 'Iron Chancellor', who proclaimed: 'On the order of the Führer, I christen you with the name *Bismarck*.' She cracked a champagne bottle against the bow, the band struck up the national anthem and the great ship began moving down the slipway. Then she stopped – stuck fast for 3 minutes before she was finally freed. The newly christened *Bismarck* then continued down the slipway and into the River Elbe.

While the crowds departed, waiting tugboats towed the newly built battleship a few hundred yards to the Steinwerder Kai West, also known as the Equipping Pier. There the process of fitting-out would begin. This involved the completion of the superstructure, the installation of the warship's machinery and weapons systems and the addition of all the fixtures and fittings which would turn the steel hulk into a fully operational modern battleship. A temporary straight stem had been fitted for the launch, and this was now replaced by what was known as an 'Atlantic stem', an elegantly raked bow that added considerable grace to the vessel. More importantly it was designed to reduce 'wetness' on the forecastle. As before, this work was carried out by the skilled shipyard workers of Blohm & Voss. The whole fitting-out process was scheduled to take 18 months.

In 1938 Admiral Raeder (Großadmiral Raeder after 1 April 1939) proposed a dramatic expansion of the fleet, and called for warship production to be stepped up. In early 1939 Hitler approved Raeder's 'Plan Z', an ambitious

ABOVE **During the fitting-out process work is under way on the completion of *Bismarck*'s forward superstructure. Although the scene looks to be a chaotic one, with electrical cabling draped over the superstructure, fitting-out was a highly organised process, where each task had its place in the busy schedule. Note the presence of a workmen's site hut on the port side of the forward superstructure.**

expansion of the Kriegsmarine to 17 capital ships, including 10 battleships and 4 aircraft carriers. On 1 April *Schlachtschiff* 'G' was launched in Wilhelmshaven, having been christened *Tirpitz*. Raeder hoped that *Bismarck* and *Tirpitz* would be just the first of several powerful battleships. Unfortunately for him events overtook the scheme, when against the großadmiral's advice Hitler ordered the invasion of Poland.

Bismarck was still tied up alongside the Equipping Pier when war was declared in September 1939. With Germany now at war, resources earmarked for Raeder's fleet were diverted elsewhere – to build tanks, aircraft and U-boats. Also, Germany was now plunged into a war with Britain and France, who between them had overwhelming naval assets. While the Chief of the Kriegsmarine contemplated how best to use its small surface fleet, *Bismarck* slowly began to take on the appearance of a real warship.

In April 1940 the first of her crew arrived to learn what they could about the workings of their new ship. As she was still a construction site they were housed in accommodation ships. In late June she was moved into a waiting floating dock to have her propellers fitted, and her *Magnetischer Eigenschutz* (Magnetic Self-Protection) system applied. Also known as a degaussing coil, this reduced the magnetic signature of the vessel, and thereby reduced the risk posed by enemy magnetic mines. In mid-July *Bismarck* was taken out of the dry dock and an inclination test was carried out to determine her metacentric height. By now the battleship was virtually ready for service. All that was needed now was for the dockyard to sort out any remaining snags and to prepare the ship for her handover to the Kriegsmarine.

On 24 August 1940, a particularly blustery day, the battleship was commissioned into the

LEFT This rare colour picture captures the moment when *Bismarck* entered the water for the first time. She came off the Blohm & Voss slipway during the launching ceremony on 14 February 1939 and floated freely on the River Elbe.

Kriegsmarine. Captain Lindemann inspected the crew, addressed them and ordered the naval ensign to be raised, while a naval band played the national anthem. At that moment the vessel officially became the KMS *Bismarck*. The only thing that spoiled the ceremony came when the liner *Vaterland* drifted into the stern of the battleship. All that was damaged, though, was pride and the battleship's after flagstaff. *Bismarck* was now a fully functioning warship, and over the next three weeks stores and supplies were stowed on board as the crew prepared for their first task – the conducting of sea trials.

LEFT *Bismarck* enters the waters of the River Elbe watched by a crowd of around 60,000 people. More onlookers cheered the sight from the far side of the harbour. In the background are the huge scaffolding frames surrounding slipways 8 and 9, while more of the Blohm & Voss shipyard can be seen behind her hull.

RIGHT During the fitting-out process hundreds of shipyard workers came aboard *Bismarck* every day, and returned home at the end of their shifts. Here many of them can be seen mustered on *Bismarck*'s quarterdeck, while one party returns to the shipyard. The photograph was probably taken during the spring of 1940.

Sea trials

In the early afternoon of 15 September 1940, *Bismarck* cast off from the Equipping Pier at the Blohm & Voss shipyard, and tugs edged her out into the middle of the River Elbe. She then began the 40-nautical mile transit of the busy river to her anchorage off Brünsbuttel. Shortly before 5.00pm she collided with the tug *Atlantik*, but neither vessel was damaged. She dropped anchor just after 7.00pm, and that night *Bismarck's* light anti-aircraft guns joined the canal defences in opening fire on a formation of British bombers as they flew overhead. No hits were recorded. The next day the transit of the canal began and proved uneventful. By 6.00pm on 17 September, *Bismarck* was tied up alongside the Scheerhafen in Kiel, the naval quay named after the German commander at Jutland. The following day the battleship was moved out to a buoy in the anchorage to conduct gun calibration tests.

On 28 September *Bismarck* slipped her mooring and headed out into the Baltic Sea. Off Gotenhafen (now Gdynia in Poland) she began an eight-week programme of sea trials. These involved the testing of her engines and performance and the appraisal of her fighting abilities. Speed trials were first conducted on 23 October, and she easily surpassed the 30-knot requirement set by the Kriegsmarine. Above all, this was a time when the crew were trained in all aspects of the battleship's operation, with what seemed like a never-ending succession of exercises, emergency drills, manoeuvres and tests of seamanship. The young sailors rose to the challenge, and the evaluators declared themselves pleased with their performance.

This praise was repeated by Großadmiral Raeder when he inspected *Bismarck* on 12 November as she lay at anchor off Gotenhafen. His visit marked the end of this intensive period of training and evaluation. After his visit, *Bismarck* moved alongside the quay and a few additions were made to her weaponry. Four new 10.5cm (4.1in) heavy anti-aircraft guns were fitted around the after

ABOVE A Kriegsmarine propaganda film crew were on hand to record the commissioning ceremony of *Bismarck*, and went on to film her preparations for active service. Here the film team are being ferried across the Kuhwerder Basin to film the ship being moved from her berth.

LEFT On the afternoon of 15 September 1940, *Bismarck* finally left the Blohm & Voss shipyard, and made her way up the River Elbe towards the open sea. Here she can be seen pulling away from the shipyard, which is on her starboard side.

THE BATTLESHIP AND THE U-BOAT

While *Bismarck* was being built, another warship was taking shape on the slipways of Blohm & Voss. On 2 January 1940 work began on construction project BV-532. This was the shipyard identifying number for a new Type VIIC U-boat, which was laid down next to *Bismarck*, on slipway 10. At the time *Bismarck* was being fitted out at the adjacent Equipping Pier (Steinwerder Kai West). The U-boat was finally launched on 7 December 1940, by which time *Bismarck* had already been commissioned, and was conducting sea trials in the Baltic Sea. *Bismarck* returned to Hamburg two days after the launch, and so the two warships lay beside each other as *Bismarck*'s crew went home on Christmas leave. She was still there on 6 February 1941 when the U-boat was commissioned into the Kriegsmarine, becoming *U-556*.

Before the ceremony, the U-boat's commander Kapitänleutnant (Lieutenant Commander) Wohlfarth paid Captain Lindemann a visit, when he had the audacity to ask the battleship's commander if he might borrow the ship's band to play at the commissioning ceremony. An amused Lindemann was happy to oblige, and so *U-556* was commissioned with great aplomb. In return, Wohlfarth offered to 'sponsor' the battleship. Lindemann agreed, and soon a hand-drawn *Patentschaft* (Sponsorship Certificate) was presented to the battleship. It showed Sir Parzifal ('Parsifal' was Wohlfarth's nickname) on the conning tower of *U-556*, protecting *Bismarck* from British Swordfish and their torpedoes. At the bottom the certificate even showed the mighty battleship being towed to safety by the tiny U-boat. The text of the *Patentschaft* read:

We, the *U-556* (500 tons) hereby declare before Neptune, the ruler of the oceans, lakes, rivers, seas, brooks, ponds and drainage ditches that we will stand beside our big brother, the battleship *Bismarck* (42,000 tons), whatever may befall her on water, land or in the air.

Hamburg, 28 January 1941
Commander and crew, U-556

Shortly afterwards *U-556* left Hamburg to begin her sea trials and crew training off Kiel and the crew cheered the battleship as they parted company. *Bismarck* briefly joined her there in March, but then the battleship sailed for Gotenhafen, and the two warships parted company for the last time. *U-556* was placed on active service on 1 April, and a month later on 1 May she began her first patrol. It lasted 30 days, during which 'Parsifal' and his crew sank seven ships – a Faeroese trawler, then three Allied merchant ships from two different convoys. On 30 May *U-556* put in to Lorient. It was from there that *U-556* left on her second and last patrol. On 27 June she was sunk in the North Atlantic, 150 nautical miles to the south of Iceland. She had been detected by British escorts and was depth charged. However, Wohlfarth and 41 of his 56-man crew survived the sinking and were rescued. They spent the rest of the war in a prison camp. Coincidentally, *U-556* was sunk exactly a month after *Bismarck* was lost.

Ironically, on 26 May, while *U-556* was on her way home from her first patrol, she received a signal sent to all U-boats within range of her to come to the aid of *Bismarck*. *U-556* was 360 nautical miles to the south-west of *Bismarck*, but the U-boat was low on fuel and had no torpedoes left. There was little she could do to help. That evening she spotted *Ark Royal* and *Renown*. In the distance Wohlfarth could see star shells lighting up the night sky during the attack on *Bismarck* by Vian's destroyers. That evening the U-boat commander wrote in his log: 'Moderate visibility, very dark night. What can I do for *Bismarck*? I can see star shells being fired, and flashes from the *Bismarck*'s guns. It is a terrible thing to be near, and not be able to do anything. All I can do is to scout, and guide in boats that have torpedoes.'

At dawn *U-556* rendezvoused with *U-74*, which took over the job of maintaining contact with *Bismarck*. As he was now desperately short of fuel, Wohlfarth's U-boat resumed its course towards Lorient. When *Bismarck* finally sank that morning her little sponsor was less than 300 nautical miles away. The choice of imagery on the *Patentschaft* was apposite. *Bismarck* was damaged by British Swordfish torpedo bombers, of the kind depicted on the certificate. Also, if she ever needed a tow, it was that evening when the two vessels were just a few miles apart. However, 'Parsifal' and his men were powerless to help.

ABOVE ***Bismarck*** **is seen making her way down the River Elbe during her maiden voyage in mid-September 1940. This slightly blurred photograph was probably taken from one of the tugs that accompanied the battleship during her voyage from Hamburg to Kiel.**

BELOW Kapitän zur See (Captain) Ernst Lindemann (1894–1941) was a highly respected captain, who was well liked by his crew. He appeared to have boundless energy, possibly because he drank coffee and chain-smoked throughout the day.

BELOW During ***Bismarck*****'s commissioning ceremony on 24 August 1940, the ensign staff at the stern of the battleship was damaged when the liner** ***Vaterland*** **was accidentally driven against the stern of** ***Bismarck*** **moments after she was launched. In this photograph taken shortly afterwards, the liner can be seen safely secured astern of the battleship, while a colour party raise** ***Bismarck*****'s naval ensign.**

ABOVE Captain Lindemann addressing the assembled ship's company from the *Bismarck*'s quarterdeck during the battleship's commissioning ceremony, 24 August 1940. Behind him the ship's band are assembled, ready to play as the ensign is raised for the first time.

RIGHT On 15 September 1940, during her maiden voyage from Hamburg to Kiel, *Bismarck* collided with one of the tugs that was guiding her down the River Elbe. A few of the tug crew fell overboard, and here one of them is hauled on board the battleship.

BELOW Seamen forming part of the watch on deck recover a stretcher carrying a sailor. While this may have been taken during a man overboard exercise, it is more likely that this photograph is dated 15 September 1940, when *Bismarck*'s crew rescued men thrown overboard during a collision on the River Elbe.

ABOVE The liner and the battleship collide. On the day of her commissioning ceremony, *Bismarck* was hit by the side of the newly launched liner *Vaterland*. After her launch she drifted across the mouth of the Kuhwerder Basin and collided with the stern of *Bismarck* as the battleship lay alongside the Equipping Pier. Fortunately no serious damage was done, and the liner was moved away to the far side of the basin.

superstructure, to augment the four mounted further forward, abaft the funnel and bridge superstructure. Also, two 10.5m stereoscopic rangefinders were added above the forward and after fire control stations.

On 5 December *Bismarck* left Gotenhafen and headed west to Kiel. There she paused to take on supplies and fuel before beginning her second transit of the Kaiser Wilhelm Canal. She arrived back alongside the Blohm & Voss Equipping Pier in Hamburg on the evening of 9 December. There shipyard engineers removed the rangefinder mounted to 'Anton' turret, as it was deemed impractical to use at high speed due to spray. The anti-aircraft gun crews continued their training while the rest of the men set to painting their ship, adopting a Baltic camouflage pattern. Captain Lindemann thanked the crew for their efforts, and told them that when they returned from leave they would be heading back to the Baltic Sea, to begin working-up exercises, ready for their first operational assignment. The period of trials and training was over. From this point on *Bismarck* would be a fully operational warship. Then, on 16 December, most of the crew were sent home on Christmas leave. For most of them it would prove to be their last.

LEFT In this photograph, taken from the roof of 'Caesar' turret, *Bismarck*'s commissioning ceremony is under way. On behalf of the Kriegsmarine, Captain Lindemann accepts the ship from the dockyard. With the raising of the naval ensign the battleship officially became the latest addition to the fleet. After the ceremony Lindemann inspected the crew, arrayed here in their various divisions.

Chapter Two

The *Bismarck* at war

KMS *Bismarck* had a brief but ultimately eventful career. She only made one sortie, in May 1941, and that ended with her sinking, but this dramatic voyage – codenamed Operation Rheinübung – ensured the German battleship's place in the history books.

OPPOSITE *Bismarck* fires on the British cruiser HMS *Hood*, 24 May 1941. *(Bundesarchiv)*

ABOVE The German battlecruiser KMS *Scharnhorst* took part in Operation *Berlin*, an Atlantic sortie whose success led to the planning of Operation *Rheinübung*.

Background

On 24 January 1941, *Bismarck* was declared ready for active operations, but the Kaiser Wilhelm Canal was blocked by a sunken merchant ship, and so *Bismarck* and her crew waited for it to be cleared. Eventually, on the morning of 6 March *Bismarck* left Hamburg for the last time, and the following day she began her transit of the canal, covered all the while by a Luftwaffe fighter escort. She grounded briefly during the passage, so when she reached Kiel on 9 March she went into dry dock, to check her hull for damage. Captain Lindemann seized this opportunity to repaint her underside, too. On 14 March *Bismarck* moved to Scheerhafen, where she took on stores and embarked her two spotter aircraft. Finally, on 18 March she sailed from Kiel to Gotenhafen to conduct more training exercises. Two weeks later Captain Lindemann learned that he and his crew were about to embark on their first operation – a long-range sortie into the North Atlantic code named Operation *Rheinübung* (Rhine Exercise). *Bismarck* and her crew were finally going to war.

RIGHT Großadmiral Erich Raeder (1876–1960) was a firm believer in the naval value of capital ships, and was convinced that *Bismarck* could wreak havoc in the North Atlantic if she could break through the British cordon around Iceland and the Faeroes.

By the spring of 1941 the conflict had been raging for a year and a half, and the German war machine had achieved great things. Poland had been overrun, as had the Netherlands, Belgium and France. In April 1940, while *Bismarck* was fitting-out, the rest of the Kriegsmarine supported the German invasion of Denmark and Norway, and now German armies were massing in the east for an invasion of Yugoslavia and Greece. Italy had entered the war as an Axis ally, and the Royal Navy was now badly stretched, fighting a naval war on two fronts – the Atlantic and the Mediterranean.

The German conquest of France provided the Kriegsmarine with new bases on the French Atlantic coast. Now U-boats could reach their hunting grounds in the North Atlantic without a long and dangerous journey across the North Sea and then around the north of Scotland.

The Battle of the Atlantic was at its height, and while Allied merchant ships were being sunk in record numbers, U-boat losses were also mounting. Admiral Dönitz, commanding the Kriegsmarine's U-boat fleet, felt he was at the brink of success – a little more pressure and the Allied convoy system would collapse from such heavy attrition. For his part Großadmiral Raeder felt that the surface fleet should play its part in the campaign. By using his powerful capital ships to disrupt British convoys, he hoped to sever Britain's vital maritime lifeline.

This support began in late January 1941 with Operation *Berlin* – a German surface sortie into the North Atlantic. Under the direction of Admiral Lütjens the *Scharnhorst* and *Gneisenau* successfully broke out into the North Atlantic between Greenland and Iceland. They then remained at large for two months, sinking or capturing 22 Allied merchant ships with a total tonnage of 116,000 tons, before putting in to Brest on the French Atlantic coast on 22 March. The success of this mission made it almost inevitable that *Bismarck* would be used in a similar way. So, as *Bismarck* was performing a second round of sea trials off Gotenhafen, Admiral Lütjens was in Berlin, discussing future operations in the North Atlantic with Großadmiral Raeder.

A department of the Kriegsmarine known as the *Seekriegsleitung* (Maritime Warfare Command, or SKL) was responsible for the planning of surface naval operations and the deployment of warships. It answered directly to Großadmiral Raeder. On 2 April its Chief of Staff, Generaladmiral Otto Schniewind, issued a new directive following its approval by Raeder. The directive underlined the strategic importance of surface ship sorties into the Atlantic, and established their objectives – the disruption of enemy convoys and the sinking of merchant ships. While Schniewind issued the directive, the policy was pure Raeder, who was a strong advocate of the offensive use of his new battleships.

With Raeder's approval, Schniewind and Lütjens began planning Operation *Rheinübung* as soon as the new directive was announced. They had hoped to have more capital ships at their disposal, and it was even envisaged that a combination of the forces of all four German capital ships – two sailing from the French coast, and two from the Baltic – could be utilised in two *Seekampfgruppen* (sea battle groups). This, though, was a risky plan, as it involved the two groups successfully breaking out into the North Atlantic, and then effecting a rendezvous on the high seas. Out there they would be beyond the reach of German air cover, and beyond the range of escorting German destroyers. The scheme proved too fraught with danger and was abandoned.

In any case, *Tirpitz* had still to complete her initial sea trials, and would not become fully operational before the start of July. *Scharnhorst*

LEFT Admiral Günther Lütjens (1889–1941) was one of the most capable senior officers in the Kriegsmarine, and had already demonstrated his abilities during Operation *Berlin*.

BELOW Captain Lindemann pictured inspecting *Bismarck*'s guard of honour as he came on board to take command of the ship during her commissioning ceremony, 24 August 1940.

To: Admiral Lütjens
From: Chief of Staff, Generaladmiral Otto Schniewind, Chief of Staff, Seekriegsleitung

As soon as the two battleships of the 'Bismarck' Class are ready for deployment, we will be able to seek engagement with forces escorting enemy convoys and, when they have been eliminated, destroy the convoy itself. As of now, we cannot follow that course, but it would soon be possible, as an intermediate step, for us to use the battleship *Bismarck* to distract the hostile escorting forces, in order to enable the other units engaged to operate against the convoy itself. In the beginning, we will have the advantage of surprise because some other ships involved will be making their first appearance, and, based on his experience on the previous battleship operations, the enemy will assume that one battleship will be enough to defend a convoy.

At the earliest possible date, which it is hoped will be during the new moon period of April, the *Bismarck* and the *Prinz Eugen*, led by the fleet Commander, ought to be deployed as commerce raiders in the Atlantic. At a time that will depend on the completion of the repairs she is currently undergoing, *Gneisenau* will also be sent into the Atlantic. The lessons learned in the last battleship operation indicate that the *Gneisenau* should join up with the *Bismarck* group, but a diversionary sweep by the *Gneisenau* in the area between Cape Verde and the Azores may be planned before that happens. Their heavy cruiser *Prinz Eugen* is to spend most of her time operating tactically with the *Bismarck* or with the *Bismarck* and *Gneisenau*. In contrast to previous directives to the *Gneisenau–Scharnhorst* task force, it is the mission of this task force to also attack escorted convoys. However, the objective of the battleship *Bismarck* should not be to defeat in an all-out engagement enemies of equal strength, but to tie them down in a delaying action, preserving her own combat capability as much as possible, so allowing other ships to attack the merchant vessels in the convoy. The primary mission of this operation also is the destruction of their enemies the merchant shipping; enemy warships will be engaged only when the objective makes it necessary and can be done without excessive risk.

The operational area will be defined as the entire North Atlantic north of the equator, with the exception of the territorial waters of neutral states. During last winter the conduct of the war was fundamentally in accord with the directives of the Seekriegsleitung … and closed with the first extended battleship operation in the open Atlantic. Besides achieving important tactical results, this battleship operation shows what important strategic effects similar sorties could have. They would reach beyond the immediate area of operations two of the theatres of war. The goal of the war at sea must be to maintain and increase these effects repeating such operations as often as possible.

We must not lose sight of the fact that the decisive objective in a struggle with England is to destroy her trade. This can be most effectively accomplished in the North Atlantic where all her supply lines converge, and where, even in the case of disruption in more distant areas, supplies can still get through by the direct route from North America.

Gaining command of the sea in the North Atlantic is the best solution to this problem, but this is not possible with the forces that at this moment we can commit to this purpose, and given the constraint that we must preserve her numerically inferior forces. Nevertheless, we must strive for local and temporary command of the sea in this area and gradually, methodically, and systematically extend it.

During the first battleship operation in the Atlantic, the enemy was always able to deploy one battleship against us, and protect both of its main supply routes. However, it became clear that providing this defence of his convoys brought him to the limit of the possibilities open to him, and the only way you could significantly strengthen his escort forces is by weakening areas important to him or by reducing convoy sailings.

LEFT ***Bismarck*** **captured on camera as she was being towed through the Kaiser Wilhelm Canal, September 1940. A towing party on the battleship's forecastle can be seen keeping an eye on the towing cable, which is passed through the starboard towing fairlead. This in turn is secured to one of** ***Bismarck*'s** **anchor cables.**

was in dry dock in Brest, having her boilers repaired. She would not be available for naval operations until late June at the earliest. On 6 June *Gneisenau* was hit during a British bombing raid on Brest, and was hit again four days later. This meant she would be out of action for several months and that of the Kriegsmarine's four capital ships, only *Bismarck* was available to take part in Operation *Rheinübung*. Still, Großadmiral Raeder felt that she was fast enough to evade the British, or if she had to engage, then she had the firepower needed to fight her way out of trouble.

By way of support, the Hipper class heavy cruiser *Prinz Eugen* was also earmarked for the operation. She carried eight 20cm (8in) guns, and was remarkably similar in appearance to *Bismarck*, so that she resembled a scaled-down version of the new battleship. Finally, Admiral Lütjens was placed in command of the operation. Despite being given detailed orders from Schniewind and Raeder, he would have full operational control during the sortie, and would decide where to break out into the North Atlantic and where to strike at enemy convoys when he got there. For the most part the scope and duration of the operation were left to his discretion. However, the orders stressed that he should avoid taking excessive risks with his ships. He had the firepower to take on most escorted convoys, but it was clear that engaging enemy capital ships was to be avoided if at all possible. Whatever damage the *Bismarck* inflicted, the most important outcome was that both German warships should return safely.

It was hoped that the operation could begin in late April, but for various reasons the project had to be delayed. Then on 22 April *Prinz Eugen* damaged her propeller, and returned to Kiel for repairs. The following day she detonated a mine dropped by British aircraft. Although the damage was minor, it meant the repairs would take longer than expected. On 26 April Lütjens met Raeder, and asked for a postponement until *Tirpitz* was ready. It was denied – the operation would go ahead around the time of the new moon. Its commencement was set for 16 May.

BELOW ***Bismarck*** **as she makes a transit of the Kaiser Wilhelm Canal on 8 March 1941. During this transit** ***Bismarck*** **briefly ran aground, and on her arrival in Kiel she went into dry dock to make sure she had not been damaged.**

Bismarck's consort during Operation *Rheinübung* was the heavy cruiser *Prinz Eugen*, one of three Hipper class warships laid down during the mid-1930s. She was named after Eugene of Savoy, the famous general of the early 18th century who fought alongside the Duke of Marlborough. Under the terms of the Anglo-German Naval Agreement (1935), Germany was allowed to build up to five 'treaty cruisers' – warships with 8in guns, as defined in the London Naval Treaty of 1930. According to the agreement work couldn't start on these 'treaty' or 'heavy' cruisers until January 1943, unless they carried lighter 5.9in (15cm) guns. So, the Kriegsmarine ordered what became the Hipper class of cruisers, which were large enough to carry 8in (20cm) guns, even though their initial design called for lighter 15cm weapons.

Prinz Eugen was the third of these cruisers to be built, her sister ships being the *Admiral Hipper* and the *Blücher*. Two more vessels were eventually built and launched as the *Seydlitz* and *Lützow*, but neither was ever completed. *Prinz Eugen* was laid down in the Germaniawerft shipyard in Kiel in late April 1936, and was launched just over two years later, on 22 August 1938. By then the decision had been taken to replace the 15cm guns with 20.3cm ones, an upgrading which was officially made in response to the announcement by the Soviet Union that they were building a new class of heavy cruisers armed with 18cm guns. The speed of this upgrade, however, revealed that Kriegsmarine designers had already planned for this contingency. Fitting-out took two years, and so she was finally commissioned into the Kriegsmarine on 1 August 1940.

Prinz Eugen was slightly larger than her two sister ships, and therefore has been described as a Hipper class (second batch) vessel – a one of a kind. She also had a different engine configuration with nine rather than twelve boilers, but generated the same amount of power as her two sisters. In addition to her main gun battery of eight 20.3cm guns, *Prinz Eugen* carried a powerful battery of anti-aircraft weapons, controlled by a sophisticated fire control system similar to that fitted in *Bismarck*. The result was a cruiser that was fast and powerful – her only real limitation was her restricted range, which made her of only limited use as an Atlantic raider.

Before Operation *Rheinübung*, *Prinz Eugen* could have been regarded as an unlucky ship. In July 1940 she was damaged during a British air raid on Kiel, which delayed her completion. While working up in

BELOW The German heavy cruiser KMS *Prinz Eugen*, commanded by Kapitän zur See (Captain) Brinkmann, was superior to her British counterparts in terms of speed, modernity and capability.

ABOVE **Kapitän zur See (Captain) Helmuth Brinkmann (1895–1983) first saw action during the First World War, and held various staff appointments before being given command of *Prinz Eugen* in August 1940. He handled her with considerable skill, and evaded his pursuers to reach Brest without incident.**

Prinz Eugen

Displacement:	16,974 tons (standard), 19,042 tons (fully laden)	
Dimensions:	Waterline length:	199.5m (654ft 6in)
	Length overall:	207.7m (679ft 1.5in)
	Beam:	21.5m (70ft 6in)
	Draught:	6.6m (21ft 8in), 7.2m (23ft 7.5in) when fully laden
Armament:	8 20.3cm guns in 4 twin turrets	
	12 15cm guns in 6 twin turrets	
	12 3.7cm anti-aircraft guns in 6 twin mounts	
	8 2cm anti-aircraft guns in single mounts	
	12 53.3cm torpedo tubes, in 4 triple mounts	
Sensors:	FMG 39 (gO) radar (later redesignated FuMO22)	
Protection:	Belt:	70–80mm
	Upper deck:	12–30mm
	Main turrets:	70–105mm
	Armoured deck:	20–50mm
	Conning tower:	50–150mm
	Torpedo bulkheads:	20mm
Aircraft:	3 Arado Ar196 float planes, and 1 catapult	
Propulsion:	9 La Mont steam boilers, 3 Brown-Boveri geared turbines, 3 propeller shafts, producing 132,000shp	
Maximum speed:	32.5kts	
Fuel oil capacity:	3,250 tons	
Range:	5,050 nautical miles at 15kts	
Complement:	1,600 men	

the Baltic before her Atlantic sortie she was also damaged by a magnetic mine as well as being plagued by mechanical problems. However, during Operation *Rheinübung* the cruiser performed well, and her guns scored several hits on the *Prince of Wales*. After successfully detaching from *Bismarck* the cruiser headed south. On 26 May she rendezvoused with the tanker *Spichern*. Engine trouble led Captain Brinkmann to call off the sortie, and after refuelling again on 28 May, this time from the *Esso Hamburg*, *Prinz Eugen* set a course towards Brest. She managed to evade the British and reached the French port safely on 1 June.

Prinz Eugen was still in Brest a month later when she was badly damaged during a British bombing raid. She was back in service by February 1942 when, together with *Scharnhorst* and *Gneisenau,* she took part in the celebrated 'Channel Dash', a bid to move the three ships to a German port. *Prinz Eugen* was torpedoed during the operation and part of her stern was lost. She was eventually repaired in Kiel and remained in the Baltic for the rest of the war. In 1946 she was used as a target ship for the atomic bomb tests staged off Bikini Atoll in the Pacific. She sank from the damage she sustained there on 22 December 1946.

ABOVE *Bismarck* is pictured lying at her mooring in Kiel Roads in September 1940, before she continued on into the Baltic to conduct her sea trials. She retained this appearance until her return to Hamburg that December, when she was repainted in a Baltic camouflage scheme.

Back in Gotenhafen preparations on board *Bismarck* continued, while in Berlin Generaladmiral Schniewind supervised the support phase of the operation – the dispatch of twelve support ships – nine tankers, two surveillance ships and a supply vessel. These were to be stationed at various points in the North Atlantic, and could be called upon to support or replenish the two warships if required. In addition six U-boats were diverted from offensive operations to act as additional reconnaissance vessels. On 5 May Adolf Hitler travelled to Gotenhafen to inspect *Bismarck* and *Tirpitz* – both of which had arrived there to conduct sea trials. Tirpitz was tied up alongside, while *Bismarck* lay at anchor in the roads. Hitler arrived at the *Bismarck* on board the tender *Hela*, and after inspecting the crew he was taken for a tour of the ship. The following day the routine of training exercises continued, and *Prinz Eugen* also arrived, having completed her repairs in Kiel. However, minor damage to *Bismarck*'s port crane meant that this had to be repaired before the operation could begin. That being the case, a new start date of 18 May was scheduled. This time there would be no further postponement. Operation *Rheinübung* was about to begin.

Operation *Rheinübung* begins

On the morning of Sunday 18 May 1941, Admiral Lütjens inspected the *Prinz Eugen* before returning to *Bismarck* with the cruiser's commander Captain Brinkmann. There he held

RIGHT On 12 November 1940 Großadmiral Raeder inspected *Bismarck* as she lay alongside in Gotenhafen, where she had just undergone work on her rangefinders. In this photograph Raeder is welcomed on board by Captain Lindemann.

an operational meeting with the two captains (Lindemann and Brinkmann), his chief of staff Captain Band and Admiral Saalwächter, commanding Group West, who had strategic control of operations in the North Atlantic. This was when Lütjens revealed his orders and declared his intention to refuel off Norway, and then break out into the Atlantic through the Denmark Strait between Greenland and Iceland. The meeting broke up and as soon as Saalwächter went ashore and Brinkmann returned to his ship, Lütjens gave the order to proceed to sea. It was 11:30 and Operation *Rheinübung* was now officially under way.

As the ship's band played the German folk song 'Muss i den', *Bismarck* slipped her lines and got under way, accompanied by *Prinz Eugen*. The two warships only went as far as the roads, where they dropped anchor to take on fuel and supplies. During the refuelling a fuel hose ruptured, leaving *Bismarck* some 200 tonnes short of her maximum capacity. Undeterred, she raised anchor and spent the afternoon conducting training exercises before returning to her anchorage. At 21:18 that evening *Prinz Eugen* weighed anchor and put to sea. In order to deceive watching enemy spies, *Bismarck* remained at anchor until 02:00 the following morning, and then followed the cruiser into the Baltic. At 11:30 the two

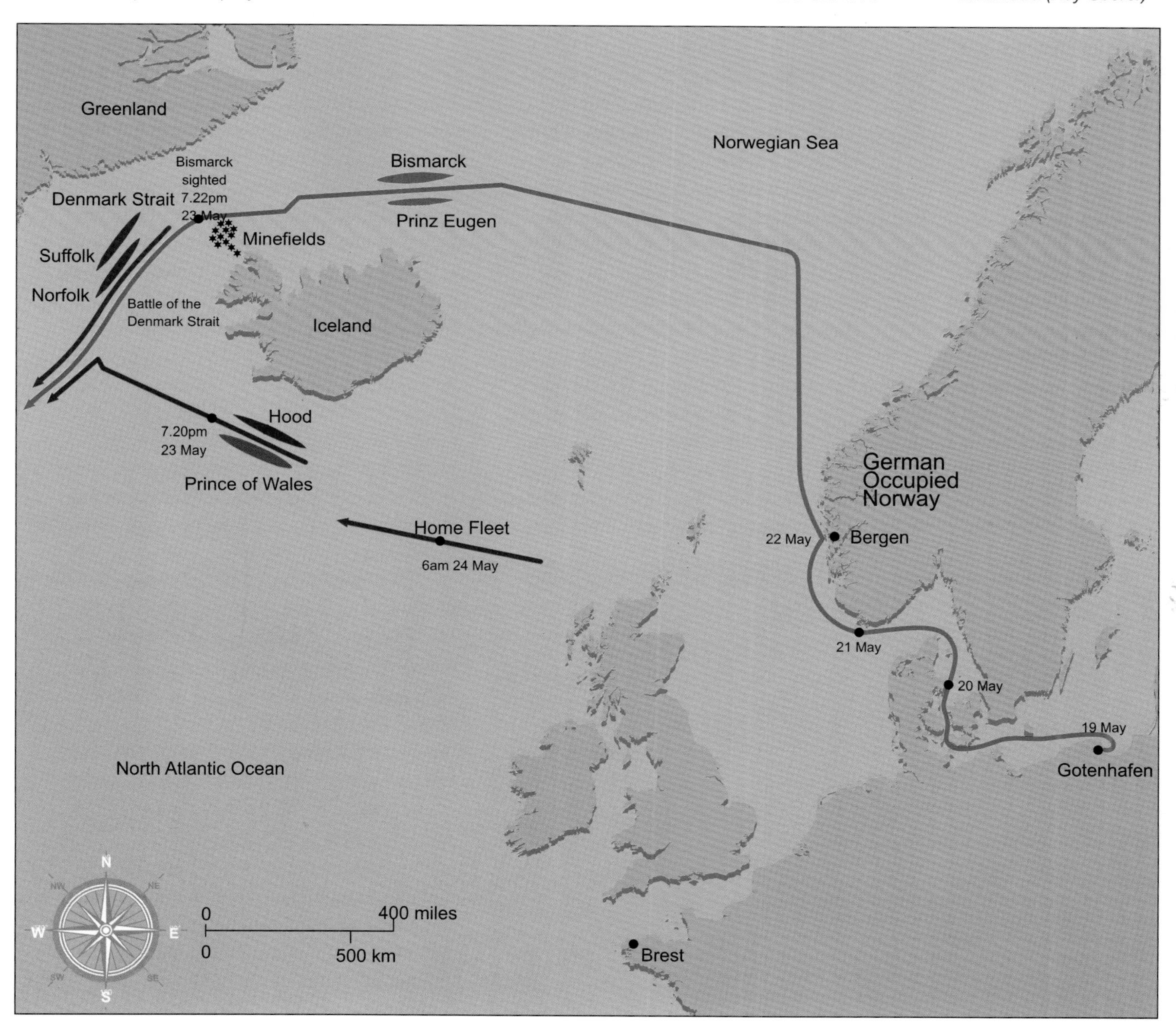

BELOW Operation *Rheinübung* – breakout. *(Roy Scorer)*

RIGHT ***Bismarck*** **being towed by** ***Prinz Eugen*****, photographed from the after superstructure of the cruiser. This towing operation formed part of the exercises conducted by the two warships off Gotenhafen before Operation** ***Rheinübung*****. From this aspect the white fake bow waves on** ***Bismarck*** **are clearly visible.**

warships rendezvoused off the white cliffs of Cape Arkona, the northern tip of the island of Rügen. There they also picked up their Baltic escort – the destroyers *Z-16* and *Z-23*.

It was while they were off this headland that Captain Lindemann used the intercom system to address the crew. He told them what they had already guessed – they were going to break out into the Atlantic and attack enemy convoys. They then continued on to the west, between the coastline of Germany and Denmark, until they entered the Fehmarn Belt, where at 22:30 they rendezvoused with a third destroyer, the flotilla leader *Z-10*, with the 6th Flotilla's Captain Schulze-Hinrichs embarked. By nightfall they were in the Langelandsbælt, and by 23:00 they had reached the southern approaches of the Great Belt, the waterway between Funen and Zealand that led north to the more open waters of the Kattegat. The small squadron made the Great Belt transit during the night and by the dawn of 20 May they reached the Kattegat without incident. So far the voyage had been uneventful.

BELOW When the Führer toured ***Bismarck*** **on 5 May 1941, the battleship was lying at anchor in Gotenhafen Roads. His tour complete, Hitler is pictured here as he is about to return to the fleet tender** ***Hela*****.**

That Tuesday morning the skies were overcast – something Lütjens welcomed as it reduced the risk of being detected by British reconnaissance aircraft. On their port side sat the low-lying coastline of German-occupied Denmark, while to starboard was Sweden, a neutral country, but one whose sympathies lay predominantly with the Allies. For that reason Lütjens decided to keep out of sight of the Swedish coast as much as he could. He knew that keeping their presence a secret would be all but impossible, but that there was no need to take unnecessary chances. He was right to be cautious – the relatively narrow seaway was busy. They passed Danish and Norwegian freighters, and both Swedish and Danish fishing boats. The risk was that one of them would report the news to the Resistance, and so it would reach the British Admiralty in London.

Around noon a flight of Swedish aircraft on patrol near the Swedish port of Gothenburg sighted the German *Seekampfgruppe*, and passed the information on to naval headquarters. An hour later, at around 13:00 they passed the old Swedish cruiser *Gotland*, which was on patrol at the entrance of the Skagerrak – she too passed on the news to

Stockholm. That evening the sighting report was surreptitiously passed on to a Norwegian colonel representing his government in exile. He in turn passed it to Captain Henry Denham, the British naval attaché in Stockholm, who immediately contacted the British Admiralty. So, by 21:00 that evening, the Admiralty knew the *Bismarck* and *Prinz Eugen* were at sea, and heading towards Norwegian waters.

Shortly after their encounter with the *Gotland* the German ships reached the edge of the Skagerrak minefield. There was a clear channel through it, but Lütjens was wary of taking it, as enemy submarines might be lurking off its western entrance. Instead he had arranged to rendezvous with a flotilla of German minesweepers, which spent the afternoon clearing a new path through the field. By 16:00 the swept channel was ready and the German ships sailed through it, out into the open water of the Skagerrak. The ships then headed north-west, towards the southern tip of Norway at Lindesnes, to the west of Kristiansund. They passed under its darkened lighthouse shortly after midnight, and once clear of the coast they turned north. Their progress, though, had not gone unnoticed. Members of the Norwegian Resistance spotted them, and late that evening they radioed the sighting to London. This augmented Captain Denham's report, and confirmed that the *Bismarck* was steaming up the Norwegian coast. In fact this was the third such report – an agent in Gotenhafen had already reported that *Bismarck* and *Prinz Eugen* had left the port.

The German warships passed Stavanger shortly before dawn on Wednesday 21 May, and three hours later the *Seekampfgruppe* altered course off Marstein lighthouse to enter the Korsfjord, the long fjord that led north towards Bergen. It had two entrances – one on either side of the island of Sund – which was something that appealed to Lütjens as he suspected the British might now be looking for him. In fact *Prinz Eugen*'s radio room intercepted a British message telling aircrews to look out for two German capital ships between Bergen and Stavanger. This was why Lütjens decided to put into the Norwegian coast – the skies were clear, and it made sense to lie low in a remote anchorage before resuming the voyage at night. Besides, the tanker *Wollin* was waiting for them near Bergen, so it meant that

ABOVE *Bismarck* entering the Grimstadfjord, pictured from the *Prinz Eugen* as the cruiser continued on up the Korsfjord to Kalvanes Bay. *Bismarck* is still painted in her Baltic camouflage scheme, but soon after she came to anchor work began to repaint the hull in an overall grey.

LEFT *Bismarck* photographed from *Prinz Eugen* as the two warships head north towards the Norwegian coast on 20 May, at the commencement of Operation *Rheinübung*.

RIGHT **This aerial photograph was taken by Flying Officer Suckling on 21 May 1941, and shows *Bismarck* at anchor in the Grimstadfjord, accompanied by smaller support vessels.**

either ship could refill their oil tanks before they began their breakout into the Atlantic.

At noon *Bismarck* dropped anchor in the Grimstadfjord, a small inlet of the Korsfjord to the south of Bergen. *Prinz Eugen* continued up Korsfjord and anchored in Kalvanes Bay, on the north-eastern corner of Sund, while the three destroyers put in to Bergen. Merchant ships were sent alongside both ships to act as shields against torpedoes, and the crews settled down to their regular anchor watch routine. Unknown to them, at 13:15 a British Spitfire flown by Flying Officer Suckling of Coastal Command flew over the Korsfjord at just over 26,000ft (8,000m), before banking over the Grimstadfjord. He wasn't spotted, and he flew on unmolested. An hour later he landed at the airfield in Wick in the north of Scotland, and his film was sent to London for evaluation. When the film was developed, the analysts found themselves looking at photographs of the two German warships. That evening the Admiralty issued a warning that a Bismarck class and a Hipper class vessel had been sighted off Bergen.

Meanwhile, the crew of the *Bismarck* spent the afternoon painting ship. Stages

LEFT **The German Führer Adolf Hitler, photographed during his inspection of *Bismarck* and *Prinz Eugen* on 5 May 1941. He saw capital ships as a propaganda tool more than a strategic one, and never fully grasped the importance of seapower.**

RIGHT **The Swedish cruiser *Gotland* was on patrol off the Skagerrak on 20 May 1941 when she spotted the German force as they steamed by. News of this sighting was immediately transmitted to Stockholm.**

were thrown over the side, and the Baltic camouflage markings were painted over, leaving the battleship grey all over, with the exception of small white wave-shaped marks at the waterline forward of 'Anton' turret, to confuse British gunnery directors. Effectively it made the battleship look shorter than it really was, and therefore would encourage the enemy gun directors to overshoot. While *Bismarck*'s crew were painting ship, their counterparts on the *Prinz Eugen* were refuelling from the tanker *Wollin* as she lacked *Bismarck*'s fuel capacity. Throughout the afternoon Luftwaffe fighters maintained watch over the two vessels, just in case the RAF launched an attack.

When he heard of the sighting, Admiral Tovey, the Commander of the British Home Fleet, placed his fleet on standby for operations against the *Bismarck*. The aircraft carrier *Victorious* was in Scapa Flow, about to sail to the Mediterranean in company with the battlecruiser *Repulse*, which was in the Clyde. This transfer was cancelled, even though the carrier only had nine Swordfish torpedo bombers and six Fulmar fighters on board – all with inexperienced aircrews. Tovey's new flagship *King George V* was readied for sea, as were five light cruisers and six destroyers. *Repulse* was ordered to join them off the north-west coast of Scotland. Meanwhile, he waited for fresh information.

Tovey also signalled Vice Admiral Holland, commander of the battlecruiser squadron, to put to sea at once with his flagship – the battlecruiser *Hood* – and the new battleship *Prince of Wales*, accompanied by six destroyers. They were to head to Hvalfjordur near Reykjavik, where they would support the line of British cruisers already on station around Iceland.

Two British heavy cruisers were already on patrol in the Denmark Strait. Rear Admiral Wake-Walker, commanding the 1st Cruiser Squadron, had his flagship *Norfolk* on station there, but on 19 May *Norfolk's* near sister *Suffolk* had put in to Hvalfjordur to refuel. *Suffolk* was ordered back on station and together these heavy cruisers would act as Tovey's first line of defence. Although their 8in guns were no match for *Bismarck*, they could shadow her using their radar, and report her movements, allowing British battleships to close in and intercept the German *Seekampfgruppe*. The light cruiser *Arethusa* was also refuelling in Hvalfjordur, and she was ordered to reinforce the light cruisers *Birmingham* and *Manchester* already on patrol between Iceland and the Faeroes. With Coastal Command patrolling the less likely gaps between the Faeroes and Shetland, and between Shetland and Orkney, Tovey was fairly certain that the German ships would be spotted if they tried to break out into the North Atlantic. His biggest fear was that his cruisers would run out of fuel before the Germans made their move. This being the case, he ordered *Birmingham* and *Manchester* to put in to Skaalfjordur in the Faeroe Islands, so they could refuel and be back on station before *Bismarck* could reach them.

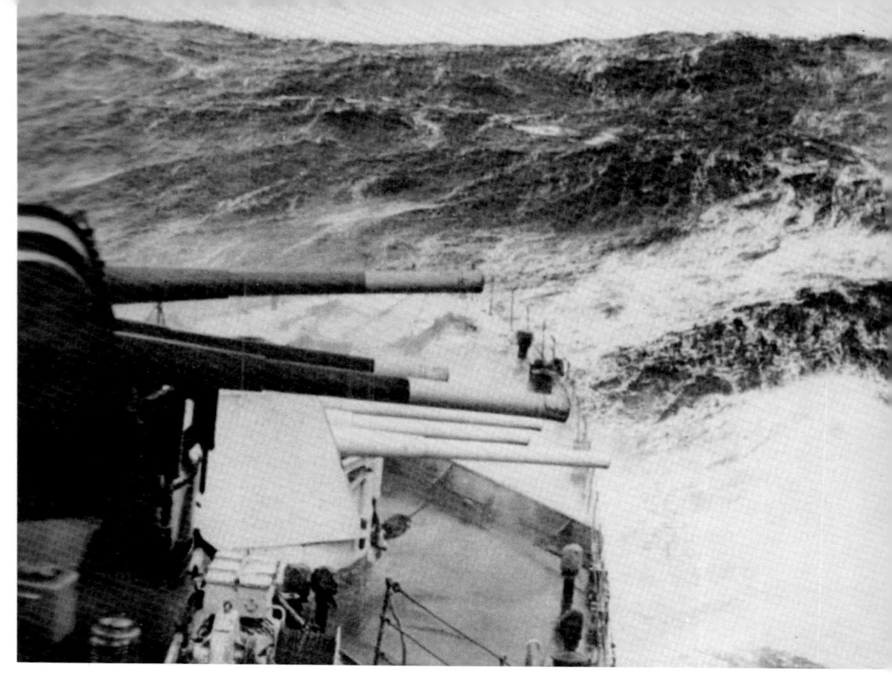

ABOVE The rough waters of the Denmark Strait, pictured from the after superstructure of the British heavy cruiser HMS *Suffolk*, while she was on patrol in this key channel during the weeks preceding the sortie by *Bismarck* and *Prinz Eugen*.

LEFT Captain Henry Denholm RN was the naval attaché assigned to the British Embassy in Stockholm. He was told of the sighting of *Bismarck* by the Swedish cruiser *Gotland* by Swedish sympathisers, and he promptly radioed the news to the Admiralty in London.

RIGHT **The British heavy cruiser HMS *Norfolk* was the flagship of Rear Admiral Wake-Walker, who also commanded *Norfolk*'s half-sister HMS *Suffolk*. Both cruisers were built during the late 1920s and lacked the speed and firepower needed to take on *Bismarck* and *Prinz Eugen*.**

Back in the Grimstadfjord, Admiral Lütjens had reached a decision. He realised that if the British did not know about his presence near Bergen, then they soon would. However, a German aerial reconnaissance of Scapa Flow showed that the bulk of the Home Fleet was still at anchor. By leaving that evening, Lütjens hoped to make it to the Atlantic before Tovey's ships could reach their blocking positions between Greenland and the Faeroes. He considered his options. There were five routes to choose from, three of which were practical. He could easily discount the narrow Pentland Firth between Orkney and the British mainland, and the gap between Orkney and Shetland – both were too close to Scapa Flow, and its attendant cluster of airbases. That left three routes – the gaps between Shetland and the Faeroes, the Faeroes and Iceland, and finally the Denmark Strait, between Iceland and Greenland.

RIGHT **Rear Admiral William Wake-Walker (1888–1945) was an experienced commander of scouting forces, and his cruisers did exactly what was required of them – shadowing *Bismarck* and reporting her course, speed and position during her breakout into the North Atlantic.**

While the Denmark Strait lay furthest from Bergen, it was also the furthest from Scapa Flow. Lütjens realised that the British would have cruisers stationed there but these could be brushed aside, and he hoped to reach the gap before any British capital ships could arrive to block his path. It had disadvantages, too. Pack ice off the coast of Greenland reduced the width of the channel from 160 nautical miles to something around half that. Known minefields off the Icelandic coast reduced its width even further. This meant that if enemy capital ships were there, then *Bismarck* and *Prinz Eugen* would have little room to manoeuvre, and therefore could not avoid a fight. Generaladmiral Schniewind favoured the next gap between Iceland and the Faeroes, which was 230 nautical miles wide, but Lütjens doubted he would be able to pass through it without a fight, as he knew it was often heavily guarded and that the British could reach it before he could. The third option – passing between the Faeroes and Shetland – was discounted as being too dangerous, as it was within range of British aircraft, and too close to Scapa Flow.

Raeder and Schniewind had left this major tactical decision up to the force commander. After weighing up all the options, Lütjens decided to head for the Denmark Strait. At 19:30 that evening *Bismarck* weighed anchor, then steamed north up the Korsfjord, where she rejoined *Prinz Eugen* and the escorting destroyers. Beyond Korsfjord they entered Hjeltefjord and then the wider waters of the Fedjefjorden. They passed the Hellisøy lighthouse at around 22:00 and entered the

Norwegian Sea. As they did, British aircraft flew over the Korsfjord, dropping flares as they searched for the two warships. By then, though, they were safely out in the open sea.

After two hours they had completely cleared the coast, whereupon the force turned due north and increased speed to 24 knots. It was now midnight. At 04:20 on Thursday 22 May the *Seekampfgruppe* had reached the latitude of the Faeroe Islands. There the destroyers were detached and ordered to make their way into Trondheim to refuel. *Bismarck* and *Prinz Eugen* were now on their own. Lütjens maintained the same course throughout the morning, but increased speed to 27 knots, which meant that by 14:00 they had reached the Arctic Circle, just above the latitude of Iceland's north coast. They kept heading north to avoid British search aircraft operating from Iceland. Then, a little after 23:00, they reached the latitude of Jan Mayen Island, and Lütjens altered course to the west, heading towards the northern end of the Denmark Strait. The German tanker *Weissenburg* was stationed close by, but Lütjens decided not to waste valuable time refuelling. He was determined to pass through the bottleneck of the Denmark Strait before the British could reinforce their cruiser patrols there.

That evening British search aircraft returned to the Korsfjord, but found both anchorages empty. So, at 22:00 on 22 May, Tovey set sail from Scapa Flow, his flagship *King George V* accompanied by *Victorious*, five light cruisers and six destroyers. A German reconnaissance aircraft had flown over Scapa Flow earlier that evening and reported that Tovey's battleships were still at anchor there, together with an aircraft carrier. The news was relayed to Lütjens that evening, just as he was altering course to the west. He must have felt confident that his departure had gone undetected, and that there would be no capital ships in the Denmark Strait when he got there. Unknown to him, Vice Admiral Holland had just received new orders to linger to the south of Hvalfjordur, at the latitude of 62° north. That way his two capital ships could react to sightings to the east or the west of Iceland. Tovey was planning to take up station to the south-east, covering the approaches on either side of the Faeroe Islands.

ABOVE A Royal Navy radar operator pictured manning his set on board a British cruiser during 1941. The superiority of their radar sets gave the British the edge over their German counterparts, and allowed Wake-Walker's cruisers to shadow *Bismarck* from a safe distance.

Dawn on Friday 23 May broke to reveal bad weather – a strong north-easterly wind and rough seas. Still the *Seekampfgruppe* sailed on throughout the day, and Lütjens would have welcomed the bad weather as it brought with it low visibility, which reduced the risk of detection from British search aircraft operating from bases in Iceland. In 1940, when Germany invaded Denmark, Allied troops occupied Iceland, which was then a Danish possession. The harbours of Hvalfjordur outside Reykjavik, Akureyri on the north coast and Seydisfjordur on the eastern side of the island were used as refuelling bases by British warships, and Allied search aircraft were based at Reykjavik. The island had

RIGHT Operation *Rheinübung* began on 18 May 1941. This photograph was taken two days later, when *Bismarck*, *Prinz Eugen* and their escorting destroyers were passing Skagen, the most northerly tip of Denmark. The photograph was taken from one of the German minesweepers that met the force there to lead them through the defensive minefield which blocked the Skagerrak.

become an Allied bastion, blocking Germany's access to the Atlantic. Lütjens knew this, and was right to be cautious. Shortly before 14:00 Lütjens ordered another course change to the south-west, from 266° to 240°. This was to avoid the increasing risk of encountering pack ice as they approached the coast of Greenland.

By 18:00 the *Seekampfgruppe* had entered the Denmark Strait. There was only a gap of 30 nautical miles between the pack ice and the British minefields, and Wake-Walker's flagship *Norfolk* lay astride this relatively narrow channel. *Suffolk* was still steaming north to join her after refuelling. The crews of the two British heavy cruisers had been warned that *Bismarck* might be attempting a breakout, and the lookouts were alert. It was foggy and the light was fading – hardly ideal conditions for a naval encounter. Then, at 19:11 radar operators on *Bismarck* spotted what appeared to be two warships on their starboard side. The crew manned their guns. Eleven minutes later a lookout on board *Suffolk* spotted a heavy cruiser through the mist, followed moments later by a battleship. The report was radioed to *Norfolk* and passed on to the Admiralty, but it was also intercepted by the radio operators on board *Bismarck*.

After sighting the German battleship, Captain Ellis of the *Suffolk* ordered his ship to turn away, so it was swallowed up by the mist. This was a sensible precaution – to risk a gunnery duel with the *Bismarck* would have been suicidal. The radar on *Suffolk* was temperamental, hence the first sighting came from a lookout, rather than from a radar contact. Wake-Walker and Captain Phillips in *Norfolk* eventually linked up with *Suffolk*, and together they shadowed the Germans from a distance. Then, at 20:30 *Bismarck* sighted *Norfolk* 6 miles away through a gap in the mist. *Bismarck* opened fire, firing

BELOW *Bismarck* is pictured here from the deck of a minesweeper as she follows another minesweeper through the swept channel leading into the Skagerrak during her voyage from Gotenhafen to Grimstadfjord.

five salvos before the cruiser withdrew into the mist and her own smokescreen. After that the British ships made sure to keep their distance, and relied on radar to shadow the enemy. Interestingly, this was the first time *Bismarck*'s guns had fired in anger, and the blast from her guns damaged her forward Seetakt radar, which meant she could only detect targets astern of her. However, Lütjens felt satisfied. He had passed through the British cruiser screen and he felt sure that nothing now lay between him and the vastness of the North Atlantic.

Unknown to him, Vice Admiral Holland was only 300 miles away when he received *Suffolk*'s signal. A quick glance at the chart revealed the situation. *Bismarck* and her consort were almost directly due north of *Hood* and *Prince of Wales*, and appeared to be steering a south-westerly course through the Denmark Strait, close to the pack ice on its western side. By heading to the north-west at 27 knots, Holland would be in a position to intercept the enemy ships soon after dawn. At 21:00 Holland ordered a change of course to 295° and increased speed. An hour later he detached his destroyers, as they were unable to keep up in the rough seas. They would follow on as best they could.

Both sides were now racing towards each other, but only the British were expecting – in fact seeking – a battle at dawn. What the British did not know was that thanks to the damage to the radar, *Bismarck* and *Prinz Eugen* had changed places, so that the cruiser was now leading, with the *Bismarck* following behind her. This manoeuvre was not detected by the shadowing British cruisers, but it would have a profound impact on the course of the coming battle. At 22:00 *Bismarck* reversed course, in an attempt to catch the pursuing cruisers. The British kept their distance and *Bismarck* soon returned to her original course.

ABOVE In this view of *Bismarck* lying at anchor in the Grimstadfjord, the chevrons which formed the core of her Baltic camouflage scheme have been painted over. The dark patches on her hull, however, suggest that the grey paint they were covered with was still not completely dry when this photograph was taken. This photograph was probably shot soon after midday. Work on the dark bow and stern sections was carried out during the afternoon.

BELOW Able Seaman Newell, a lookout on board HMS *Suffolk*, was the first member of Wake-Walker's cruiser group to spot *Bismarck* as she attempted to pass through the Denmark Strait on the evening of 23 May 1941. The German battleship was glimpsed through a gap in the fog at a range of 7 nautical miles, and Captain Ellis promptly turned away, so his cruiser was hidden by the fog.

The Battle of the Denmark Strait

During the night Holland turned on to a more westerly heading of 240°, just in case the Germans altered course during the night. On board his two ships the crews went to action stations at 04:00, while on *Prince of Wales* civilian contractors worked through the night to sort out the mechanical problems that still plagued her 14in gun turrets. As dawn approached on Saturday 24 May 1941, the British lookouts peered intently through the darkness towards the north, the direction from which the German ships would appear. Then, at 05:37 a lookout on board the *Hood* spotted smoke on the northern horizon. It was on the battlecruiser's starboard beam, as the British ships were now steering 240° at 28 knots. In fact, on board *Bismarck*, the hydrophone team had already detected two fast-moving ships approaching from the south-east. At 05:29 the forward fire control position on board *Bismarck* detected smoke on the south-eastern horizon. The British were easier to see against the lightening sky, hence the 8-minute gap between the two sightings.

Both sides were now 15 nautical miles apart, and both were already at action stations – in fact, thanks to the British cruisers, the Germans had been at full alert all night. So, three pairs

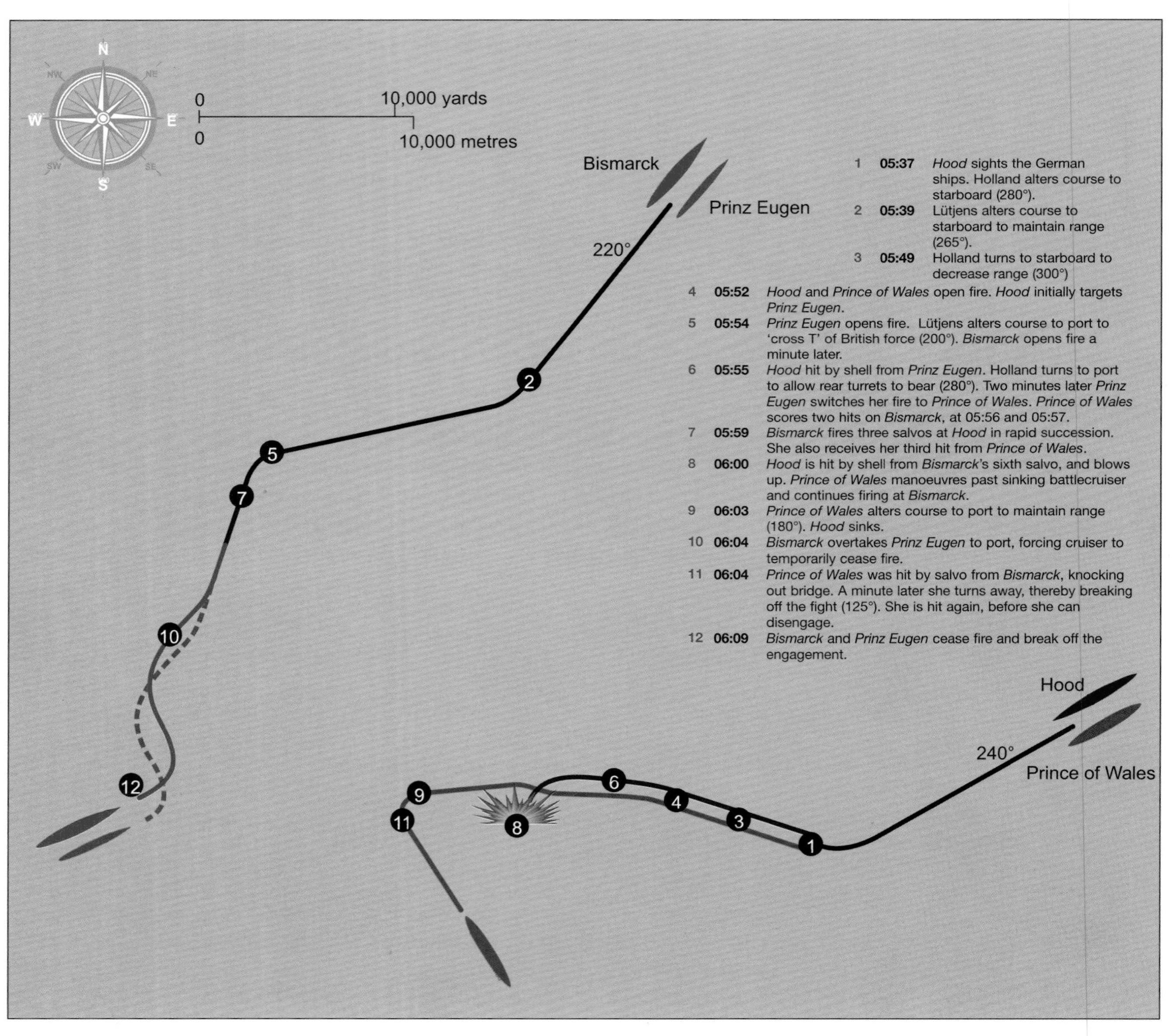

BELOW The Battle of the Denmark Strait. *(Roy Scorer)*

LEFT The venerable British battlecruiser HMS *Hood*, lying peacefully at anchor in Scapa Flow. This vast anchorage served as the wartime base of the British Home Fleet.

of warships were in the area, even though the British cruisers were too far astern of *Bismarck* to intervene. Of the others, *Prinz Eugen* was ahead of *Bismarck*, and *Hood* was followed by *Prince of Wales*. As the two groups of ships approached each other, the British were heading towards the south-west, with the Germans steaming towards them from the north, approaching Holland's ships at what was almost a right angle. This meant that if they maintained their present course the British would 'cross the T' of the Germans, and would therefore be able to fire all their guns at the enemy, while only the forward guns of the *Prinz Eugen* could fire back in return. Lütjens remained unconcerned, as his gunnery advisers considered the approaching ships to be light cruisers.

Hood was armed with eight 15in guns, which had a theoretical range of 15 miles, but a maximum practical range of 12½ miles. *Prince of Wales* astern of her had ten less-powerful 14in guns, but turret problems were still hindering her combat effectiveness. Holland knew that if the range decreased the hit probability increased, and importantly his own flagship would become less vulnerable. At long ranges shells have a high arc of fire, and so fall on their target almost vertically. At ranges of less than 9 miles the arc is much shallower, and so shells would tend to hit a warship's belt armour rather than her less well-protected deck. This being the case, Holland decided to close the range as quickly as possible.

At 05:37 Holland ordered a turn of 40° to starboard, putting his ships on to a new course

LEFT The British battleship HMS *Prince of Wales*, pictured off Colombo in late November 1941 while en route to Singapore. Six months earlier, when she engaged the *Bismarck*, she had only just been commissioned, and her turrets were still not fully operational.

RIGHT A rare colour photograph of the British battlecruiser HMS *Hood*, taken before the outbreak of war. She was elegant and impressive, but her beautiful lines hid the fact that her armoured protection was woefully inadequate compared to more modern capital ships such as *Bismarck*.

of 280°. At the time the Germans were steering a course of 222° – heading towards the south-west, with *Prinz Eugen* preceding *Bismarck*. This turn towards him must have alarmed Lütjens. Only capital ships would consider such a move. His gunnery teams would have noted the enemy speed was 28 knots, a rate which only Britain's battlecruisers or new King George V class battleships could attain. This meant they matched *Bismarck* for speed, leaving him no option but to fight. Although the crew were already at their stations, General Quarters was sounded on board *Bismarck*. Two minutes after Holland's course change Lütjens did the same, turning his ships 33° to starboard, on to a new heading of 265°. That meant that while the two pairs of ships were still converging, the rate of closure was slowed, giving Lütjens more time to react.

RIGHT Vice Admiral Lancelot Holland (1887–1941) was the titular commander of the Battlecruiser Squadron attached to the Home Fleet, but in practice he served as Vice Admiral Tovey's deputy. He had recently returned from the Mediterranean, and hoisted his flag in *Hood* shortly before she sailed from Scapa Flow to intercept *Bismarck*.

On *Hood*, Holland's gunnery teams noticed the change, and at 05:49 the vice admiral ordered another change of course, this time a 20° turn to starboard, on to a new heading of 300°. This more acute angle of approach meant that only the front guns of the British ships could bear on the enemy – a reversal of the situation when the two sides had first sighted each other. Now the British were 'crossing the T' of the Germans. By 05:52 the range had decreased to 12 miles, and the *Hood* opened fire on the lead enemy ship with her two forward turrets. A minute later *Prince of Wales* did the same, firing at the second German warship. Holland had ordered both ships to fire at the left-hand enemy ship, but Captain Leach's gunnery officer on *Prince of Wales* correctly identified the second ship as *Bismarck*, and so Leach ignored his instructions and fired on her instead. The problem was, at that range and angle, the silhouette of both German warships was remarkably similar. It was only after *Hood* fired her first salvo that her gunnery officer realised the mistake, and Holland ordered *Hood* to switch her fire to *Bismarck* – the right-hand ship. However, for some reason the order was not passed on for several vital minutes.

Prince of Wales's first salvos landed well astern of *Bismarck*, while *Hood*'s first two salvos fell short of *Prinz Eugen*. When they saw the size of the shell splashes the Germans were left in no doubt they were facing capital ships armed with guns of comparable size to *Bismarck*'s. At 05:55 Lütjens finally gave the order to open fire. The range was now 11 nautical miles, and the enemy ships and

the smoke above them could now be seen with the naked eye. *Prinz Eugen* fired first, aiming at *Hood*. While her 20.3cm guns lacked the punch of the other three ships, Captain Brinkmann hoped to cause some damage through plunging fire. At that range shells took about 50 seconds to reach their target, but no hits were recorded. However, her second salvo was ranged perfectly, and a 20.3cm shell struck *Hood* between her after funnel and the mainmast, hitting an anti-aircraft ammunition locker and starting a small fire.

Then the *Bismarck* opened fire, and her first salvo fell a little short of *Hood*. The range was closing so fast that the fire control teams of both sides had to make constant adjustments, making it hard to determine the range. Then, at 05:56, *Prince of Wales* scored a hit on *Bismarck*, when a 14in shell struck her port side forward of her main armoured belt. The shell penetrated the hull and exited through her starboard side. The hit caused a small oil leak and minor flooding. *Hood*'s gunnery was less accurate, and her fourth, fifth and sixth salvos all missed *Prinz Eugen*. At 05:55 Holland ordered another course change, this time turning 20° to port, on to a new course of 280°. He was worried that the Germans would be able to slip past him into the Atlantic, and this move made this less likely. However, it still was not enough of a turn to allow the British ships to clear their arcs and bring their after guns into action. The range had now decreased to just 10 miles.

At 05:57 *Prinz Eugen* fired two more salvos at *Hood* – she could fire one off every 30 seconds – but both missed. *Bismarck* was

ABOVE In this dramatic reconstruction of the sinking of HMS *Hood*, the battleship *Prince of Wales* surges past her, as the forward two-thirds of the battlecruiser begin to sink. Members of *Prince of Wales*'s crew who witnessed the scene recall being shocked into silence by the spectacle.

LEFT Several photographs were taken of *Bismarck* from *Prinz Eugen* during the Battle of the Denmark Strait, fought on the morning of 24 May 1941. The cruiser was ahead of the battleship for most of the action, and was well placed to record *Bismarck*'s role in her first engagement.

LEFT During the Battle of the Denmark Strait, after *Hood* blew up, *Bismarck* overhauled *Prinz Eugen* on her port side. This photograph shows *Bismarck* about to overtake the cruiser, while firing her main guns at the *Prince of Wales*. The blast from *Bismarck*'s guns was so close that it temporarily altered the camera's light settings, effectively turning day into night.

CENTRE HMS *Hood* was a battlecruiser – the only one in her class – and entered service in 1920. Battlecruisers carried the same armament as battleships, but traded armoured protection for speed. The flaws of the concept were revealed at Jutland, but unlike the fleet's other remaining battlecruisers, *Repulse* and *Renown*, *Hood* was never rearmoured to conform to the standards expected of modern battleships. Nevertheless, in 1941 she was still a powerful warship, and her belt armour was considered adequate defence against *Bismarck*'s guns. Her Achilles heel, though, was her weak deck armour, which was particularly vulnerable to long-range plunging fire.

BOTTOM In this historic photograph taken from *Prinz Eugen*, the salvos fired from the German ships can be seen falling around their British counterparts. *Hood* is behind the twin white shell splashes on the right, while the location of *Prince of Wales* is marked by the funnel smoke and shell splashes further to the left. At this stage the range between the protagonists was approximately 10 nautical miles.

more fortunate, and a 38cm shell from her third salvo reportedly struck *Hood*'s main fire-control position, although British observers deny this. If it was a miss it was a close one. In return *Hood* fired another salvo at *Prinz Eugen*, missing again, while *Prince of Wales* struck *Bismarck* with a salvo, striking her amidships below the waterline, causing minor flooding in her No. 4 electric plant and No. 2 boiler room. On *Bismarck*, Lütjens ordered *Prinz Eugen* to switch her fire to the British battleship (which he believed to be Tovey's flagship *King George V*), leaving *Bismarck* to concentrate on the battlecruiser, which by now had been identified as *Hood*. He also ordered Brinkmann to reduce

RIGHT **Shells from *Hood* fall dangerously close to the stern of *Prinz Eugen* during the opening minutes of the Battle of the Denmark Strait. *Hood* opened fire on the lead ship thinking she was *Bismarck*, and it took several crucial minutes before this mistake was recognised.**

CENTRE ***Bismarck* is approximately 1,200m astern of *Prinz Eugen* in this photograph, taken at approximately 05:57 on 21 May 1941. *Bismarck* was firing her main guns at HMS *Hood*, which was approximately 10 nautical miles away off her port bow at the time.**

BOTTOM **This historic photograph, taken from *Prince of Wales* at 06:01 on 21 May 1941, shows the British battlecruiser *Hood* exploding. Two plumes of smoke – one larger than the other – mark the spot where *Hood* was ripped apart. The smaller plume probably came from the initial magazine explosion in the stern of *Hood*, while the larger plume to the right was slightly further forward, when the main magazines went up. The smudge of smoke to the left of these two plumes marks the location of the battleship *Prince of Wales*. *Hood* was approximately 8.6 nautical miles away from the photographer at the time.**

speed, to allow *Bismarck* to overtake the cruiser, and therefore avoid their fire crossing.

The range was still closing rapidly, and within a few minutes *Hood* would have passed through her 'zone of vulnerability', where she was at risk from plunging fire hitting her poorly armoured deck. So, at 05:59, Holland ordered another change of course – another 20° turn to port, on to a new heading of 260°, to clear fully the arc of fire of his after guns. At that point *Bismarck* fired three salvos in quick succession – 30 seconds apart. Having straddled the battlecruiser with her third salvo, her gunnery officers were confident that they now had the enemy's range. This coincided with *Hood*'s latest turn to port. The fourth and fifth salvos missed the battlecruiser, landing just off the *Hood*'s starboard beam – exactly where she would have been if she hadn't begun her turn. *Hood*, *Prince of Wales* and *Prinz Eugen* also missed with their latest salvos.

RIGHT After the destruction of *Hood*, both *Bismarck* and *Prinz Eugen* concentrated their fire on *Prince of Wales*. This photograph, taken from the German cruiser, shows *Bismarck* engaging *Prince of Wales* during the closing minutes of the battle, shortly before the British battleship broke off the action. A shell splash from *Prince of Wales*'s penultimate salvo can be seen falling astern of *Bismarck*.

Then, at 06:01, *Bismarck's* fifth salvo reached *Hood*. The venerable battlecruiser was 860ft 7in (262.3m) long, which meant that as she completed the turn, her stern swung into the area where the German shells were landing. One of these 38cm shells struck *Hood* behind her mainmast, close to her after turret. It easily penetrated her 2in-thick deck armour, and exploded in a magazine serving her after 4in guns. Although the exact sequence of events may never be known, this explosion ignited the main magazine of 'X' turret, which exploded, blowing the turret into the air amid an incredible pillar of fire. This ripped the stern off the ship. Shocked observers in *Prince of Wales* saw a large spurt of flame appear behind the *Hood*'s mainmast, followed a fraction of a second later by an enormous explosion and a much larger pillar of smoke and flame which completely obscured the battlecruiser's stern. Captain Leach ordered an immediate turn to starboard, to avoid colliding with whatever was left of *Hood*.

On the bridge a survivor recalled that the hit went largely unobserved, but the helmsman reported that the steering had gone. Then the ship began to sink. As the survivor stepped into the sea from the bridge wing he looked back and saw Vice Admiral Holland, still sitting in his command chair, about to go down with his ship. As *Bismarck*'s sixth salvo landed astern of the sinking ship, the battlecruiser's stern section rose in the air and hung there momentarily. The front three-quarters of *Hood* kept moving forward through momentum alone, until her bow also began to rise out of the water, so that the remains of the stricken ship formed a gigantic V shape in the water. Then the bow and stern sections slipped below the water.

RIGHT *Bismarck* pictured firing at *Prince of Wales* as she overhauled *Prinz Eugen* on the cruiser's port side. The picture was taken at approximately 06:04. This salvo struck the British battleship at the base of her after funnel, causing her to break off the action a minute later.

ABOVE The King George V class battleship *Prince of Wales*, photographed while passing up the west coast of Orkney. This photograph was taken shortly after she returned to service once the damage inflicted by *Bismarck* and *Prinz Eugen* had been repaired.

Within 3 minutes of the shell striking her there was nothing left of *Hood*, save a scattering of wreckage. Of her 1,421-man crew, there were just 3 survivors.

The suddenness of the *Hood*'s destruction took everyone by surprise. On *Bismarck* observers claim the fireball they created seemed large and close enough to touch, while on *Prince of Wales* the crew were stunned by the disaster. Nevertheless, there was no time to pause – the battle was still being fought. *Norfolk* was a distant observer of the tragedy, and it passed the appalling news on to the Admiralty. On board *Prince of Wales*, Captain Leach and his men soon found themselves targeted by both German ships. The range was now down to just 8 miles. At 06:02 a salvo from *Prince of Wales* straddled *Bismarck*, but caused no damage. Almost simultaneously the British battleship was hit on the bridge, killing or wounding almost everyone inside. Captain Leach was only stunned, but realised that the battle had become too one-sided. Two of his forward guns had malfunctioned, reducing the number of guns which could bear to just four. 'X' turret had also jammed completely. It was at that point that Leach decided to withdraw.

At 06:03 *Prince of Wales* turned hard to port, beginning a turn of 160° away from the enemy. She also laid a smokescreen. This didn't protect her from the shells, though. *Bismarck's* ninth salvo hit the British battleship twice – once on the waterline belt, and the other on her secondary gun control position, which was knocked out. She was also hit in the stern by a shell from *Prinz Eugen*. What may have saved *Prince of Wales* was a German lookout on *Prinz Eugen* who thought he spotted an approaching salvo of torpedoes. Both German ships immediately turned to port on to a course of 270°. *Prince of Wales* was still being hit – *Bismarck* scored one superstructure hit on her boat deck, while *Prinz Eugen* scored two hits – one on the stern and the other on a secondary ammunition locker, but the shells failed to explode. However, by now all three ships were steaming away from each other, although the Germans were now turning back on to their original course of 220°.

At 06:09 Lütjens ordered his ships to cease fire. The battle had lasted just 17 minutes and claimed the lives of more than 1,500 men. Britain had lost the venerable *Hood* – the most famous and elegant warship in the Royal Navy, while her new destroyer had been outfought by *Bismarck*. Lütjens had every right to be pleased, as he had won a spectacular victory. When the damage reports reached him he learned that the two structural hits from *Prince of Wales* had caused nothing more than minor structural damage. However, the third hit had struck *Bismarck* below the waterline, causing a leak in her port fuel tank. *Prinz Eugen* was unscathed. As the German ships sped on into the North Atlantic *Bismarck's* crew tried to repair the damage, while engineers tried to evaluate just how serious the leak actually was. While Captain Lindemann wanted to pursue the *Prince of Wales*, Lütjens refused to – his mission was to attack convoys, not sink enemy battleships. Instead he altered course to 200°, with *Prinz Eugen* taking the lead. This was because *Bismarck* was still being shadowed by Wake-Walker's two cruisers, and with *Bismarck* astern they would keep a respectful distance from her.

The pursuit

At 06:32, Lütjens sent a signal to the headquarters of Kriegsmarine Group North, based in Wilhelmshaven. It read: 'Battlecruiser, probably *Hood* sunk. Another battleship, *King George V* or *Renown*, turned away damaged.' The next signal went to General Saalwächter of Kriegsmarine Group West, based in Paris, and said: '*Hood* destroyed within five minutes in gunnery duel at 06:00 this morning. *King George V* turned away after hits. My speed reduced. Stem down due to hit in foreship.' The signal to Group North was augmented within half an hour with a position. Their signal read: 'Have sunk a battleship approximately 63° North, 32° West.' Signalling the two commands was important – Group North controlled operations as far as the Denmark Strait, while operations in the Atlantic were supervised from Paris. Interestingly, Lütjens only passed on the information about the damage to *Bismarck* in his signal to Group West.

He realised that *Bismarck* had lost sufficient fuel oil to restrict her cruise in the Atlantic. That morning he would have received damage reports from both captains. While *Prinz Eugen* had emerged unscathed, Lindemann would have reported that of the three hits *Bismarck* had suffered, only the one in the bow was a cause

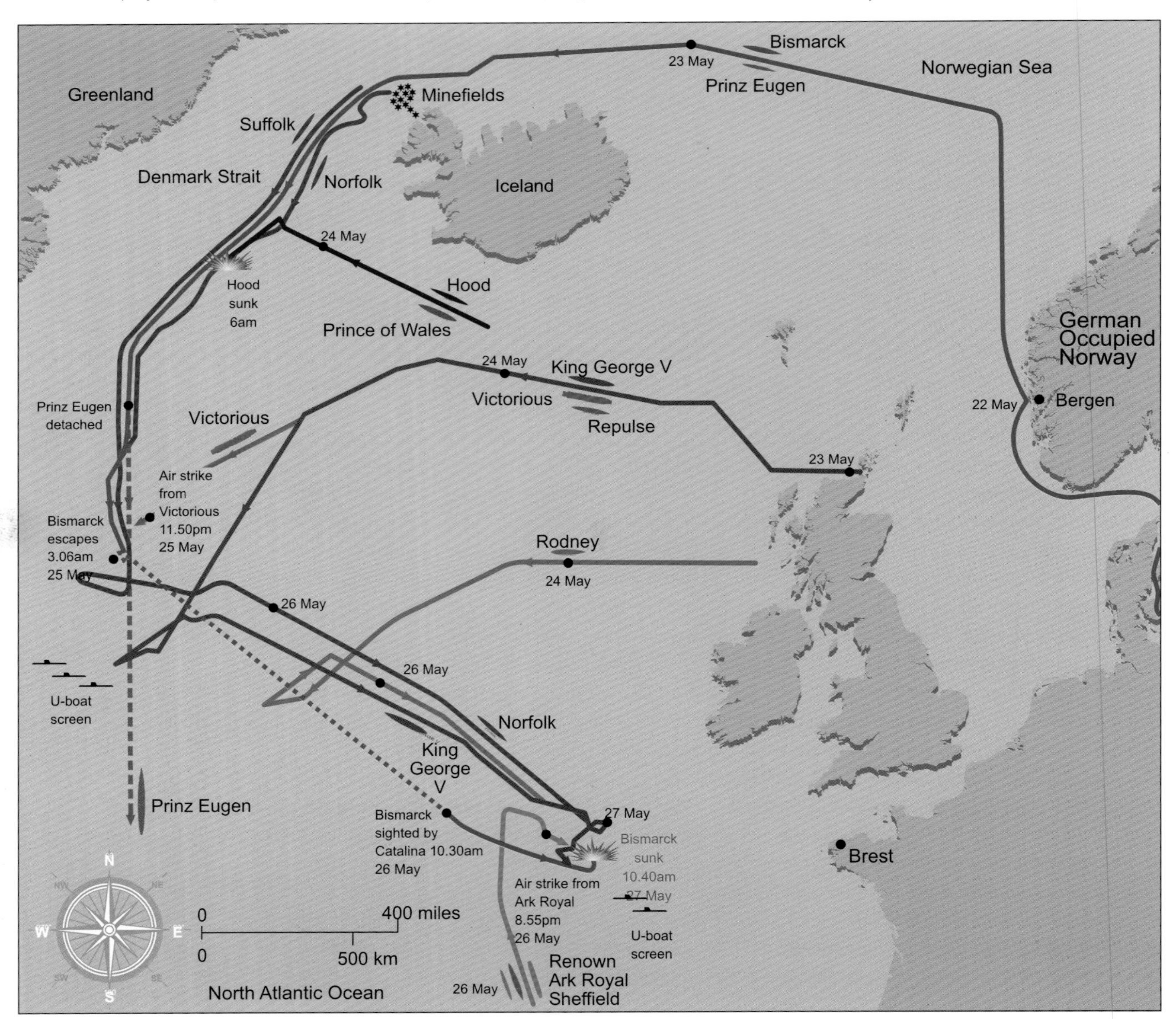

BELOW Operation *Rheinübung* – pursuit. *(Roy Scorer)*

LEFT ***Bismarck*** **photographed from** ***Prinz Eugen*** **shortly after the Battle of the Denmark Strait. She is riding visibly low in the water at the bow – the result of a hit scored by a 14in shell from** ***Prince of Wales*** **which ruptured a fuel tank and caused flooding in her bow compartments.**

for concern. The forecastle was flooded, the bow was riding 3° lower in the water than usual, and there was a 9° list to port. Maximum speed was now reduced to 28 knots. Lindemann flooded empty tanks in the stern to balance the ship. No. 2 boiler room was shut down when damage control parties failed to stem the flooding there. Worst of all, a combination of the fuel leak and the severing of fuel links with the bow tanks meant that the battleship had her fuel stocks reduced by approximately 1,000 tons. Lindemann recommended returning to Bergen, but Lütjens refused to countenance the idea. Instead he decided to head for Saint-Nazaire, on the French Atlantic coast.

Just after 08:00 Lütjens sent a signal directly to Berlin, stating his intention 'To proceed to St. Nazaire. Prinz Eugen cruiser warfare.' In other words, he planned to detach Brinkmann's heavy cruiser, so it could continue hunting enemy convoys. Meanwhile, *Bismarck* would head towards Saint-Nazaire alone. The French port was approximately 1,600 nautical miles away – the equivalent of 70 hours at 24 knots. That meant that given the additional time needed to shake off her pursuers, *Bismarck* could probably reach the safety of the port by the early morning of Tuesday 27 May. Even if she was delayed, by then she would at least be within range of sufficient Luftwaffe air cover to deter any British pursuit.

As the two German ships ran southwards on a heading of 220°, the damaged *Prince of Wales* joined Wake-Walker's two heavy cruisers, and together they shadowed the Germans from a safe distance, approximately 15 miles astern of *Bismarck*. However, a sea mist had returned and contact could only be maintained by radar. Behind them the destroyer *Electra* picked up three survivors from *Hood*, and took them to Hvalfjordur. *Norfolk* sent regular updates to Vice Admiral Tovey, who was moving in from the north-east to intercept the Germans. British dispositions were altered.

BELOW **HMS** ***Victorious*** **was an Illustrious class fleet aircraft carrier, which entered service on 14 May 1941, just weeks before she was called upon to launch an air strike against** ***Bismarck*****. Although she was capable of carrying 36 aircraft, during the operation she only had a single squadron of antiquated Swordfish torpedo bombers embarked, crewed by inexperienced trainee pilots.**

RIGHT The capital ships of Vice Admiral Tovey's Home Fleet are pictured in the North Atlantic during their attempt to intercept *Bismarck*. The photograph was taken from the quarterdeck of the flagship *King George V*, while astern of her are the battlecruiser *Repulse* and the aircraft carrier *Victorious*.

The three light cruisers east of Iceland were moved to the Denmark Strait, in case the German ships slipped back the way they had come. That morning the battleship *Rodney* and three destroyers were detached from a convoy, and sent eastwards to join the chase. So too was the elderly battleship *Ramillies*, while the battlecruiser *Renown* in Halifax, Nova Scotia, was ordered to sea to help protect the two convoys left unscreened by this redeployment. The cruisers *Edinburgh* and *Gloucester* were ordered to assist Tovey, while Vice Admiral Somerville's Force H based in Gibraltar, was placed on alert, ready to intercept *Bismarck* if the need arose. His force consisted of the aircraft carrier *Ark Royal*, the battlecruiser *Renown* and the light cruiser *Sheffield*.

RIGHT Vice Admiral Sir John Tovey (1885–1971) commanded the British Home Fleet, and was the man responsible for bringing *Bismarck* to bay. A veteran of the Battle of Jutland in 1916, Tovey was a thorough professional, and was well respected by his men. His performance during the hunt for the *Bismarck* was exemplary as he directed his scattered forces in pursuit of the German battleship.

By 14:40 Tovey realised that it was unlikely that he was going to intercept *Bismarck*, so he sent the faster aircraft carrier *Victorious* on ahead of the rest of his force, hoping it could get close enough to *Bismarck* to launch an air strike. Given the very limited range and performance of the Fairey Swordfish, that meant closing to within 80 nautical miles. To the south-west, Lütjens signalled Captain Brinkmann that he planned to detach his cruiser. The signal read: '*Bismarck* will turn away on a westerly course during rain squalls. *Prinz Eugen* to maintain course and speed unless forced to turn away, or three hours after *Bismarck* has turned. Thereafter, release to refuel from *Belchen* or *Lothringen*, then conduct independent cruiser warfare. Execute on signal 'Hood.' By then he had already changed course to 180° – due south.

At 18:39, Lütjens set his plan in motion. After making the signal 'Hood' *Bismarck* suddenly turned through 180°, taking the British by surprise, and emerging from a fog bank just 9 miles from *Suffolk*. *Bismarck* opened fire, forcing the cruiser to turn away. *Prince of Wales* and *Norfolk* fired in support, but *Bismarck* disengaged. *Suffolk* had the best radar of the three British ships, and this distraction meant Brinkmann was given the chance he needed. *Prinz Eugen* increased speed and again escaped unnoticed. Three hours later he turned to circle around the British ships, and again escaped undetected. It was a brilliantly executed manoeuvre, and as dusk grew closer, *Bismarck* sailed on alone into the gathering darkness.

RIGHT A Fairey Swordfish torpedo bomber of the kind flown by the Fleet Air Arm crews from *Victorious* and *Ark Royal*. This lumbering biplane had a top speed of 124 knots, making it much slower than most contemporary torpedo-carrying aircraft. They had a range of 455 nautical miles, and could remain in the air for 5½ hours.

Lütjens reported the successful detaching of *Prinz Eugen* at 19:14. Shortly before 21:00 he sent another signal to Paris, stating his intention to head directly to Saint-Nazaire, due to a shortage of fuel. Unknown to him, 120 miles away Captain Bovell of *Victorious* was almost within range of an airstrike. This was a dangerous business, as for the most part the aircrews were completely inexperienced, the sea conditions were bad, which made launching and recovery fraught, and the strike had to be carried out in the dark. At 22:10 nine Swordfish

RIGHT The British aircraft carrier *Ark Royal* formed the key element of Vice Admiral Somerville's Force H, which was based in Gibraltar. She was designed to carry 60 aircraft with a mixture of Albacore fighters and Swordfish torpedo bombers. Although these were all obsolete biplanes, on the afternoon of 26 May 1941 they were all the Royal Navy had to prevent the *Bismarck* from reaching Brest.

LEFT *Bismarck* pictured during her run to the south after the Battle of the Denmark Strait on 23 May 1941. This blurred photograph, taken in rolling seas from the quarterdeck of *Prinz Eugen*, was the last picture taken of the battleship from the German cruiser.

RIGHT **After the sinking of the *Bismarck*, Flying Officer Dennis Briggs from RAF Coastal Command described his sighting of *Bismarck* during a radio interview for the BBC. He told how his co-pilot Ensign Smith spotted something through the clouds, and how they dropped down to 2,000ft to take a closer look. As they radioed in the sighting report, *Bismarck* opened fire on them, forcing them to break contact.**

torpedo bombers took off from *Victorious*, and led by Lieutenant Commander Esmonde, they headed off in the direction of *Bismarck*. Actually they were vectored towards Wake-Walker's ships, who directed them towards *Bismarck*, which was 14 miles to the south.

The attack that followed was watched by the neutral crew of the US Coastguard cutter *Modoc*, which the Swordfish flew over on their way to the target. One of the biplanes became lost in the clouds and fog, but at 23:33 the remaining eight aircraft began their assault, attacking from the north-east before splitting to run at the ship from either beam. *Bismarck* began to zigzag, and her anti-aircraft guns sent up a wall of flak. With a top speed of around 80 knots when carrying a torpedo, a Swordfish attack called for steady nerves when faced by such a barrage. This, though, worked to the aircrews' advantage, as most of the flak burst ahead of them, their low speed confusing the German gunners. Then the *Bismarck*'s main guns joined in, firing at a low elevation (-8°), so that huge shell splashes erupted in front of the British biplanes.

Amazingly just one Swordfish was hit, but it survived the attack and limped back to *Victorious*. One of the 18in torpedoes struck the *Bismarck*, hitting the battleship on her starboard side, but causing no significant damage, despite killing one sailor and injuring six more. This fatality – Oberbootsman Kirchberg – was *Bismarck*'s first casualty. However, the manoeuvring to avoid the torpedoes had ripped off the matting used to cover the hole in *Bismarck*'s forecastle. Flooding began anew, and amidships the water in No. 2 boiler room caused it to be

RIGHT **Vice Admiral Somerville's Force H at sea. In the foreground is Somerville's flagship HMS *Renown*, with HMS *Ark Royal* on her starboard beam. In the distance is the light cruiser HMS *Sheffield*. While the battlecruiser *Renown* lacked the firepower needed to stop *Bismarck*, *Sheffield*'s radar was powerful enough to track the German battleship, and would help direct *Ark Royal*'s aircraft towards her during their crucial air strike.**

RIGHT On the morning of 26 May, Flying Officer Dennis Briggs of Coastal Command and his US Navy co-pilot located the *Bismarck*, which opened fire on their Catalina flying boat. This sighting gave the British a slim chance to intercept the German battleship before she reached the safety of Brest.

temporarily shut down. For an hour speed was reduced to 16 knots, but by 01:00 *Bismarck* had picked up speed again, and was making 20 knots. All of the aircraft managed to land back on *Victorious*, although a Fulmar fighter sent up to relay signals was forced to ditch in the sea and her two-man crew were lost. The other aircrews from *Victorious* must have considered themselves fortunate to have survived.

At 01:30 *Prince of Wales* closed to within 10 miles and briefly engaged *Bismarck*, just to keep up the pressure. Then the British battleship fell back, and she and her two accompanying cruisers began zigzagging, as they were warned that U-boats were operating in the area. This gave Lütjens the opportunity he was looking for. At 03:00, *Suffolk* was completing a zigzag leg to port, when *Bismarck* suddenly increased speed to 27 knots, and turned away to starboard. At 03:06 radar contact was lost as *Bismarck* escaped to the west. Expecting the British to fan out in pursuit, he then looped around to the north, and finally turned to the north-east. He crossed the path of the British ships 20 miles astern of them, before settling on to a new course of 130°. The British had now completely lost contact with *Bismarck*, which was now free to head towards the French coast.

At dawn on Sunday 25 May aircraft from *Victorious* conducted a widespread aerial

RIGHT The flight deck of HMS *Ark Royal* during pre-war flying operations. It took time to launch 15 or so Swordfish biplanes and to form them up in formation. This meant that on 26 May 1941, after the aircraft returned from their abortive first attack and after rearming and refuelling their planes, there was just enough time to launch one more hastily planned airstrike before nightfall.

LEFT After her rudder was damaged by the torpedo launched from the Swordfish, *Bismarck* steered an extremely erratic course. Captain Lindemann did what he could to compensate for this by using his engines, but as this aerial photograph shows, he was unable to steer a straight course. This picture was taken soon after dawn on 27 May 1941.

search, while British surface ships joined in using their radar. It seemed as though *Bismarck* had vanished. For almost 24 hours the British had no clear idea where she might be. Tensions were high as both Tovey and the Admiralty tried to outguess Lütjens. If damage had been sustained, she could well head to Saint-Nazaire – the only French port with a dock large enough to house *Bismarck*. Otherwise she could be anywhere in the North Atlantic. That was when Lütjens made his first serious mistake. At 09:30 he broke radio silence and sent a lengthy situation report to Group North and to Berlin, outlining his damage. This signal was detected by the British, who worked out that *Bismarck* was now to the south-east of Tovey's flagship. Unconcerned by all this, Captain Lindemann ordered his crew to erect a fake funnel, to confuse enemy reconnaissance aircraft.

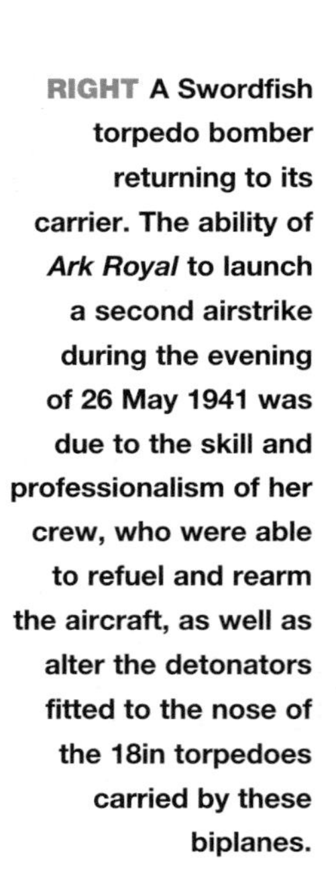

RIGHT A Swordfish torpedo bomber returning to its carrier. The ability of *Ark Royal* to launch a second airstrike during the evening of 26 May 1941 was due to the skill and professionalism of her crew, who were able to refuel and rearm the aircraft, as well as alter the detonators fitted to the nose of the 18in torpedoes carried by these biplanes.

Staff in the British Admiralty could see just how desperate the situation now was. Tovey was too far to the west, and unlikely to intercept *Bismarck*. Wake-Walker's cruisers had returned to Iceland to refuel, and both *Victorious* and *Prince of Wales* were about to do the same. Force H had been ordered northwards from Gibraltar early that morning, while *Rodney* was approaching Tovey from the west, as was the light cruiser *Edinburgh*. A heavy cruiser, *Dorsetshire*, was steaming up from the south-west. There were seven transatlantic convoys at sea, and where possible these were diverted away from this vast naval arena. What had begun as a search had now turned into a pursuit, even though *Bismarck* still remained undetected as night fell.

This changed at 10:30 on Monday 26 May. Earlier that morning two Catalina PBY flying boats had taken off from Loch Erne in Northern Ireland, to join in the search. At 10:25 Flying Officer Briggs and his US co-pilot Ensign Smith spotted a warship and closed in to take a clearer look. When it opened fire they identified her as *Bismarck*. They radioed in a sighting report – *Bismarck* had been spotted. At the time she was steaming at 20 knots to conserve fuel,

ABOVE The British light cruiser HMS *Sheffield* was armed with twelve 6in guns as well as torpedoes, and while this was a useful enough armament for many naval missions, engaging a modern battleship was not one of them. However, she carried a powerful radar suite, and therefore was able to shadow *Bismarck* during 26 May, broadcasting reports of her course, heading and speed.

RIGHT Each Fairey Swordfish carried a single 18in Mark XII torpedo. Produced in 1937, these torpedoes weighed 702kg (1,548lb), and had a range of 1,370m (1,500yd) at a speed of 40 knots. Their warhead consisted of 176kg (388lb) of TNT.

BELOW **HMS *Rodney* was an ungainly looking warship, thanks to her high citadel superstructure and the grouping of her three triple turrets in front of it. Only 'B' turret was superimposed – 'A' and 'C' turrets were not, which meant 'C' turret could only fire at targets on the battleship's beam. This is why *Rodney*'s captain was sure to steer a course which 'cleared his arcs', allowing all of his guns to bear on *Bismarck*.**

on a course of 130°. In the Admiralty it was quickly realised that Tovey would be unable to intercept *Bismarck* unless she could be slowed down. To the north, a flotilla of five destroyers commanded by Captain Vian was also out of range. Only Force H was in a position to intercept, being 150 miles to the east of *Bismarck*. However, Somerville's flagship *Renown* was too badly outgunned to consider sending her into battle against *Bismarck*. That left the fragile Swordfish torpedo bombers embarked on the carrier *Ark Royal*.

Somerville turned *Renown* on to a parallel course to *Bismarck*, 120 miles to the north. He sent *Sheffield* in nearer to pick *Bismarck* up on radar, and ordered *Ark Royal* to close with the German battleship, and to launch an airstrike. Shortly before 15:00, 15 Swordfish took off from *Ark Royal*, under the command of Lieutenant Commander Stewart-Moore. At 16:10 the aircraft spotted a warship, and dived in to attack it. Unfortunately they were attacking *Sheffield* rather than *Bismarck* – a mistake that was only realised after the first wave had launched their attack. Fortunately no hits were scored, and the shamefaced aircrews returned to *Ark Royal*. There the planes were refuelled and rearmed. However, there was only time for one more strike before nightfall. At 19:10 the aircraft took off again. *Bismarck* was 100 miles to the south-east, and so it was 20:40 before the target was sighted. This time it really was *Bismarck*, which opened up a heavy barrage of flak.

Once again the aircraft split up to strike the battleship from both port and starboard. The first wave of five aircraft attacked at 20:47. One torpedo hit was scored on the port side, but no serious damage was caused and the aircraft all escaped unscathed. All five torpedoes launched by the second flight also missed. That left the final flight of five aircraft, which, as before, divided their attack – three aircraft attacking from port and two from starboard. Four torpedoes missed, but the final one struck the battleship in the stern on her starboard side, just forward of her rudder. *Bismarck* had been weaving to avoid torpedoes throughout these attacks, and when the torpedo struck her rudder was turned 15° to port. The explosion jammed the

LEFT **Vice Admiral Tovey's flagship *King George V* was a sister ship of *Prince of Wales*, and therefore she carried ten 14in guns. While these guns were of slightly smaller calibre than those carried by *Bismarck*, there were more of them, and the British battleship was fitted with a modern array of fire-control equipment and radar. This made her a powerful adversary.**

rudder and flooded the steering compartment.

The aircraft flew off – amazingly none of them had been shot down – while on *Bismarck* the damage-control teams worked to free the rudder. Meanwhile, the battleship kept turning slowly to port. Captain Lindemann tried to counteract the turn using his engines, but this was only partially successful. When the aircrews returned to *Ark Royal* they felt they had failed, until *Sheffield* reported the *Bismarck* was circling to port. The torpedo had managed to hit the *Bismarck*'s Achilles heel. If the battleship had not been turning, the torpedo would have glanced off her armoured belt and caused minimal damage. Instead, it hit what was probably *Bismarck*'s one vulnerable spot. Until that last torpedo hit, *Bismarck* was heading towards Saint-Nazaire, and no British warship was in a position to stop her. Now she was helpless and the Home Fleet were closing in.

RIGHT **While the aircrews from *Victorious* had an unsuccessful baptism of fire against *Bismarck*, they saw further action in the Mediterranean, where *Victorious* played her part in the vicious convoy battles fought during the relief of Malta. This shows her in action during Operation *Pedestal* (1942). She also saw service in the Arctic and the Pacific, and enjoyed a long post-war career. *Victorious* was finally retired from service in 1968.**

The night battle

Tovey was closing in from the north with the battleships *King George V* and *Rodney*, as well as the heavy cruisers *Norfolk* and *Dorsetshire*. He decided to avoid a night battle, and instead chose to engage *Bismarck* after dawn. He estimated that even by making his approach at an economical speed, his battleships would have to break off the action by 10:00, in order to make it back to Scapa Flow before they ran out of fuel. To keep the Germans occupied during the night he decided to send in Captain Vian's 4th Destroyer Flotilla to launch hit-and-run attacks against *Bismarck* under cover of darkness.

At 22:38 Vian's five destroyers – *Cossack* (flagship), *Maori*, *Zulu*, *Sikh* and the Polish *Piorun* approached *Bismarck* from either beam, and from astern. Once *Bismarck* opened fire they withdrew, only to return 45 minutes later, this time launching a torpedo attack which was aborted due to *Bismarck*'s accurate gunnery. Then Vian gave his commanders permission to attack on their own initiative. *Zulu* made a run at 01:20, but her torpedo attack was aborted owing to bad visibility. *Cossack*, *Maori* and *Sikh* then made torpedo runs, and two destroyers later claimed one hit each, but in fact no

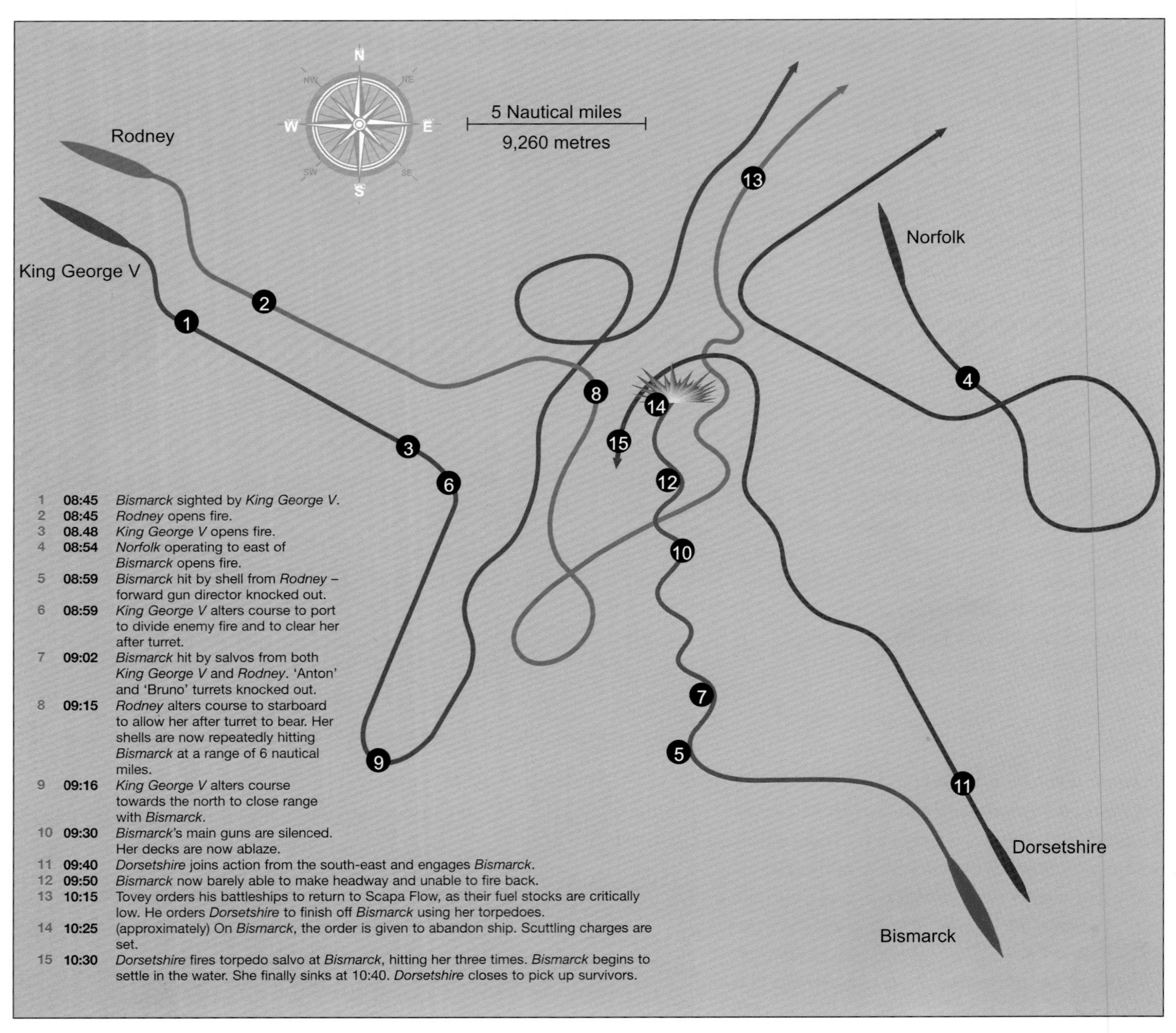

BELOW *Bismarck*'s final battle. *(Roy Scorer)*

ABOVE HMS *Maori* (F-24) took part in the nocturnal attacks on *Bismarck* during the night of 26/27 May 1941. She carried four 21in torpedoes and fired them all at the target, but scored no hits. She was lucky to survive the engagement, as her captain reported that *Bismarck*'s fire was both extremely heavy and very accurate.

BELOW Captain Philip Vian (1894–1968) commanded the destroyers that attacked *Bismarck* during the night of 26/27 May 1941. He was an excellent commander of destroyers, and he made skilled use of his force that evening, denying the *Bismarck*'s crew any rest before their final battle.

torpedoes struck their target. This claim was probably made because *Bismarck* stopped in the water at 01:48, and remained there for an hour as damage-control teams tried to free her rudder. The destroyers shadowed the battleship for most of the night, forcing the weary Germans to remain at their battle stations.

On board *Bismarck* all attempts at repairing the rudder were unsuccessful. It was now clear that *Bismarck* was doomed. Plans to fly an Arado float plane to France with the ship's logs and the crews' last letters were foiled due to the poor weather. They were still 500 miles from Saint-Nazaire, but Group West promised tugs and fuel as well as air cover, even though these would never reach *Bismarck* in time. Just before midnight Lütjens radioed Group West, informing them of the damage, and just before 03:00 he sent a final message to Hitler. It read: 'We fight to the last in our belief in you, my Führer, and in the firm faith of Germany's victory.' The reply was: 'All of Germany is with you.' By now it was clear to everyone on board that they were on their own, the enemy was closing in, and this would be a fight to the death.

Götterdämmerung

Dawn on Tuesday 27 May unveiled a grey, leaden sky and a lumpy sea, with strong Force 8 winds. Visibility was good, though, and so at 07:53 *Norfolk* spotted *Bismarck* away to the south-east, at a range of 16 miles. The sighting was relayed to Tovey on *King George V*, and at 08:45 the two British battleships spotted their prey. *Bismarck* was 12½ miles away, heading in a roughly northern direction, making

THE FATE OF *BISMARCK*'S SURVIVORS

After *Bismarck* sank, the heavy cruiser *Dorsetshire* rescued 86 survivors from the water, before the rescue was abandoned following the mistaken sighting of what might have been a U-boat. Rope ladders, heaving lines and scrambling nets had been lowered, and British sailors helped the German sailors as best they could. However, many had been burned or injured and the oil-coated men found it difficult to grip the ropes. When *Devonshire* steamed away, hundreds more survivors were left behind. The destroyer *Maori* picked up another 25 of these, bringing the total of survivors rescued by the British to 111. One of these, Maschinengefreiter Lüttich, later died of his wounds on board *Dorsetshire*. He had lost an arm during the final battle and was severely burned. On 29 May he was buried at sea. Later, *U-74* surfaced amid the floating debris and rescued three more survivors, who were floating in a rubber dinghy. That evening the weather trawler *Sachsenwald* rescued two more men from a rubber raft. They were taken on board and eventually, like their comrades on *U-74*, they made it back to Germany.

Of the 110 *Bismarck* survivors rescued by the Royal Navy all recall how they were treated well by their captors and were given the same good rations and cigarettes as the British sailors, as well as fresh clothing and medical attention.

The senior surviving officer from *Bismarck* was Korvettenkapitän von Müllenheim-Rechberg, who was given a whisky, before remonstrating with Captain Martin of the *Dorsetshire* for his abandonment of the search. Years later, in his memoirs, Müllenheim-Rechberg admitted that Martin had no choice but to act the way he did. After all, his priority was the safety of his own ship and men. On 30 May the *Dorsetshire* arrived in Newcastle, where the survivors were put ashore. *Maori* went on to Leith near Edinburgh, reaching there later the same day.

The survivors were now placed in the hands of the British Army, who treated them with less compassion than the British sailors. The survivors were transported by train to London, where they were held in a prison compound in Knightsbridge. From there they were moved to a larger camp in Cockfosters, in north London. Some of the survivors were questioned in the nearby Combined Services Interrogation Centre, and the results formed the core of a British intelligence report into the sinking, which also provided useful information on *Bismarck* herself. After that, the officer survivors were moved to a camp near Penrith. In the spring of 1942 the *Bismarck* survivors were reunited and shipped across the Atlantic to Canada. There they sat out the war until their repatriation to Germany in 1946.

BELOW This German painting by Claus Bergen, entitled *Wreath in the North Sea*, was painted in 1936 to represent a wreath laid from a German U-boat over the site of the Battle of Jutland, two decades after the battle took place. However, it perfectly encapsulates the nature of maritime commemoration, where nothing remains to mark the spot where a ship and her crew were lost.

ABOVE **HMS *Rodney* pictured in action against *Bismarck* during the German battleship's last battle. Fire from her powerful armament of nine 16in guns was well directed, and after 12 minutes she scored her first hit on *Bismarck*. Many more would follow as *Rodney* and *King George V* went on to silence *Bismarck*'s guns. An original painting by Paul Wright.**

10 knots. *Rodney* altered course slightly to increase the distance between the two British battleships and at 08:47 she opened fire with her nine 16in guns. The salvo fell short. *Bismarck* turned using her engines so all her guns could bear on *Rodney*, and a minute later she replied – her first salvo. At 08:48 *King George V* opened fire, and 6 minutes later *Norfolk* joined in. *Bismarck* was surrounded by shell splashes, which slightly reduced the effectiveness of the British gunnery. Still, the range was decreasing steadily, and at 08:59 a 16in shell from *Rodney* knocked out *Bismarck*'s main gun director. This was to be the first of many damaging hits on the German battleship as the British warships found their range.

At the same moment *King George V* altered course to starboard, allowing her after turret to open fire. Mechanical problems plagued 'Y' turret throughout the battle, reducing the power of the battleship's broadside. At 09:02 a 16in shell struck *Bismarck*'s 'Bruno' turret, putting it out of action and temporarily silencing 'Anton' turret. That meant *Bismarck* could only fire back with her two after turrets. Fires had broken out on *Bismarck*'s upper deck, and the battleship was now wreathed in smoke. Still, she was fighting back, and her after turrets engaged Tovey's flagship and then *Rodney* using their own after director. Then at 09:15 a 14in shell from *King George V* put this last director out of action, which meant that *Bismarck*'s after turrets could only be fired under local control. Both *Rodney* and *King George V* had altered

RIGHT **This is one of a small collection of photographs shot during *Bismarck*'s final battle. This picture was taken from the heavy cruiser *Dorsetshire* at around 10:05, and features the battleship *Rodney* in the middle distance. *Bismarck* is largely obscured under a pall of smoke.**

ABOVE Royal Navy gunners pictured at their stations inside one of *Rodney*'s three triple turrets. This photograph was clearly not taken at action stations, as none of the gunners are wearing anti-flash protection hoods. While the loading process was largely automated, these gunners were on hand to make sure the hydraulic system operated smoothly.

course again to ensure all their guns had a clear line of fire. *Rodney* was now just 6 miles from her target, a range that made it difficult to miss the stricken battleship.

At 09:21 'Dora' turret was silenced when a shell exploded inside her right gun barrel. Five minutes later *Bismarck*'s final main turret was silenced when 'Caesar' turret was hit. The crew of 'Anton' turret had worked feverishly to bring their guns back into action, and a minute later at 09:27 *Bismarck*'s forward turret opened fire again. She managed three salvos before the turret was finally knocked out at 09:30. A few secondary guns were still firing under local control, but by now *Bismarck* was ablaze from stem to stern, and she was being battered by a ceaseless barrage of shells. Observers reported that the battleship seemed to be lit by an orange glow. At 09:40 the heavy cruiser *Dorsetshire* joined in, adding the weight of her 8in shells to the devastation.

However, *Bismarck* was still afloat. While her superstructure was now badly battered – and on fire – her thick belt armour protected her lower hull, and watertight integrity was maintained. By 09:45 *Bismarck* was still moving but barely making headway, still facing roughly towards the north. Rodney was now just 2 miles off her port bow, while *King George V* was 6 miles off her port beam. *Norfolk* and *Dorsetshire* lay off the battleship's starboard beam. It was becoming clear that *Bismarck* was not going to sink through gunnery hits alone. Tovey realised that his two battleships were reaching the point where they had to break off, or risk running out of fuel before reaching Scapa. This meant *Bismarck* had to be sunk within the next few minutes. At 09:56 *Rodney* fired a torpedo at *Bismarck*, and scored a hit, just to add to the battleship's woes. Still she remained afloat.

Finally, at 10:15, Tovey ordered his battleships to break off the action. He would use *Dorsetshire* to finish off *Bismarck* with torpedoes as *Norfolk* had already expended all of hers. As the rest of the fleet disengaged, *Dorsetshire* moved in for the kill. There is some controversy over what happened next. At 10:30 the cruiser fired two torpedoes at *Bismarck*. However, 15 minutes earlier, the order to abandon ship had already been given on *Bismarck*. Both Lütjens and Lindemann had been killed during the battle, so the order was given by the battleship's first officer, Commander Oels. His fear was that what remained of *Bismarck* would be captured by

BELOW This photograph is probably the last one ever taken of *Bismarck*. The photographer on board *Dorsetshire* recorded the moment when the German battleship began to sink, shortly after the cruiser had fired a spread of torpedoes at her. The location of *Bismarck* is marked by a plume of smoke, and small-calibre shell splashes, presumably fired from the two circling British cruisers.

the British, so a simultaneous order was given to scuttle the ship. Explosive scuttling charges had already been rigged, with 9-minute fuses. Bulkhead doors were left open to ensure maximum damage, while sea cocks and flooding valves were also opened.

At that point Oels was killed by an explosion, possibly triggered by one of *Dorsetshire*'s torpedoes. The British cruiser fired a third torpedo at 10:36, which hit her port side. A minute later *Bismarck* began listing heavily to port, until the water reached her upper deck. At 10:36 she finally rolled over and capsized. She began to sink. Many of her crew in the water were pulled under as she sank, while hundreds of others were still trapped inside her hull. At 10:40 the *Bismarck* – pride of the German nation – finally slipped beneath the waves. All that remained of her was a sea filled with debris and a huge slick of oil. Hundreds of men remained in the oil-covered water, and *Dorsetshire* edged in to pick up survivors, accompanied by the destroyer *Maori*.

Survivors were hauled from the water, or scrambled up the boarding nets rigged over the cruiser's side. At that moment a lookout spotted what he thought was a periscope in the water. Captain Martin of *Dorsetshire* knew that U-boats were racing to *Bismarck*'s aid, and he felt his duty to his own men outweighed any humanitarian duty to *Bismarck*'s survivors. With this in mind, he gave orders to get under way again and, accompanied by *Maori*, they departed. In all, the two British ships rescued 111 men from the water that morning, although one man soon died of his wounds. Unfortunately hundreds more were left to their fate. Over the next 24 hours five more men were rescued by *U-74* and the German weather ship *Sachsenwald*, which meant that 115 men of *Bismarck*'s 2,200-strong crew survived the sinking. *Hood* had been avenged and British naval supremacy had been restored, but the human cost of Operation *Rheinübung* had been high on both sides. The most moving epitaph for *Bismarck* was delivered by her nemesis, Vice Admiral Tovey. He wrote: 'The *Bismarck* had put up a most gallant fight against impossible odds, worthy of the old days of the Imperial German Navy, and she went down with her colours flying.'

THE DIARY OF A SURVIVOR

During the questioning of *Bismarck* survivors in the camp in Cockfosters, one survivor produced a diary of events, covering the sortie of *Bismarck* into the Atlantic. This account was published in the classified report entitled *German Battleship Bismarck: Interrogation of Survivors*, produced by the British Government in August 1941. The diary was written by 25-year-old Maschinenmaat (Mechanician 2nd Class) Wilhelm Gräf (1915–75). His post was in the after turbine room, and he abandoned ship when ordered, and was rescued by *Devonshire*. What is strange is that he mentions engagements that didn't happen, doesn't record the hits suffered by *Bismarck,* and muddles events. He was an engineer and had to rely on the word of others about what was happening 'topside'. This explains the numerous errors. Interestingly the last entry occurs just a few hours before the final attack by *Ark Royal*'s Swordfish, on the evening of 26 May. As Gräf was stationed aft, close to where the rudder damage occurred, then presumably he was too busy to continue writing his diary.

On **Monday 19 May 1941** we prepared for sea at 02:00, in the harbour of Gotenhafen, and proceeded at 27 knots on a westerly course.

At 09:30 The ship proceeded northward of Bornholm (Danish)

At 11:30 We proceeded from 9 to 12 knots into Kiel Bay. The following ships assembled: *Bismarck*, *Prinz Eugen*, two mine 'bumpers' [minesweepers], destroyers *Friedrich Eckholt* and *Hans Lody*. The squadron passed the lightship *Fehenarm Belt* at 21:00. From this point course was steered to the Great Belt.

On Tuesday morning, **20 May 1941**, the mine bumpers parted company and one destroyer from the 'Narvik Flotilla' joined up with us. Course was continued at 17 knots through the Kattegat to Skagen, three minesweepers ahead of us.

At 13:45 Three drifting mines were sunk by fire, and the alarm was given 'close watertight doors'. After this the minesweepers parted company and the three destroyers acted as screen for the *Bismarck* and *Prinz Eugen*.

At 20:30 Watches were set.

At 20:50 The squadron passed Kristiansand, three destroyers ahead, then *Bismarck* and *Prinz Eugen* in line ahead.

At 22:42 The last German minefield was passed, and British reconnaissance aircraft sighted in Bergen.

21 May 1941 Off Bergen on the Norwegian coast.

02:45–08:30 Clear for action.

At about 11:15 we enter a fjord to the southward of Bergen and anchored a distance of from 500 to 600 metres from the shore.

Alarm. Enemy aircraft from 13:30 to 13:45. The weather was perfectly fine so that we could lie on the forecastle in sports kit. The fjord is surrounded by rocks.

18:30 Prepared for sea again, and sailed at 19:45. One

ABOVE ***Bismarck*** **pictured lying at anchor in Norway's Grimstadfjord after her crew had begun the process of changing her camouflage scheme. The fake bow waves were retained, but after this picture was taken the stern waves were painted over, and the darker sections at the bow and stern were painted to match the mid-grey colour of the hull. The two supply ships were on hand to act as a shield, in case of an unexpected British aerial attack.**

hour later we were off the entrance to the Sogne Fjord. We dropped the pilot there and proceeded at 24 knots.

22 May 1941

03:00 The destroyers parted company. We proceeded on a northerly course, and at 07:00 we came in sight of Trondheim.

12:45 Submarine alarm. Proceeded the whole day at 24 knots. In the evening at 21:00 we were in 68° North, 2° West.

23 May 1941

01:00 Our course is 266°. Proceeded through the Denmark Strait between Iceland and Greenland.

04:00 Speed 27 knots. Ship's position 180 miles north-east of Iceland.

07:10 Position 68° North, 11° West.

10:30 Position 68° North, 15° 30' West.

12:00 The clock was put back one hour.

12:40 Course 250°, speed 24 knots.

19:00 Clear ship for action. One cruiser of the London class in sight. She proceeded on a parallel course at 24 knots. *Bismarck*

RIGHT Throughout 21 May 1941, as ***Bismarck*** **lay at anchor in the Grimstadfjord to the south of Bergen, German aircraft flew combat air patrols over the area to protect the battleship from both enemy reconnaissance raids and aerial attack. In this photograph an Me 110 can be seen banking over the fjord at low altitude.**

ABOVE ***Bismarck*** **begins her maiden voyage down the River Elbe towards the North Sea, 15 September 1940. Tugs accompanied her during her voyage downriver, and one of them collided with the battleship, but there was no serious damage done.**

Armoured protection

Upper belt	145mm (5.71in)
Main belt	320mm (12.6in)
Main turrets	130–360mm (5.12–14.17in)
Secondary turrets	20–120mm (0.79–4.72in)
Upper deck	50–80mm (1.99–3.15in)
Armoured deck	80–120mm (3.15–4.72in)
Conning tower	220–360mm (8.66–14.17in)
Torpedo bulkhead	45mm (1.77in)
Number of protected watertight compartments	17 out of 22 compartments
Maximum armour thickness	380mm (14.96in) – belt 110mm (4.33in) – deck
Protected length	170.7m (560ft) – 70 per cent of hull length
Weight of armour	19,082 metric tonnnes

Propulsion

Maximum speed	30.1 knots
Maximum speed (as designed)	28 knots
Propulsion system	Steam turbine
Turbines	3 Blohm & Voss geared steam turbines
Boilers	12 Wagner high-pressure boilers
Propellers	3 three-bladed 4.7m diameter (15ft 5in)
Rudders	2
Power output	150,170shp (steam horsepower)
Power output (as designed)	138,000shp
Maximum shaft revolutions	278 per minute
Range	9,280 nautical miles at 16 knots 8,525 nautical miles at 19 knots 6,640 nautical miles at 24 knots 4,500 nautical miles at 28 knots
Fuel oil capacity	7,400 metric tonnes

Armament

Main armament	8 × 38cm (14.96in) SK-C/34 L52 guns, in four twin turrets
Secondary armament	12 × 15cm (5.9in) SK-C/28 L55 guns in six twin turrets
Tertiary armament	16 × 10.5cm (4.1in) SK-C/33 L65 anti-aircraft guns in eight twin mounts
Light anti-aircraft protection	16 × 37mm (1.46in) SK-C/30 L83 flak guns in eight twin mounts 18 × 20mm MGC-38 L65 flak guns; ten in single mounts, eight in two quadruple mounts

Aircraft

Aircraft	4: 2 Arado Ar-196A-2 float planes 1 Arado Ar-196A-3 float plane 1 Arado Ar-196A-4 float plane
Catapults	2: Carried amidships – 16m (52.5ft) long, but extendable to 24m (78.7ft)

Sensors and fire-control equipment

Radar	3 × FuMG40G (gO) radars
Fire direction rangefinders	5 × 10.5m base rangefinders 1 × 7m base rangefinder 2 × 6.5m base rangefinders 4 × 4m Type SL-8 rangefinders 2 × 3m night rangefinders

Miscellaneous specifications

Searchlights	7
Cranes	4 (2 large, 2 small)
Boats	9 (3 motor yawls, 4 picket boats, 2 captain's boats)
Anchors	4 (3 bow, 1 stern)

Complement

Crew	2,200 during Operation *Rheinübung*

General arrangements
Plan view

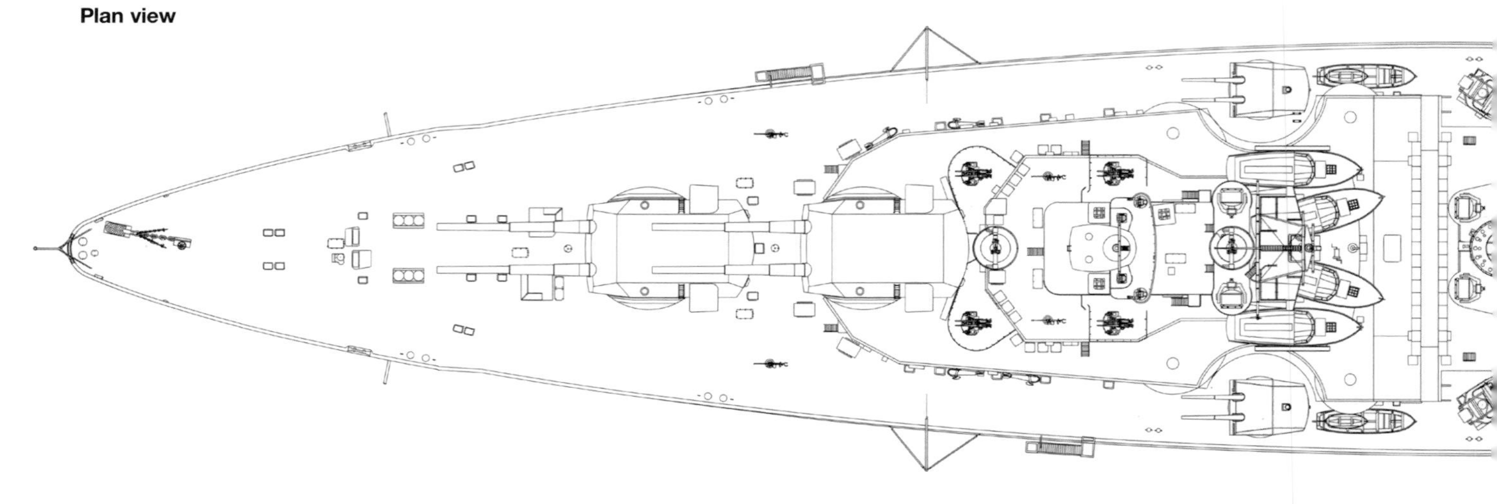

General arrangements
External profile starboard

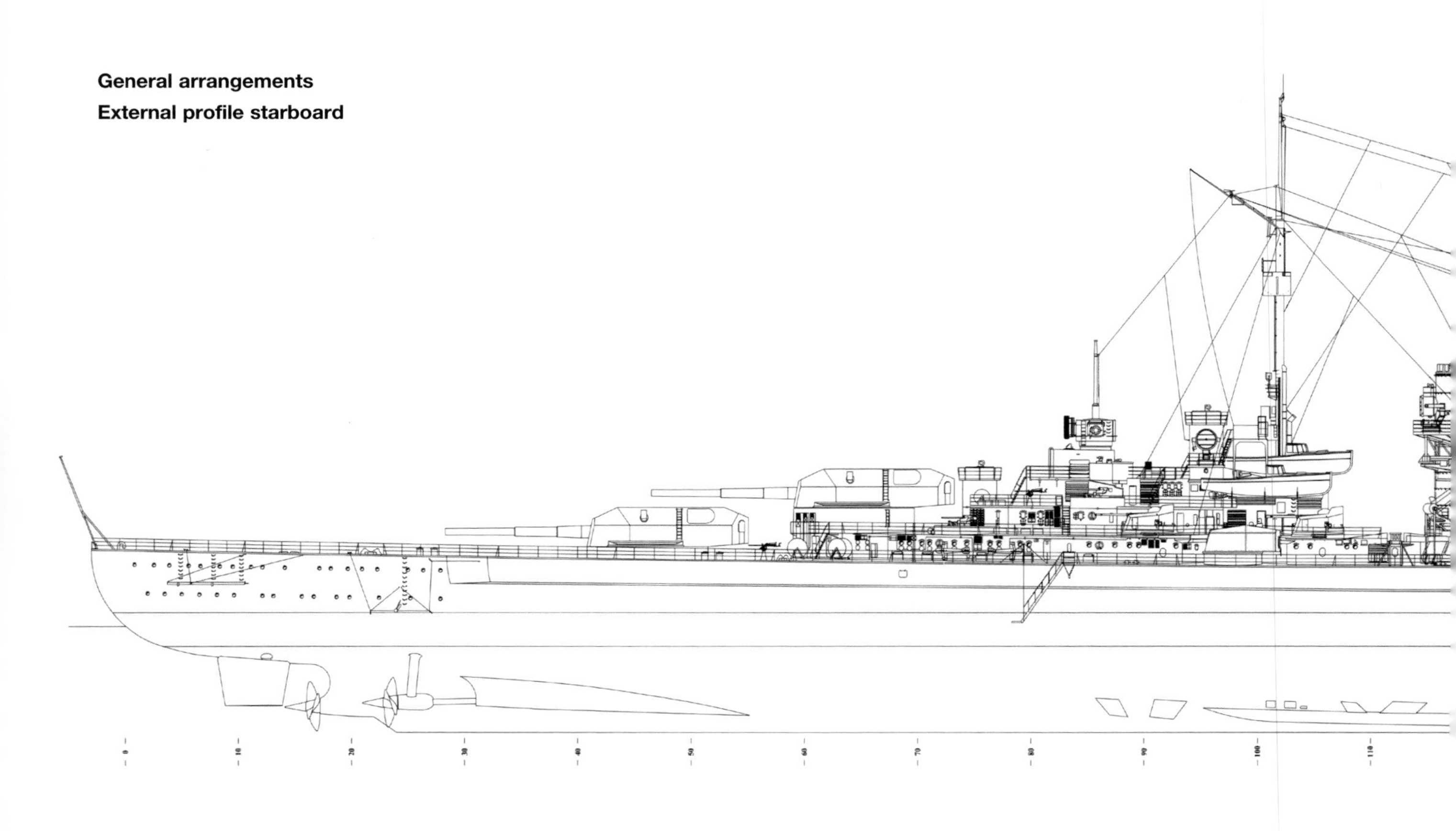

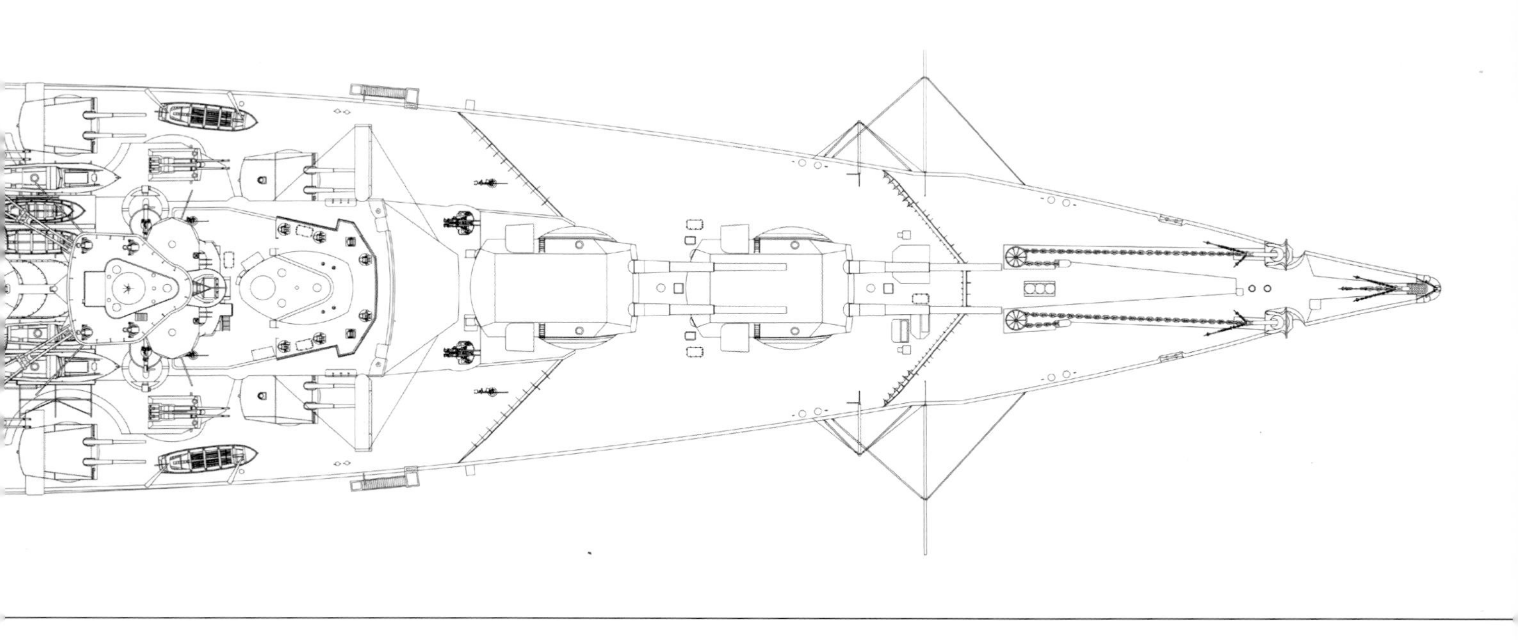

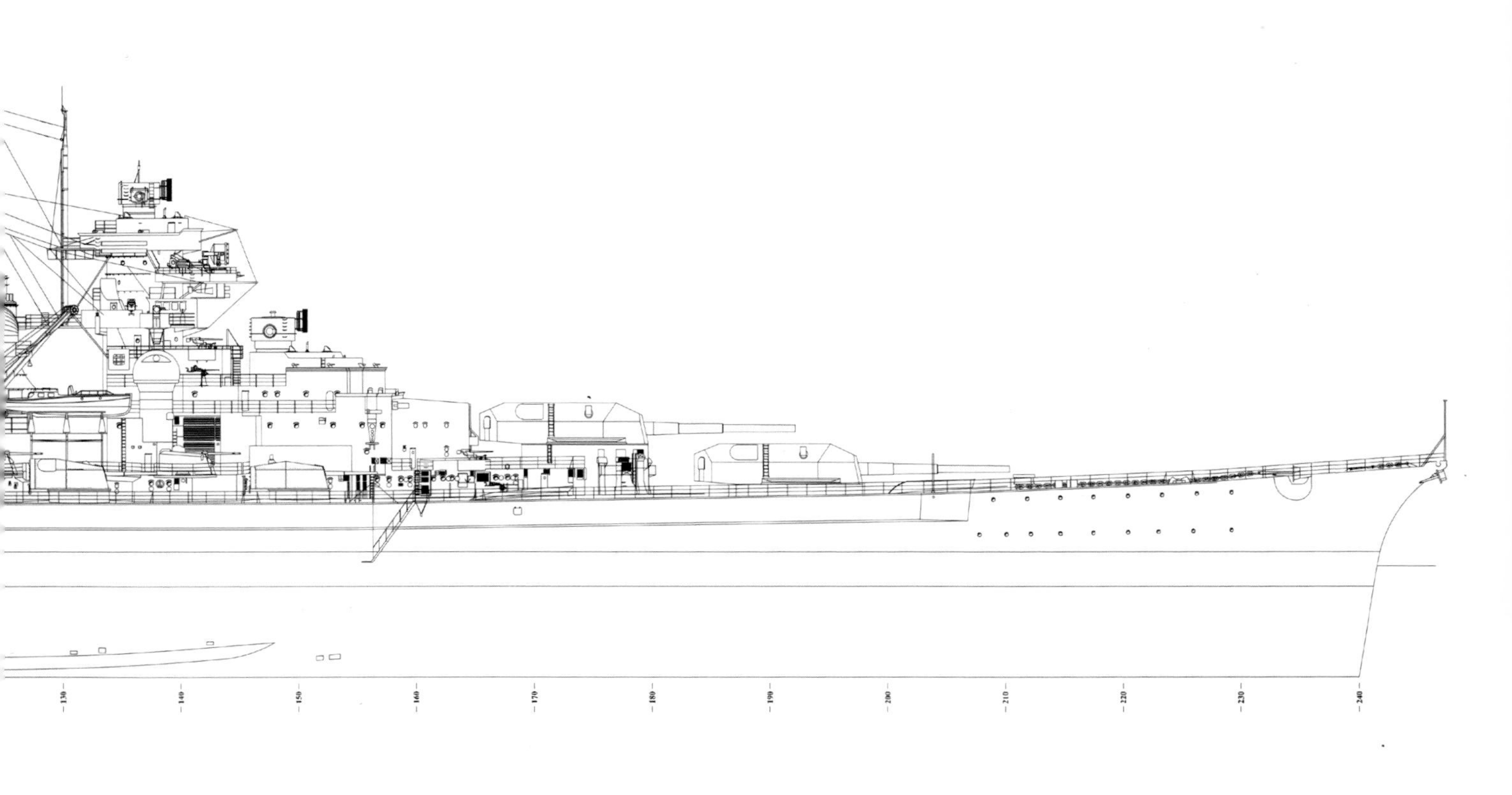
130
140
150
160
170
180
190
200
210
220
230
240

General arrangements

Bow

(© Conway/Bloomsbury Publishing Plc)

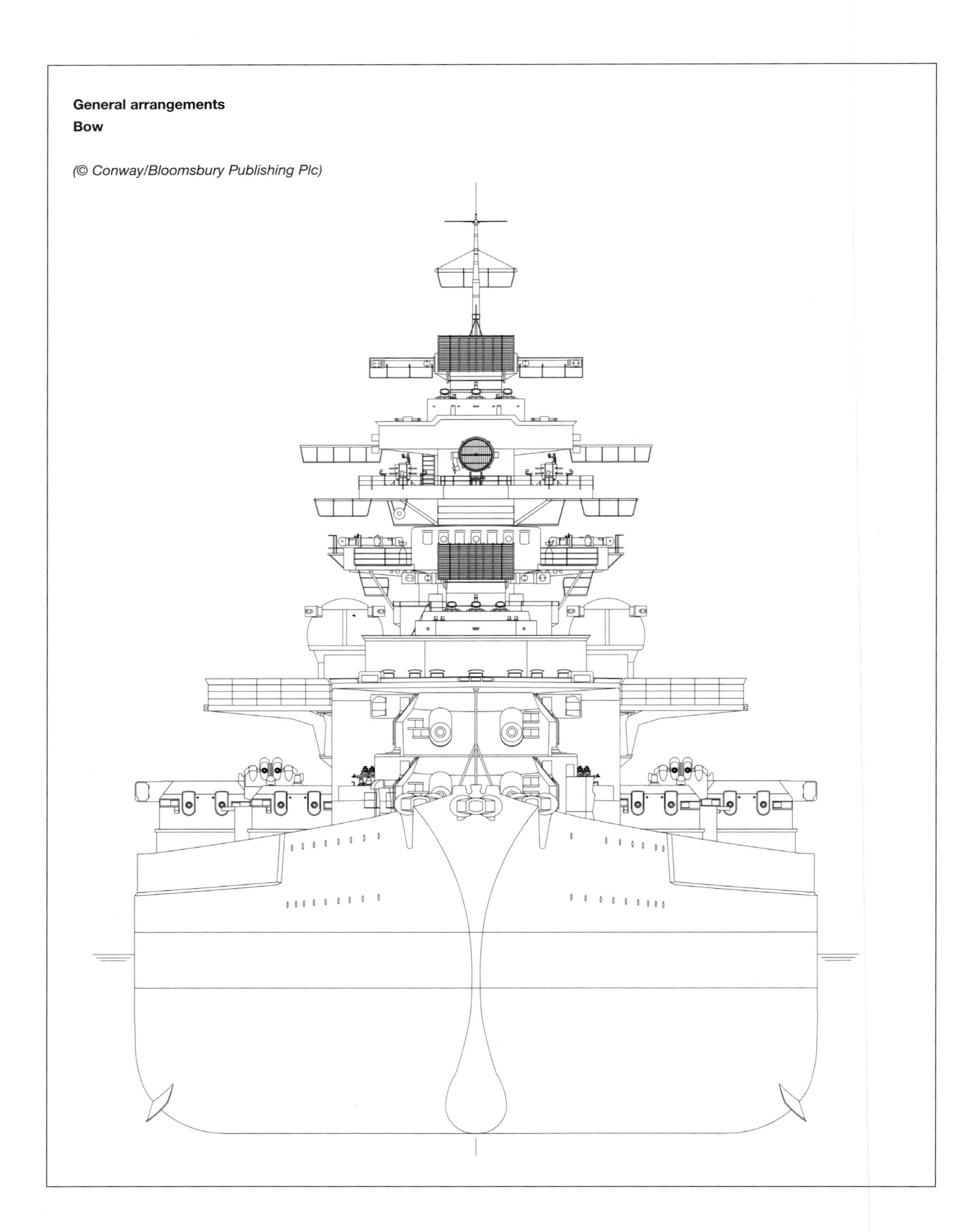

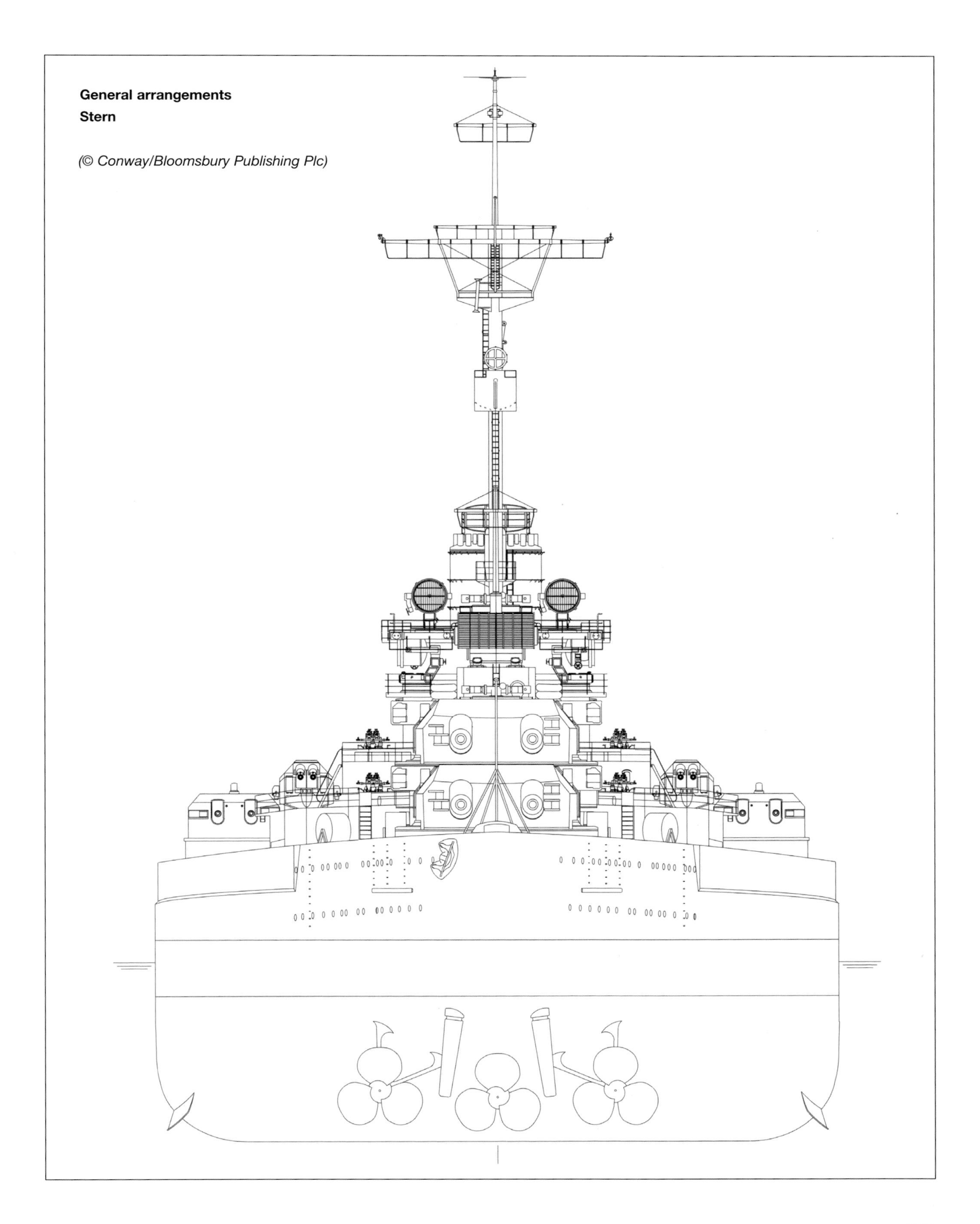

(© Conway/Bloomsbury Publishing Plc)

ABOVE The elegant clipper bow of *Bismarck*, photographed during her fitting-out at the Blohm & Voss shipyard in Hamburg. She lies alongside the shipyard's Equipping Pier, not far from the slipway where she was launched.

Orientation

A sailor boarding *Bismarck* in port would do so by way of a removable accommodation ladder spanning the gap between the battleship and the quayside. Alternatively, if he boarded the vessel from a boat, he would come aboard on one of two entry ladders rigged over the leeward side of the ship. The principal one was located near

secondary turret PI or SI, while the second – usually reserved for officers – led on to the upper deck forward of 'Caesar' turret. On occasion a third entry ladder could be fitted beside the main entry ladder.

Once on board, the ship represents a somewhat bewildering appearance, filled with passageways, companionways and compartments. Essentially, though, accommodation space was located below the upper deck, with the crew berthing forward and officers accommodated towards the stern. Non-commissioned officers berthed in both areas, depending on their speciality, with engineers tending to berth aft. The wardroom was located beneath the upper deck below the mainmast, while accommodation for both the admiral and the captain was split between the forward and after superstructure.

Clearly the lower decks of the ship were for the most part occupied by machinery spaces, but further forward were various storerooms and refrigeration spaces. Similarly, space beneath the main turrets was taken up by the turret barbettes, and below them the magazines and shell-handling spaces. Still below decks but beneath the forward and after superstructure were the ship's utilitarian compartments – laundry rooms, the sick bay, a pharmacy, administrative offices, various work rooms, radio rooms, workshops and damage-control spaces. *Bismarck* even had a forge, a welding shop and an X-ray lab.

The after superstructure contained cabins for senior officers, including the admiral and captain, and administrative offices used by the admiral's flag staff. Forward of this were the hangars, where *Bismarck*'s four aircraft were housed. Forward of the funnel was the forward superstructure. It was dominated by the foretop, the towering superstructure that was topped by a fire-control position, a rangefinder and a radar. Elsewhere in the superstructure were other command and control spaces, such as an air tracking station, a weather room, a communications office and the day cabins of both the admiral and the captain. Further forward still, beneath the forward fire-control position and the bridge, were other key compartments, ranging from a sound location room and a VHF radio room, to a room where the ship's band could practise. Effectively *Bismarck* was a large floating township of over 2,000 inhabitants, and every compartment in the ship served a purpose. Together they housed the greatest weapon of war Germany would ever produce.

BELOW *Bismarck* photographed after her voyage down the River Elbe on 15 September 1940 as she lay off the western entrance to the Kaiser Wilhelm Canal. That evening she fired her guns in anger for the first time – at British bombers passing overhead on their way to Kiel.

GENERAL ARRANGEMENTS

Deck profile – internal

1. Barbette 38cm turret 'Dora'
2. Barbette 38cm turret 'Casar'
3. Barbette 38cm turret 'Bruno'
4. Barbette 38cm turret 'Anton'
5. Mainmast
6. Foremast
7. Rudder Indicator
8. HA Rangefinder
9. 10.5m Rangefinder/FuMO 23 Radar
10. 7.0m Rangefinder/FuMO 23 Radar
11. Officers' Cabins
12. NCOs' Cabins
13. Rudder Machine Room
14. Stores
15. Engineers' Deck
16. Seamen's Kitchen
17. Engineers' Washroom
18. NCOs' Mess Deck/Reserve Hospital
19. Combat Dressing Station
20. 38cm Powder/ Cartridge Room
21. 38cm Shell Room
22. After Artillery Post
23. Signal Platform
24. Admiral's Mess
25. Lobby
26. Aircraft Hangar
27. Officers' Mess
28. Officers' Pantry
29. Shoemaker's Workshop
30. Engineers' Mess Deck
31. Storage Locker
32. Radio Room C
33. Searchlight Work Room
34. Engineers' Workshop
35. Workshop Store Room
36. Electrical Engineers' Workshop
37. Flak Work Station
38. Welding Shop
39. Forge Shop
40. Turbine Room
41. 3.7cm and 10.5cm Magazine
42. After Flak Plotting Office
43. Foretop Artillery Post
44. Air Tracking Station
45. Searchlight Platform
46. Funnel
47. Communications Centre
48. Admiral's Bridge

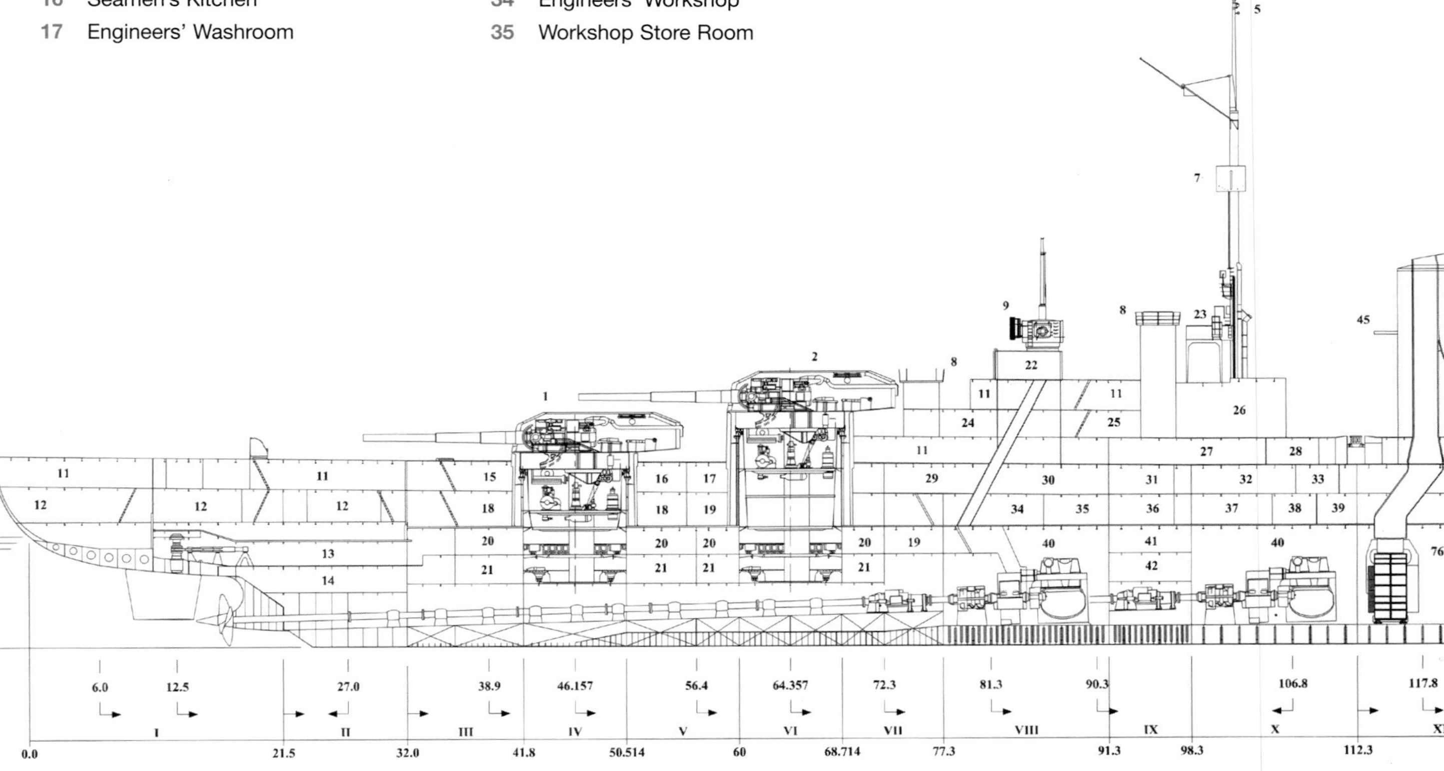

49 Weather Radio Room
50 Admiral's Sea Cabin
51 Forward Artillery Post
52 Combat Message Centre
53 Chart House
54 Bridge Shelter
55 Bridge
56 Sound Location Room
57 VHF Room
58 Music Practice Room
59 Signal Store Room
60 Fan Room
61 Copy Room
62 Gun Crew Standby Room
63 Ammunition Transfer Room
64 Pharmacy
65 Hospital Store Room
66 X-Ray Room
67 Sick Bay
68 Wash Drying Room
69 Bakery
70 Forward Seamen's Pantry
71 Laundry Room
72 Forward Canteen
73 Flak BU Work Station
74 Flak Telephone Switchboard
75 Gas Protection Store Room
76 Boiler Room
77 10.5cm Magazine
78 Control Station
79 Forward Flak Switchboard Room
80 3.7cm Magazine
81 10.5cm Shell Room
82 Auxiliary Machine Room
83 Forward Artillery Switchboard Room
84 Forward Artillery Plotting Office
85 Forward DC Switchboard Room
86 Forward Gyro Compass Room
87 Cooling Compressor Room
88 NCOs' Washroom
89 Forward Seamen's Washroom
90 NCOs' Pantry
91 NCOs' Mess Deck
92 Cool Room
93 Canteen Store Room
94 Administration Store Room
95 Seamen's Mess Deck
96 Potato Storage Room
97 Sports Equipment Storage
98 Capstan Machine Room
99 Sailmaker's Store
100 Bosun's Store
101 Rope Store
102 Radio Store
103 Carpenter's Store
104 Paravane Tube

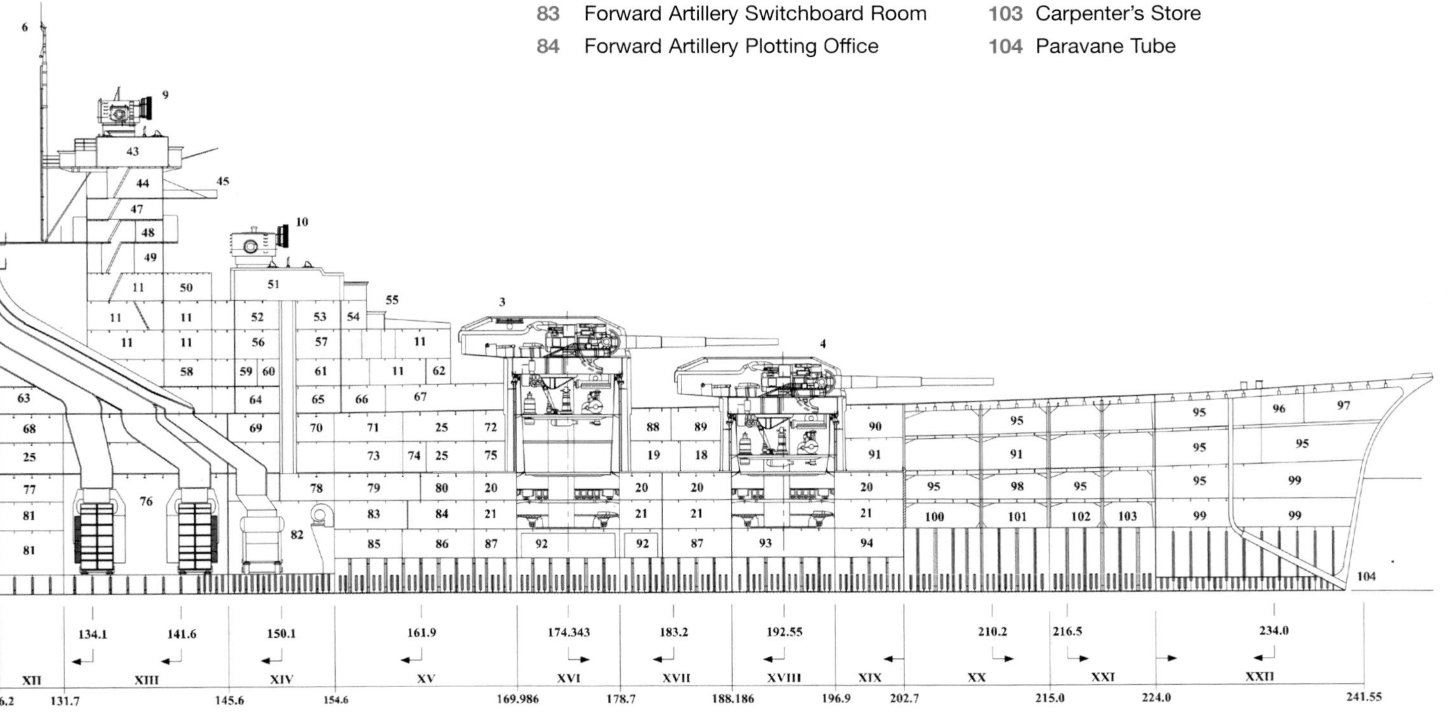

Upper deck

1 Barbette 38cm turret 'Dora'
2 Barbette 38cm turret 'Casar'
3 Barbette 38cm turret 'Bruno'
4 Barbette 38cm turret 'Anton'
5 Barbette 15cm turret Port III
6 Barbette 15cm turret Port II
7 Barbette 15cm turret Port I
8 Barbette 15cm turret Starboard III
9 Barbette 15cm turret Starboard
10 Barbette 15cm turret Starboard I
11 2cm Gun Base
12 Crane Base
13 Flagstaff
14 Stern Anchor Hawse
15 Deck Hatch
16 Skylight
17 Fairlead
18 Bollards
19 Capstan
20 After Accommodation Ladder
21 Swing Boom
22 Forward Accommodation Ladder
23 Breakwater
24 Boat Boom
25 Bow Anchor Hawse
26 Jack Staff

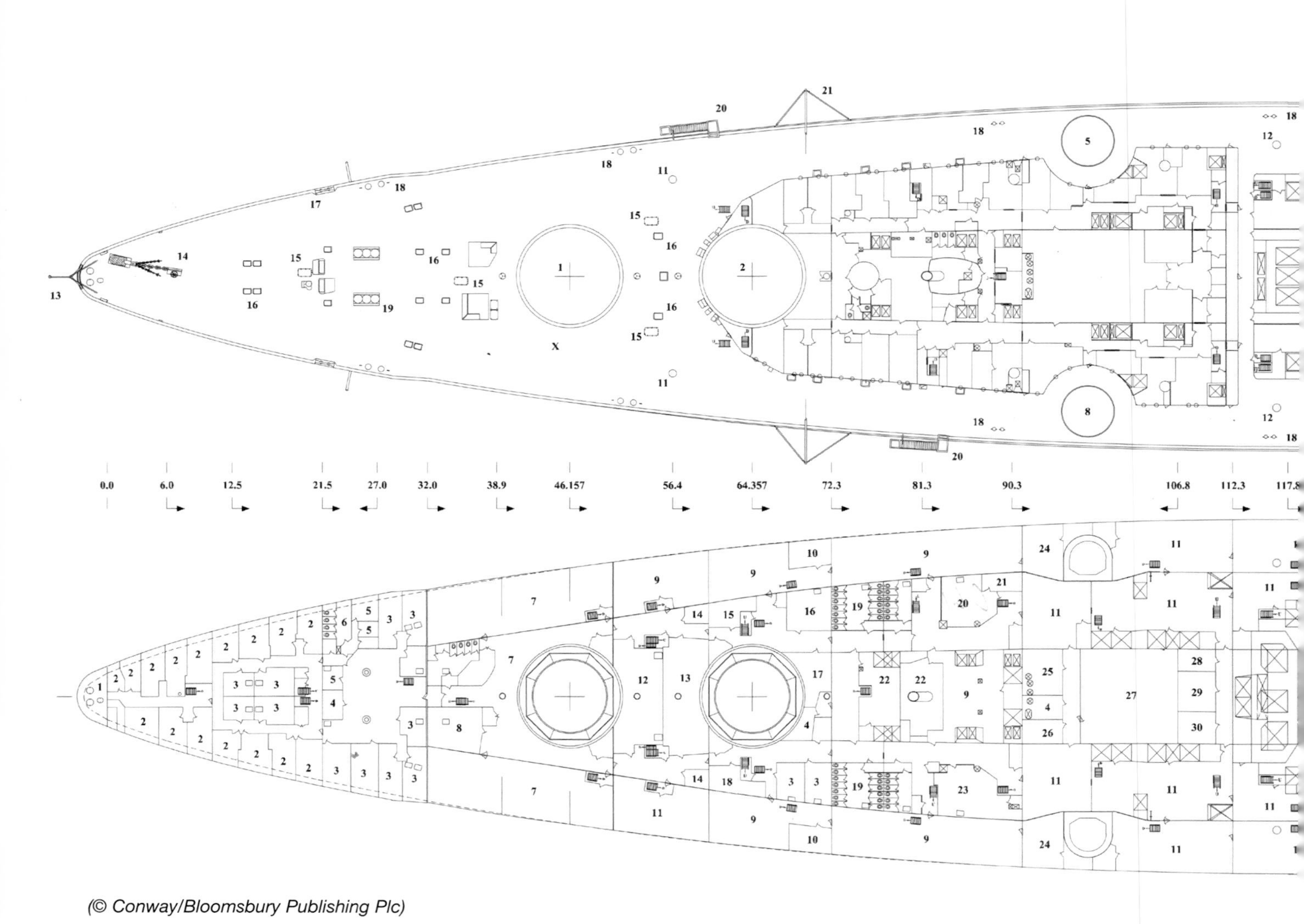

(© Conway/Bloomsbury Publishing Plc)

Battery deck

1 Smoke Generator Room
2 Officers' Cabin
3 Cabin for 2 NCOs
4 Storage Locker
5 NCOs' Washroom
6 NCOs' Head
7 Engineers' Deck
8 Engineers' Pantry
9 Engineers' Mess Deck
10 Fuel Oil Control Station
11 Seamen's Mess Deck
12 Seamen's Kitchen
13 Engineers' Washroom
14 Hammock Store
15 After Seamen's Pantry
16 NCOs' Kitchen
17 Watch Officers' Mail Room
18 Seamen's Mail Room
19 Seamen's Head
20 Aft Canteen
21 Mineral Water Storage Room
22 Shoemaker's Workshop
23 Seamen's Washroom
24 Cooks' and Waiters' Cabin
25 Deck Storage Room
26 Artillery Office
27 Radio Room C
28 Potato Storage Room
29 Searchlight Work Room
30 Potato Prep Room
31 Wash Drying Room
32 Gun Storage Locker
33 Boom Defence Store Room
34 Bakery
35 Forward Seamen's Pantry
36 Bakery Cold Storage
37 Laundry Room
38 Dishwashers
39 Lobby
40 Forward Canteen
41 Forward Seamen's Kitchen
42 NCOs' Mess Deck
43 NCOs' Pantry
44 Carpenter's Workshop
45 Sports Equipment Storage

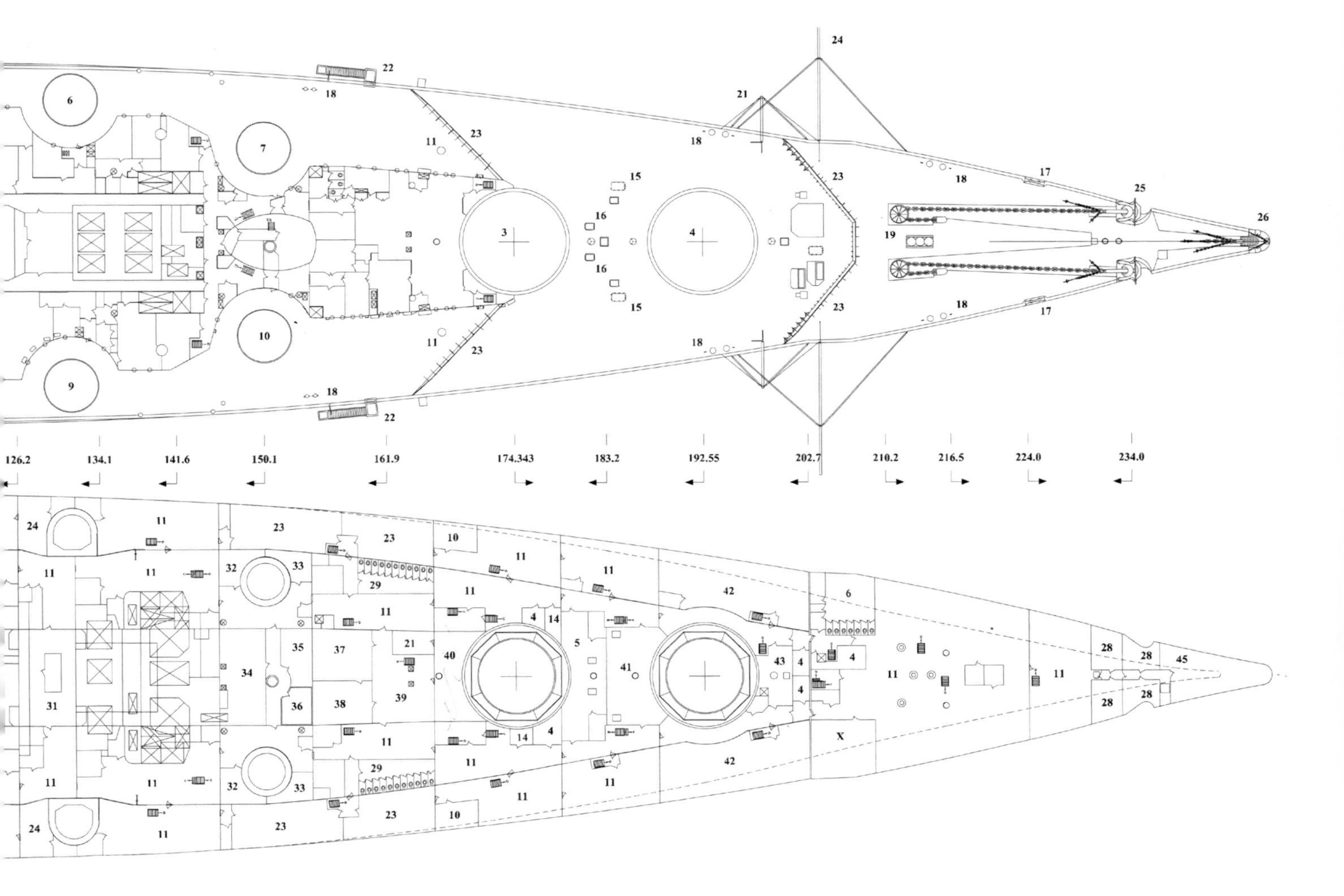

Main armour deck

1 Barbette 38cm turret 'Dora'
2 Barbette 38cm turret 'Casar'
3 Barbette 38cm turret 'Bruno'
4 Barbette 38cm turret 'Anton'
5 Barbette 15cm turret Port III
6 Barbette 15cm turret Port II
7 Barbette 15cm turret Port I
8 Barbette 15cm turret Starboard III
9 Barbette 15cm turret Starboard II
10 Barbette 15cm turret Starboard I
11 Cabin for two NCOs
12 NCOs' Mess Deck
13 NCOs' Pantry
14 Cabin for four NCOs
15 NCOs' Cabin
16 Engineers' Mess Deck
17 NCOs' Mess Deck/Reserve Hospital
18 Storage Locker
19 Combat Dressing Station
20 Seamen's Mess Deck
21 Central Control
22 Artillery Workshop
23 Artillery Store Room
24 Engineers' Workshop
25 Workshop Store Room
26 Engineers' Store Room
27 Seamen's Writing Room
28 Electrical Engineers' Workshop
29 Electrical Engineers' Store Room
30 Flak Work Station
31 Welding Shop
32 Forge Shop
33 BU Work Station
34 Hot Water Supply Room
35 Pumpmaster's Store Room
36 Air Compressor Room
37 Printing Room
38 Optical Device Storage Room
39 Sport Storage Room
40 Ventilator Work Station
41 Musical Instrument Store Room
42 Hammock Store
43 SVF Room
44 Flak BU Work Station
45 Flak Telephone Switchboard
46 Artillery BU Work Station
47 Artillery Telephone Switchboard
48 Administration Office Store Room
49 Chart Room
50 Gas Protection Store Room
51 Instrument Store Room

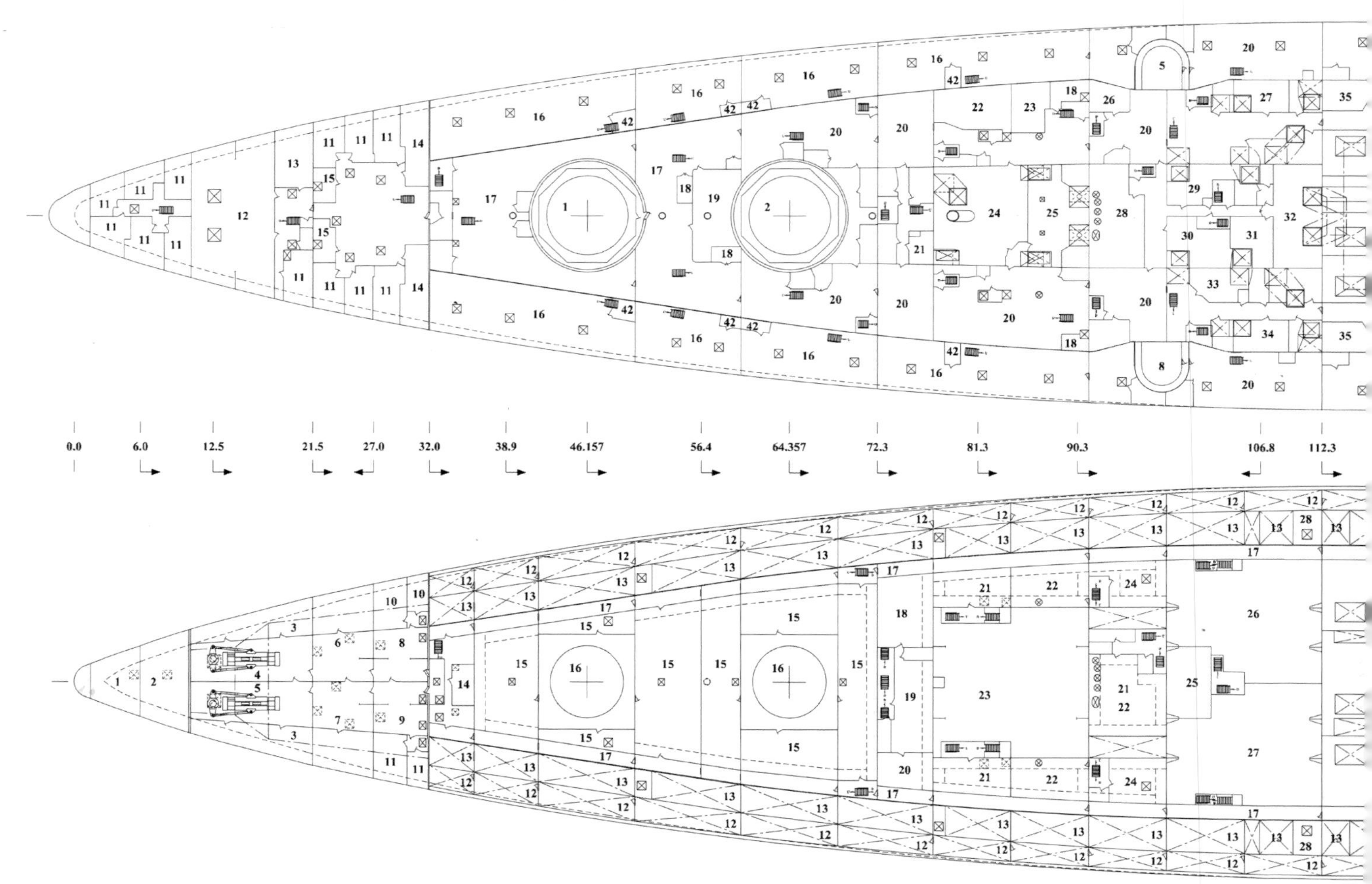

(© Conway/Bloomsbury Publishing Plc)

Upper platform deck

1 Store Room
2 NCOs' Store Room
3 Empty Room
4 Rudder Gear Room No. 2
5 Rudder Gear Room No. 1
6 Rudder Machine Room No. 2
7 Rudder Machine Room No. 1
8 Manual Steering Room No. 2
9 Manual Steering Room No. 1
10 Admiral's Store Room
11 Captain's Store Room
12 Trim Tank
13 Oil Fuel Tank
14 Dry Store
15 38cm Powder/Cartridge Room
16 38cm Powder/Cartridge Handling Room
17 Passageway
18 Aft Artillery Plotting Office
19 Artillery Reserve Switchboard Room
20 Aft Artillery Amplification Room
21 3.7cm Magazine
22 10.5cm Magazine
23 Centre Turbine Room
24 15.0cm Cartridge Room
25 Machinery Platform
26 Port Turbine Room
27 Starboard Turbine Room
28 Access Compartment
29 High Cell
30 Port Boiler Room No. 1
31 Centre Boiler Room No. 1
32 Starboard Boiler Room No. 1
33 Feed Water Tank
34 Port Boiler Room No. 2
35 Centre Boiler Room No. 2
36 Starboard Boiler Room No. 2
37 15cm Cartridge Handling Room
38 Control Station
39 Radio Room B
40 Forward Flak Switchboard Room
41 Forward Flak Control Centre
42 Transformer Room
43 Seamen's Mess Deck
44 Detention Cell
45 Storage Room

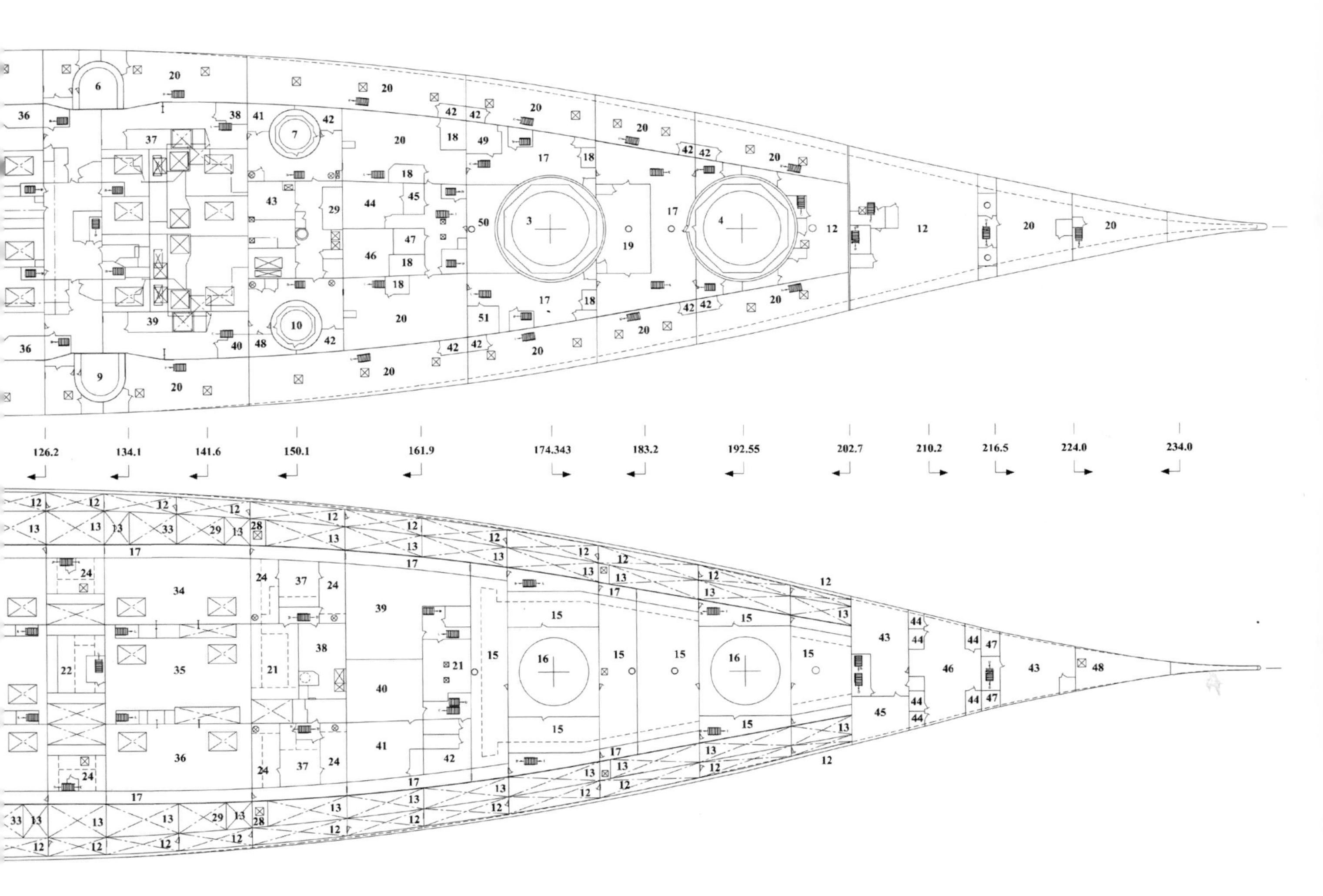

Middle platform deck

1 38cm Shell Handling Room 'Dora'
2 38cm Shell Handling Room 'Casar'
3 38cm Shell Handling Room 'Bruno'
4 38cm Shell Handling Room 'Anton'
5 Trim Tank
6 Officers' Store Room
7 Oil Fuel Tank
8 Paint Store
9 Meat Storage Room
10 Passageway
11 Spirit Store
12 Pump Room
13 38cm Shell Room
14 Canteen Storage Room
15 Flak Switchboard Room
16 Aft Regulator Room
17 Aft Artillery Reserve Switchboard Room
18 Air Conditioning Room
19 Centre Turbine Room
20 Dry Store
21 Gyro Compass Room
22 Aft DC Switchboard Room
23 Aft Central Gun Training Room
24 15cm Shell Room
25 After Flak Plotting Office
26 Port Turbine Room
27 Starboard Turbine Room
28 Port Boiler Room No. 1
29 Centre Boiler Room No. 1
30 Starboard Boiler Room No. 1
31 10.5cm Shell Room
32 Port Boiler Room No. 2
33 Centre Boiler Room No. 2
34 Starboard Boiler Room No. 2
35 Auxiliary Machine Room
36 Forward Artillery Reserve Switchboard
37 Bread Storage Room
38 Forward Artillery Switchboard Room
39 Forward Artillery Plotting Office
40 Forward Artillery Amplification Room
41 Radio Room A
42 Paint Store
43 Pyrotechnic Store
44 Chain Box
45 Bosun's Store
46 Rope Storage
47 Radio Store
48 Carpenter's Store
49 Sailmaker's Store

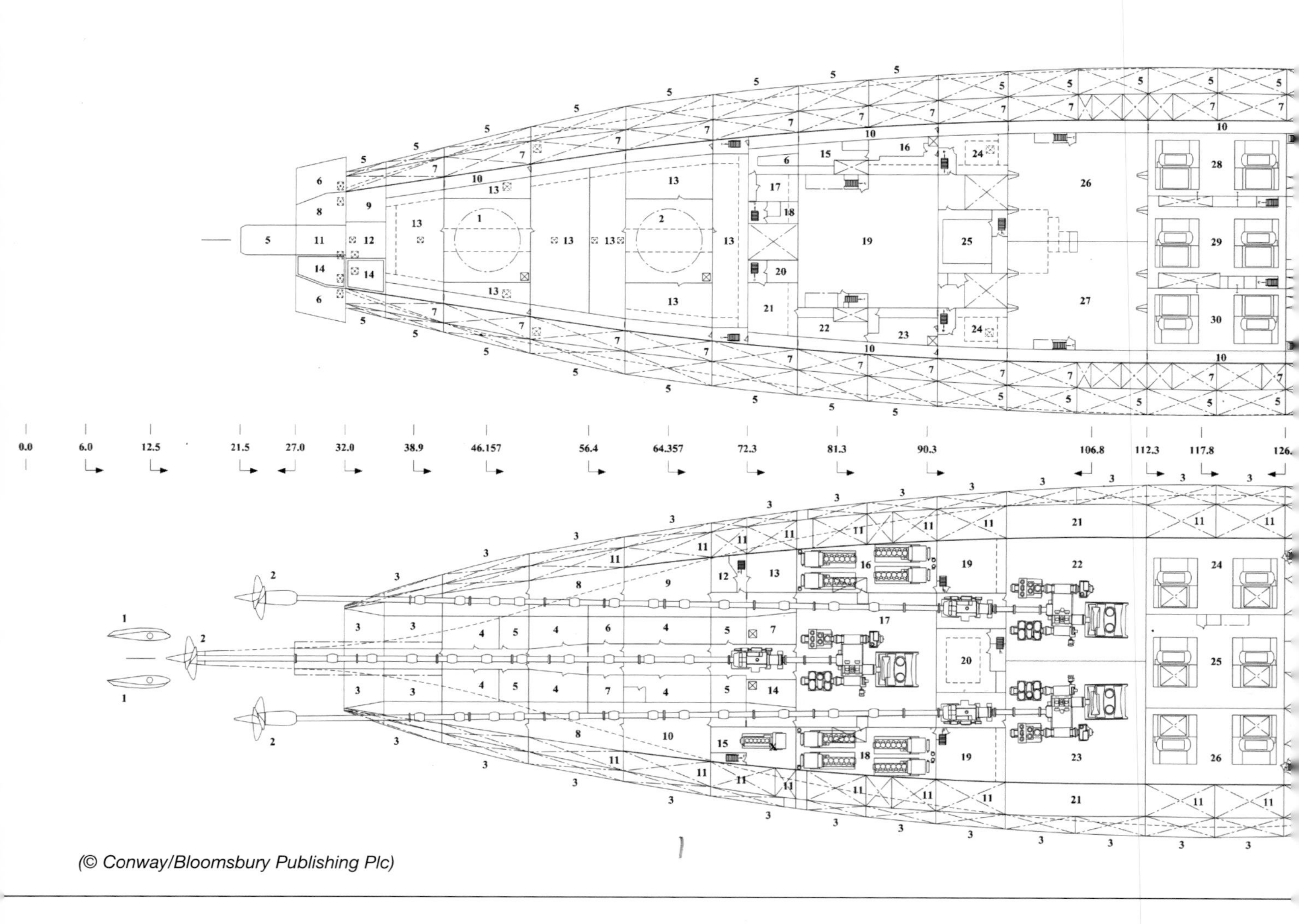

(© Conway/Bloomsbury Publishing Plc)

Lower platform deck

1 Rudder
2 Propeller
3 Trim Tank
4 Machinery Store Room
5 Pump Room
6 Fresh and Wash Water Pump Room
7 Fuel Store
8 Shaft Tunnel
9 Cooling Machinery Room
10 Fuel Pump Room
11 Oil Fuel Tank
12 Damage Control Centre
13 Electrical Store
14 Artillery Store
15 Diesel Motor Room
16 Electrical Generator Room No. 1
17 Centre Turbine Room
18 Electrical Generator Room No. 2
19 Electrical Switchboard Room
20 Aft Flak Switchboard Room
21 Fuel Room
22 Port Turbine Room
23 Starboard Turbine Room
24 Port Boiler Room No. 1
25 Centre Boiler Room No. 1
26 Starboard Boiler Room No. 1
27 10.5cm Shell Room
28 Port Boiler Room No. 2
29 Centre Boiler Room No. 2
30 Starboard Boiler Room No. 2
31 Electrical Generator Room No. 4
32 Auxiliary Machine Room
33 Electrical Generator Room No. 3
34 Cool Room
35 Ballast Pump Room
36 Forward DC Switchboard Room
37 Forward Central Gun Training Unit
38 Forward Gyro Compass Room
39 Regulator Room
40 Cooling Compressor Room
41 Bosun's Store
42 Bread Store Room
43 Meat Storage Room
44 Canteen Store Room
45 Clothing Store Room
46 Administration Store Room

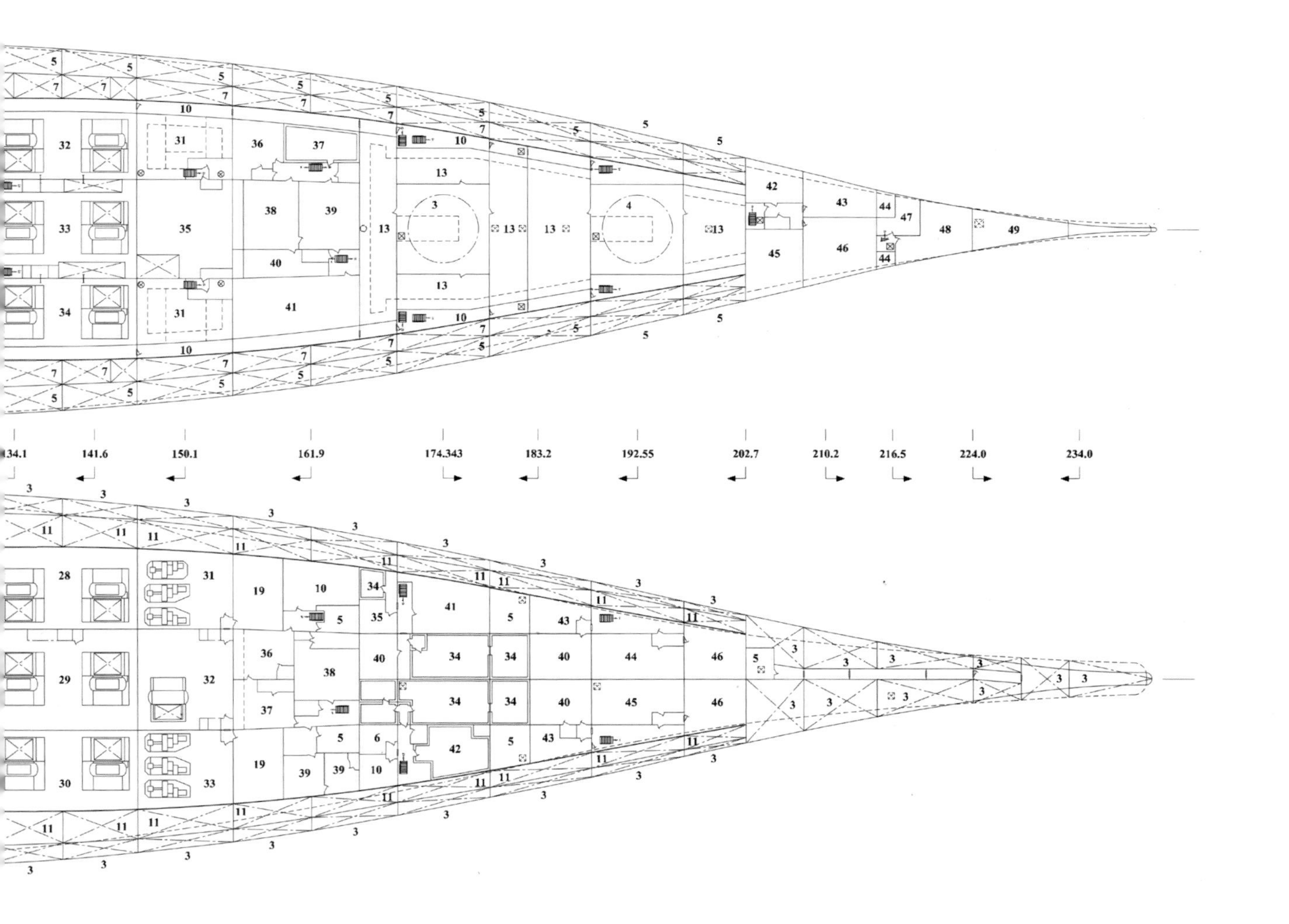

ABOVE For her launch the hull of *Bismarck* was fitted with two masts bearing the national flag, as well as two ensign staffs fore and aft, linked by bunting. The tugs were on standby to tow the battleship around the corner of the shipyard to the Equipping Pier.

Hull construction

Bismarck's hull was constructed using principles which had long been established for German warship production. The steel frames of the ship ran forward from the stern. Locations on the hull were identified by ship frame numbers, which were numbered from the stern forward. So, between ship's frame numbers 47.6 to 154.6, the keel ran along the centreline of the ship, effectively forming its backbone. The stempost – the very front of *Bismarck* – was officially designated frame 239. Between frames 154.6 and 224 the keel was replaced by a centreline longitudinal bulkhead. A total of 24 transverse watertight bulkheads divided the hull into 22 compartments, which again were numbered from the stern forward in Roman numerals. Therefore watertight compartment X, which contained two turbine rooms serving the port and starboard propellers was further forward than compartment VIII, where the centreline turbine room was located.

The transverse watertight bulkheads at frames 41.8, 50.5, 60 and 68.71 helped support the weight of the two after turrets 'Caesar' and 'Dora', while those at 169.99, 178.7, 188.89 and 186.9 performed the same function for the two forward turrets 'Anton' and 'Bruno'. These bulkheads extended from the bottom of the ship to the underside of the armoured deck, but did not extend beyond the torpedo bulkhead, which separated the innards of the ship from the space occupied by fuel and water tanks as well as the empty space between these and the outer hull, which served as an anti-torpedo space.

This torpedo bulkhead extended vertically

RIGHT *Bismarck* pictured on her return to the Blohm & Voss shipyard in December 1940. She was moored at her old berth on the Equipping Pier, and the ship was repainted in a Baltic camouflage scheme. Afterwards, most of the crew were allowed to return home on Christmas leave.

from the double bottom to the upper deck. It also provided a degree of splinter protection for the aftermost two pairs of 15cm turret barbettes. Two additional longitudinal bulkheads ran between 'Bruno' and 'Caesar' turrets to provide additional protection, and extended vertically from the armoured deck to the upper deck.

The ship had a double bottom which started at frame 46.157, where it was 1,200mm thick, and increased to 1,700mm at frame 72.3. This deeper double bottom continued as far as frame 154.6, where the bottom tapered slightly to a depth of 1,500mm. The outer hull itself was 16 to 26mm thick. A bilge keel ran from frame 88.8 to 141.1, with a maximum depth amidships of 1,000mm.

The hull was framed longitudinally as well as vertically. Apart from the horizontal frames mentioned above, nine longitudinal frames also ran along each side of the hull, parallel to the keel, which divided the ship lengthwise instead of across its beam. These were numbered in Roman numerals as well as the side of the ship, with Port I and Starboard I being closest to the keel itself. Longitudinal frame VIII on both sides of the ship ran between the watertight bulkheads between frames 21 and 202.7 – the two ends of the armoured citadel. It was continuous with the top of the torpedo bulkhead, and extended above the 'turtle-deck' slope of the armoured deck. In addition a centreline bulkhead separated No. 2 and No. 3 turbine rooms (serving the port and starboard shafts) in watertight compartment X, between frames 98.3 and 112.3. This bulkhead extended vertically from the inner double bottom to the armoured deck, and was designed to prevent more than one turbine being damaged if a torpedo or shell penetrated a turbine room.

Above the armoured deck *Bismarck* was divided by 34 transverse bulkheads, whose height depended on their location within the hull.

ABOVE A steel plate is attached to the inner ship's side of *Bismarck* during her fitting-out. This 320mm-thick panel is the first of many that will eventually comprise *Bismarck*'s main armoured belt. The face-hardened panels used for this were made from Krupp cementite new-type steel – just about the toughest type of steel in existence.

Protection

The principles behind the design and layout of the *Bismarck*'s protective armour followed the tenets established by the German Navy before the First World War. The first dreadnoughts of the Bayern class were laid down in 1913, and two of them entered service in 1916–17 – too late to participate in the Battle of Jutland. Like other German dreadnoughts, their armoured protection consisted of plates of Krupp cemented steel armour, which formed an armoured belt that extended from the forecastle

LEFT The final armoured belt was attached to *Bismarck* after her launch, as the added weight would have made her journey down the slipway extremely difficult. This photograph was taken during the late spring or early summer of 1939, and shows that the work of attaching the armoured belt is almost complete.

ABOVE **During the spring and summer of 1939 work went on fitting the armoured belt to *Bismarck*'s hull – or rather 70 per cent of it. Forward and aft of the main gun turrets, *Bismarck*'s armoured protection was much less substantial. Once the armoured belt was in place, work would begin mounting the battleship's turrets. Simultaneously, *Bismarck*'s superstructure was taking shape and, by the end of the summer, most of its key elements were in place. In this view the hull is dwarfed by the dockyard's 250-ton crane.**

to the quarterdeck, but which left the bow and stern unprotected. This belt was thickest in the 'citadel', which stretched between the forward and after turrets. This citadel protection was 350mm thick, and similar levels of protection were provided to the turret barbettes and the conning position.

A similar general configuration was adopted for the battlecruisers of the Scharnhorst class, although armour thicknesses and placement differed slightly from the original Baden class scheme. The argument was that these new capital ships were most likely to see action in the North Atlantic and the Norwegian Sea, and possibly in the waters of the Baltic or North Sea. This meant that visibility was likely to be limited, particularly during the winter months, and so the probability was that most surface actions would be fought at ranges of less than 15km (9½ miles). This was not unlike the ranges the Baden class were expected to fight at, and so the design criterion remained the same. This meant an emphasis on belt armour to offer protection against relatively close-range fire, rather than deck armour, which offered better protection from longer-range plunging fire.

The same general configuration was also used for *Bismarck*. The difference was that her armoured plates were made from a new type of Krupp cemented steel, an improved face-hardened steel known as Krupp cementite, neue Art (new type), abbreviated as 'KC n/A'. Post-war tests showed it was superior to earlier Krupp cementite steel, and to most other battleship steel protection of the period. The belt protection of *Bismarck* extended to just forward and aft of the turrets, from frame 32 to frame 202.7, and varied in thickness above and below the main belt. Additional protection was provided for the main turrets and barbettes, the secondary turrets, the conning tower (bridge) and the forward and after fire-control positions.

The main (lower) belt was 320mm thick, and extended close as far as the waterline, 9.2m (about 30ft) above the keel. Below the waterline the belt tapered to a thickness of 170mm and extended for 1.4m (just over 4½ft) below the main belt, and 7.8m (about 25½ft) above the keel. It was backed by a 60mm-thick layer of teak, and the wood backing was secured in place using armour-grade bolts. Above the main belt was the citadel belt, where the armour extended as far as the upper deck. Here the armour was also constructed using KC n/A, and was 145mm thick. Additional lighter protection was provided on both ends of the main belt, extending as far as the bow forward, and as far as the rudder housing aft. This extra protection was just 60mm thick forward, and 80mm thick aft.

The deck armour was provided by homogenous Wotan hart steel (abbreviated as Wh). Like most battleships of this period the armoured deck was located below the upper deck, and ran right across the beam of the ship, at the level of the waterline. Its edges where it met the belt armour were sloped downwards at a 22° angle, so that the belt and the armoured deck merged below the waterline. This 'turtle deck' arrangement was fairly standard in German armoured warships. It provided an extra level of protection against shells that might be able to penetrate the armoured belt. They were then faced with a thick additional armoured surface. The combination of the two made the battleship all but impervious to close-range fire.

LEFT **This revealing photograph shows *Bismarck*'s port quarter during the autumn of 1940. The armoured belt is in place, although the outer hull still resembles a patchwork quilt of steel plates. The lower superstructure is now in place, and 'Dora' turret has been mounted on top of its barbette.**

For the most part this armoured deck was 80mm thick. Amidships this increased to 95mm, and it was 110mm thick over the magazines. It was also 110mm thick at the outer sloping sides – the 22° slope that gave the armoured deck its turtle-like appearance. This sloping armour increased to 120mm around the magazines. The armoured deck conformed to the length of the armoured citadel, but a lesser degree of armour extended beyond it to offer some additional protection to the battleship's bow and stern. The bows were protected by a relatively thin splinter belt just 20mm thick. Further astern the deck armour actually increased to 110mm again to protect the rudders and propellers. The protection offered by this armoured deck was augmented by additional thinner layers of deck plating on the upper deck level (which was 50–80mm thick), and the battery deck, which was 20mm thick. Taken together, this offered a formidable degree of protection against plunging fire.

This belt and deck armour formed an armoured citadel, designed to protect everything below it from plunging fire, and to its sides from direct fire against the hull itself. It was closed off by transverse watertight bulkheads at the two ends of the citadel, at frames 32 and 202.7. The forward of these two bulkheads (at frame 202.7) was 145mm thick, while that at the end of the citadel (frame 32) had a thickness of 220mm. In both cases this tapered to 100mm when it reached the height of the upper citadel belt, just below the upper deck. Elsewhere inside the citadel, transverse watertight bulkheads varied in thickness from 110mm to 180mm, but in all cases these tapered to 100mm just as the bulkheads did at either end of the armoured citadel. Of *Bismarck*'s 22 watertight bulkheads, 17 of them were located within the armoured citadel, and were regarded as armoured bulkheads in their own right.

Bismarck had other forms of lateral protection as well as her armoured belt. An inner torpedo bulkhead ran inboard of the armoured belt along the whole length of the armoured citadel (from frame 32 to frame 202.7). This was 45mm thick and built using Wh steel. It created a void from the bottom hull plates to the armoured deck, while other longitudinal bulkheads divided this space into three compartments – two inner ones and one outer one. These longitudinal spaces were, of course, further divided by the transverse armoured bulkheads. The result was the creation of three longitudinal series of compartments. The two innermost ones were used as tanks for feed water and fuel oil, while the outer space remained empty, although it could be filled with sea water in order to balance the ship as a countermeasure to flooding.

The upper deck was lightly armoured using Wh steel. It extended from frame 10.5 to frame 224, and was 50mm thick, except around turrets 'Caesar' and 'Bruno', and around the secondary turrets where deck thickness was increased to 80mm. This formed a first line of protection for the internal spaces between the upper deck and the armoured belt. This armour was completely hidden by the teak of the upper deck.

The main turrets themselves were extremely well protected using KC n/A steel, and each had a front glacis 360mm thick, with a 320mm rear and 220mm sides. These sides were angled halfway up the side of the turret. The sloping front of the turret above the guns was 180mm thick, while the turret roof was built from steel plate 130mm thick. The barbettes were also extremely well protected, and were 220mm thick. For the two turrets 'Bruno' and 'Caesar' – those superimposed above the lower forward and aft turrets – the barbette thickness increased to 340mm for the upper barbette, which was the portion exposed between the upper deck and the base of the turret.

The secondary turrets were less well armoured, and all of them had a front face 100mm thick. The sides, rear and base ring of these turrets was 80mm thick, while turret roof – including its forward slope – was just 40mm thick. The barbettes serving these six turrets were just 20mm thick, but these received additional protection from the upper armoured belt (145mm thick), and the main belt armour (320mm).

Fire-control positions were also well protected. The foretop fire-control position was only lightly armoured using 50mm face-hardened (FH) steel plate, as any greater degree of protection would add too much topweight to the vessel. However, the forward and after fire-control positions were heavily armoured, with 200mm FH plates forward, and 150mm-thick plates aft. The upper surfaces were protected by 10mm and 50mm of plate for the forward and aft positions respectively. Communications between these two positions and the guns was protected inside an armoured tube, which ran down to the armoured citadel, and was 220mm thick for the forward fire-control position, and 50mm thick for the after position. From the citadel these communication links continued on to the main gun turrets.

BELOW The fitting of *Bismarck*'s three bronze propellers was undertaken when the battleship was moved into a dry dock situated beside the Blohm & Voss Equipping Pier. This view also gives a clear view of her twin rudders. It was the starboard of these that was hit by the aerial torpedo launched from a Swordfish, which jammed the rudder to port, and prevented *Bismarck* from reaching the safety of a French port.

Finally, the conning tower was heavily armoured, with a 350mm-thick glacis and sides, and a 220mm-thick roof.

Propulsion

Despite original plans to use turbo-electric drive propulsion on *Bismarck*, a combination of practical problems and a need to avoid excess weight led to her being fitted with a more conventional steam turbine system. During the inter-war period, the Kriegsmarine had been experimenting with new forms of high-pressure steam plants, with a favourably large ratio of performance to weight. In 1937 these Wagner water tube boilers were fitted in a batch of new destroyers, and their excellent performance led to this system being earmarked for *Bismarck*.

The battleship was fitted with 12 high-pressure Wagner Hochdruck water tube boilers, produced by Blohm & Voss. These generated a steam pressure of 70kg/cm^2 and functioned at a temperature of 480°C. They were mounted in six boiler rooms, lined three abreast, in two watertight compartments (XI and XIII), just forward of the turbine rooms. In each of these six boiler rooms one boiler was mounted in front of the other. Effectively, this meant that the boilers were arranged three abreast across the width of the ship, with two such rows in each watertight compartment.

The three boiler rooms in compartment XI were designated No. 1 port, centre and starboard boiler rooms respectively, while those in compartment XIII were similarly labelled, but designated No. 2 boiler rooms. In between the two watertight compartments containing the boilers lay compartment XII, where the auxiliary boiler machine rooms were located. All of these boilers were fired by Saacke burners.

These boilers produced high-pressure steam, which in turn was used to provide thermal energy to a series of Curtis geared steam turbines. These were also produced by Blohm & Voss. Unlike some other contemporary warships, *Bismarck* was not fitted with a cruising turbine. The turbines were divided into groups, each consisting of a high-pressure (HP), a low-pressure (LP), and an intermediate-pressure (IP) turbine, linked to a high-pressure astern and a low-pressure astern turbine by means of a single reduction gearbox. Each of these three groups or sets effectively constituted the turbine power supply for one of *Bismarck*'s three propeller shafts.

Each turbine group was housed in its own turbine room, an after one in the centreline of compartment VIII, and two adjacent and parallel to each other, a little further forward in compartment X. In between were the shaft alleys for the port and starboard propeller shafts, and a damage-control centre.

In a compound turbine arrangement like this, high-pressure steam was extracted in a number of stages. The speed at which turbine blades rotate is directly proportional to the velocity of the high-pressure steam which strikes them. Without introducing the steam in stages, the blades would spin far too quickly, resulting in vibration and damage to the machinery. *Bismarck*'s HP, IP and LP turbines had 40, 15 and 9 stages respectively, resulting in a far more workable rotation speed. The HP turbine used a Curtis turbine wheel, named after the Curtis Marine Turbine Company, which patented the design in 1906. The HP astern turbine also used a Curtis wheel, and was housed inside the larger IP turbine. Similarly, the LP astern turbine was housed inside the main LP turbine casing. This assembly, with its attendant condensers and other operational machinery, relied on a highly responsive gearbox to direct thermal pressure where and when it was required.

At full power each turbine could generate 46,000shp, but to avoid damage to the machinery, power output was governed at a maximum of 38,000shp. These three turbine sets powered three propeller shafts, each ending in a three-bladed propeller. The port and centreline propellers turned anti-clockwise, while the starboard one rotated clockwise, when viewed from astern. Due to their gearing these three propellers had a maximum rotation rate of 278 revolutions per minute (rpm). This in turn propelled the ship at a maximum speed of just over 30 knots. However, normal cruising speeds were much lower, in order to conserve fuel. It was estimated that the boilers could generate enough steam to power the turbines and turn the propellers in just under 20 minutes, if starting from cold.

Electricity was used to provide energy for a range of things within *Bismarck*, including powering the weapons and steering, lighting within the ship, operating ventilation fans, cranes, and numerous other pieces of less vital equipment, from the bridge to the galley and beyond. Electrical power to the ship was provided by four electrical generator plants, two located in watertight compartment VIII, on either side of the centre turbine room, and two more just forward of the boiler rooms, in watertight compartment XIV. Between these two was the auxiliary machinery room. There were also two electrical switchgear rooms, located in watertight compartment IX, outboard of the port and starboard propeller shaft alleys.

In compartment VIII, *E-Werke* (electrical plants) No. 1 and 2 (on the starboard and port sides respectively) each contained four 500kW DC diesel generators. Electrical plant No. 3 on the starboard side of compartment XIV had three 690kW DC turbo generators in it, while electrical plant No. 4 on the port side contained two 690kW DC and one 460kW AC turbo generators. In addition there was a diesel motor room in watertight compartment VII outboard of all three shaft tunnels on the starboard side. It housed a single Type MWM RS 38 S diesel engine. Supplied by Motorenwerke Mannheim AG, this six-cylinder engine had a regular output of 460kW of AC current, which could be increased to 550kW for short periods if required. Together, these generators provided the ship with 7,910kW of electrical power, using a 220-volt supply.

BELOW This rare but slightly out-of-focus view of the stern of *Bismarck* was taken during her fitting-out, when the battleship lay inside Floating Dry Dock No. 6 at the Blohm & Voss shipyard in the early summer of 1940. In this picture her starboard rudder has been fitted, but her port one has not yet been put in place.

Cross-section of *Bismarck* at compartment XIII, abreast of the funnel – frame 126.2 looking aft.

1 Funnel
2 Searchlight Splinter Cover Closed
3 Searchlight Splinter Cover Open
4 160cm Searchlight
5 10.5cm SKC/33 Dopp LC/ 31 Flak Gun
6 Aircraft Hangar No. 3
7 Aircraft Hangar No. 2
8 Midshipmen's Work Room
9 Barber Shop
10 Cabin for two Midshipmen
11 Seamen's Mess Deck
12 Boiler Uptake
13 Air Compressor Room
14 Passageway
15 Starboard Boiler Room No. 1
16 Centre Boiler Room No. 1
17 Port Boiler Room No. 1
18 Boiler

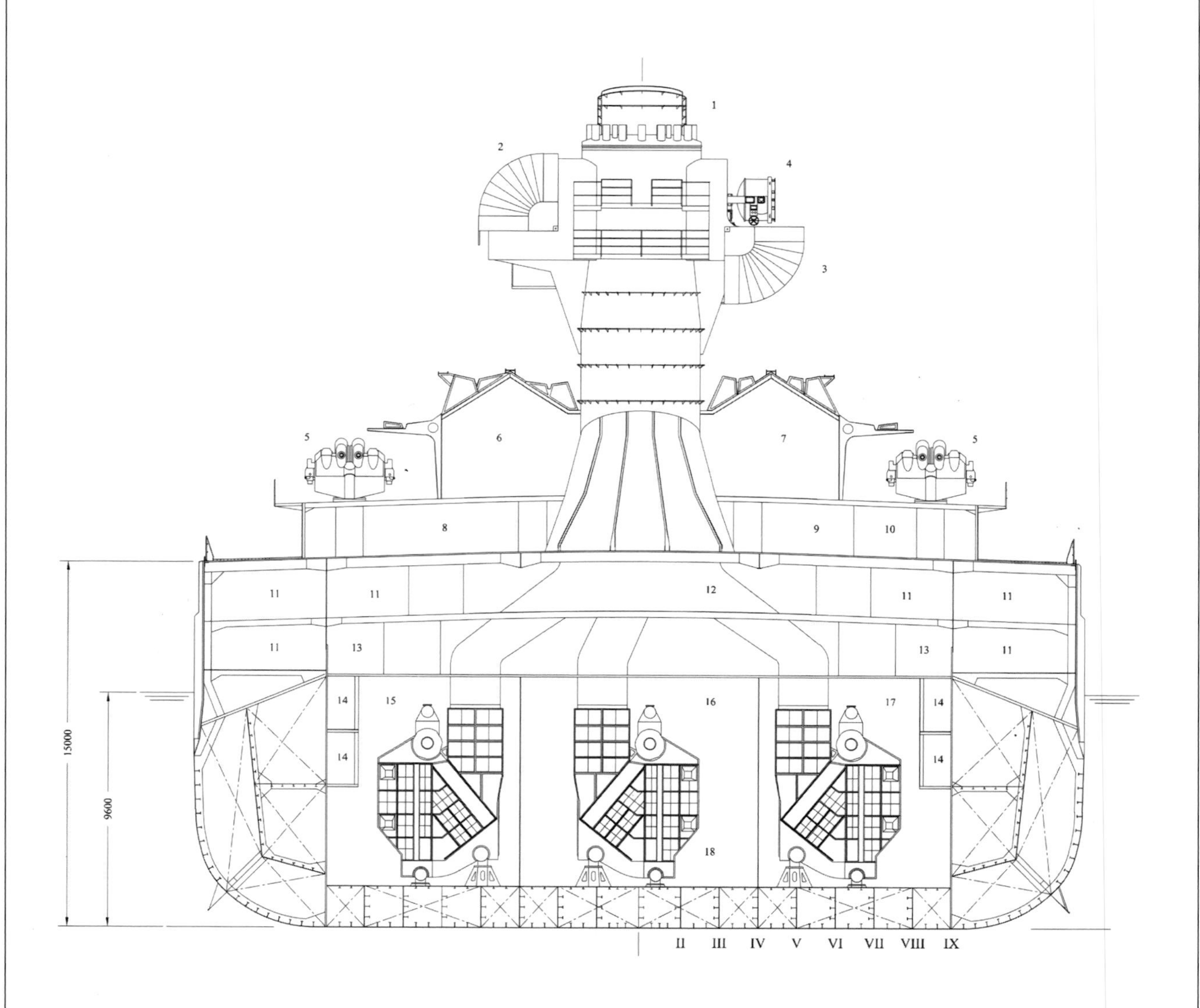

Cross-section of Anton turret and barbette.

1. Exhaust Fan Trunking
2. 10.5m Rangefinder (Removed Winter 1940/41)
3. Breech Slot
4. Main Ammunition Hoist Sheaves
5. Local Gunsight Telescope
6. Rammer
7. Loading Tray
8. Barbette
9. Turret Support Trunk
10. Auxiliary Ammunition Hoist
11. Machinery Space
12. Cartridge Hoist Rail
13. Cartridge Handling Room
14. Shell Hoist Rail
15. Shell Handling Room
16. Elevation Gear Arc
17. Turret Bearing Track
18. Elevation Rack and Pinion
19. Hydraulic Hoist Motor
20. High-pressure Air Cylinder
21. Main Ammunition Hoist
22. Revolving Cartridge Ring
23. Cartridge Ring Rollers
24. Revolving Shell Ring
25. Shell Ring Rollers

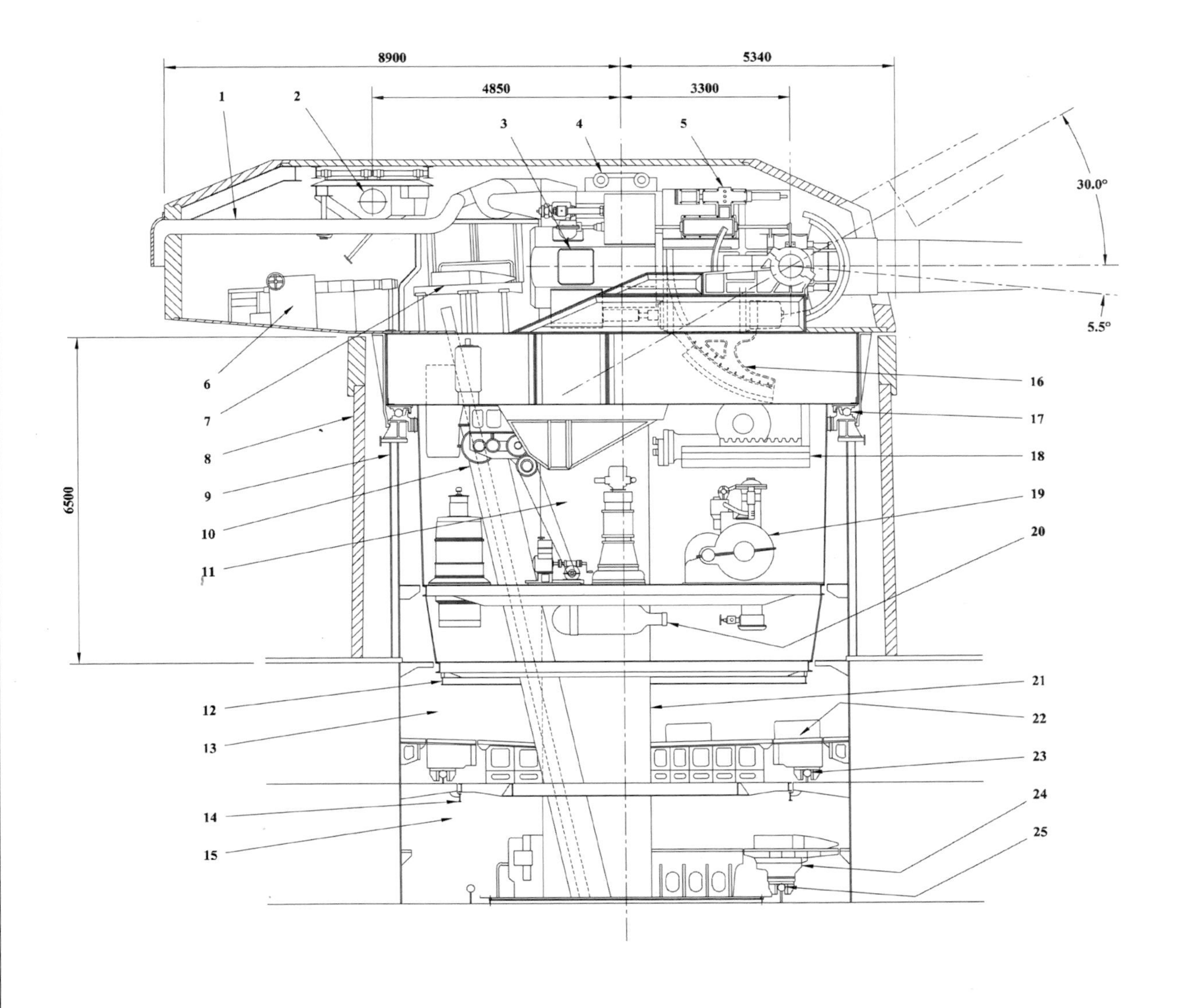

(© Conway/Bloomsbury Publishing Plc)

Armament

Main guns

Bismarck carried a powerful main armament of eight 38cm (14.96in) guns, mounted in four twin turrets. These were the primary reason for her existence. Their task was to engage and destroy enemy surface targets or, if occasion demanded, to bombard targets on shore. These guns were the largest pieces of ordnance ever carried in a German warship. Larger 40cm (16in) guns were designed, but the battleships for which they were intended were never built. The official designation for the ordnance carried on *Bismarck* was 38cm – SK-C/34; SK was an abbreviation of *schnelladekanone* (quick-firing cannon), while C/34 referred to the *construktionsjahr* (year of construction – or rather design), in this case 1934.

38cm – SK-C/34	
Gun weight	110.7 tonnes (108.95 tons)
Bore	38cm (14.96in)
Calibre	51.66
Length (overall)	19.6m (64ft 4in)
Length of bore	18.4m (60ft 4in)
Length of rifling	16m (52ft 6in)
Powder charge	212kg (467.4lb)
Rate of fire	3.3 rounds per minute (1 round every 18 seconds)

BELOW Ventilation gratings pierce the side of the upper barbette of 'Bruno' turret. 'Bruno' and 'Caesar' turrets were superimposed – raised up on these elevated barbettes to allow the guns to fire over the top of 'Anton' and 'Dora' turrets.

The 38cm gun mounted in *Bismarck* has been portrayed as a descendant of the similar-sized guns carried on the Bayern class dreadnoughts of the First World War, but in fact this weapon was completely different from its predecessors. Designed in 1934, these were high-velocity weapons, and were regarded as being more accurate than similar-sized ordnance used by other navies. This built on a high reputation enjoyed by German weaponry during the First World War, and both guns and gun mountings used on *Bismarck* benefited from a combination of long-standing expertise and recent technological development.

These guns were mounted in four twin turrets, which were designated Drh L C/34 turrets, the abbreviation Drh L standing for *Drehscheiben-Lafette* (turntable mounting), while as before C/34 referred to the *construktionsjahr*. Designed in 1934 specifically for 38cm guns, the turrets were manufactured by Krupp. According to long-standing German naval tradition, these turrets were given names rather than being identified by letters or numbers. Consequently, from bow to stern *Bismarck*'s four main gun turrets were referred to as 'Anton', 'Bruno', 'Caesar' and 'Dora'. All were mounted on the ship's centreline, with 'Anton' and 'Bruno' turrets being placed forward of the superstructure at frames 192.55 and 174.34 respectively, while 'Caesar' and 'Dora' turrets were placed aft of it, at frames 64.35 and 46.16. 'Bruno' and 'Caesar' turrets were also superimposed (or raised up) above and behind 'Anton' and 'Dora' turrets, to ensure a clear field of fire ahead or astern.

Compared with 15in turrets on other contemporary warships, those mounted on *Bismarck* were large and commodious, and the two barrels in each turret were spaced slightly further apart from those in the turrets used by other navies. This reduced the risk of interference from the two barrels, which could lead to a projectile being diverted from its course of flight. Each turret was mounted on a roller track, on which the turret could rotate. The turrets used hydraulic power for training and elevation, provided by two electrically powered hydraulic pumps fitted in each turret. Electrical power was also used to provide auxiliary power, and to augment the gun-training mechanism, the shell hoists and to power the loading mechanism.

The shell fired by these 38cm SK-C/34 guns came in three forms – the armour-piercing (AP) shell, and two varieties of high-explosive (HE) shell. During the Battle of the Denmark Strait on 24 May *Bismarck* fired 93 armour-piercing shells, which were designated 38cm Psgr. L/4,4 (m.Hb). Psgr stood for *Panzersprenggranate* (armour-piercing shell), L/4,4 refers to the length of the shell in calibres, while m.Hb referred to *mit Haube* (with cap). The cap had a ballistic cap, used as a windshield when in flight. These shells were base fused, which meant that the fuse sat at the base of the shell. These armour-piercing rounds were intended to be fired at heavily armoured targets such as enemy battleships, and were designed so that they penetrated the target's armour before exploding. This way the shell could cause the maximum possible damage to the target ship's vitals, such as her machinery spaces and magazines. They were less useful against lightly armoured targets, as the shell was likely to pass through the target without exploding.

Bismarck carried two types of HE shell. The 38cm Spgr. L/4,5 Bdz (m.Hb) stood for *Sprenggranate* (explosive shell), L/4,5 length in calibres, and *Bodenzünder* (base fused), with cap. These shells had considerably less penetrative power than AP shells, but they carried a larger explosive charge, and consequently their destructive power was greater. These shells were used against less-well-armoured enemy warships such as cruisers or destroyers. These are what *Bismarck* fired at *Norfolk* and *Suffolk*. Another variant of HE shell was the 38cm Spgr. L/4,6 Kz (m.Hb), which was similar to the previous shell type, apart from its fuse – the designation Kz referring to *Kopfzünder* (nose-fused). This type of shell exploded on impact with a target, and therefore had very poor penetrative capabilities. It was primarily designed to be fired against unarmoured targets, such as enemy merchantmen. If *Bismarck* had managed to attack an enemy convoy, this is the shell she would have used.

Bismarck carried 1,004 shells when she sailed from Gotenhafen at the start of Operation *Rheinübung*. These would have been divided equally among her four main magazines, with

ABOVE The port side waist of *Bismarck*, looking aft from beside 'Bruno' turret towards secondary turret SI. In this picture, crewmen can be seen carrying out a range of tasks, including taking on stores and performing maintenance to the bridge rail.

BELOW The arrangement of *Bismarck*'s bow anchor cables can be seen in this view of her forecastle. The two capstans serve the port and starboard bow anchor cables, which disappear through their respective navel pipes into the cable lockers, located beneath the capstans on the battery deck. A large bollard lies between the capstans on the centreline. From the capstans, the cables ran forward to the open hawsepipes where the anchors were housed, one on either side of the bow.

During the Battle of the Denmark Strait on 24 May 1941, *Bismarck* was hit three times. At 5.56am *Prince of Wales* fired a salvo at *Bismarck* at a range of 10½ nautical miles. She scored one hit when a 14in shell struck the port bow of the German battleship. The shell penetrated *Bismarck*'s thin bow armour between watertight compartments XX and XXI on her upper platform deck. The armour was just 60mm thick at that point, and the shell passed through the ship, including the bow armour on the starboard side. There it exited the battleship without exploding.

A minute later at 5.57pm *Prince of Wales* scored another hit, by which time the range had closed to 9.3 nautical miles thanks to the rapid closing speed of both ships. This time a 14in shell struck *Bismarck* amidships, just below the waterline, in watertight compartment XIV. At the point of impact the shell struck the hull below the main armoured belt and penetrated the thinner layer of 170mm-thick armour beneath it. It then plunged through the empty void compartment just inboard of the hull, and the fuel oil compartment behind it. The shell finally exploded when it came into contact with the torpedo bulkhead, which was 45mm thick. This breached the bulkhead, causing flooding in the adjacent internal compartment, electrical plant No. 4. There was also some minor flooding in the adjacent watertight compartment XIII, in No. 2. boiler room.

BELOW The British Mark XII 18in torpedoes dropped from *Ark Royal*'s Swordfish torpedo bombers were set deep so they would strike the hull of the *Bismarck* below her armoured belt, approximately 6-7 metres below her waterline.

This hit also caused a leak from the oil fuel tank penetrated by the shell before it exploded.

Finally, at 5.59am *Prince of Wales* fired a salvo at *Bismarck*, which was now 8.1 nautical miles away. A 14in shell struck *Bismarck* high on the port side of her after superstructure, forward of the mainmast, at the front edge of the boat deck, above the hangar. The shell didn't explode before it continued on into the water on the starboard side of the battleship. The only damage caused by the shell was to one of *Bismarck*'s four picket boats, which was effectively destroyed.

On board *Bismarck*, damage-control crews worked to assess the damage. The most serious hit was the first one. It flooded two compartments, and caused an oil leak. The flooding made the bow of *Bismarck* ride slightly low in the water, at an angle of 3° lower than normal. The battleship was also listing 9° to port. This in turn caused the tips of the starboard propeller to appear above the waterline. To compensate for this, Lindemann ordered the flooding of the empty starboard side outer compartments in sections II and III, at the stern of *Bismarck*. That restored the battleship's trim, by lowering her stern and starboard side. The result was that the battleship rode slightly lower in the water, but at least she was on an even trim, and her list had been countered. A more serious problem was the loss of fuel, both to the bow and amidships fuel tanks.

It was soon clear that *Bismarck* had lost sufficient fuel to limit her long-term cruising abilities. Divers were sent into the flooded compartments to assess the damage. They were then ordered to try to connect the forward fuel tanks – the ones forward of the ruptured ones – to the fuel tanks further aft. After all, they contained almost 1,000 tons of fuel oil. *Bismarck*'s full bunkerage was 7,900 tons. Unless these tanks could be reached, and connected to the rest of the fuel tanks, then this precious fuel reserve was effectively lost. Two attempts were made. The first was to connect the tanks to those astern of section XIII – behind the amidships hit. When this was unsuccessful a fuel line was run along the upper deck, but this failed when it was found impossible to securely couple the line to the bow tanks. As a result *Bismarck* had effectively lost a significant portion of her fuel stocks.

Another problem was the two waterline holes on *Bismarck*'s port side. Of these the amidships one was the most serious, as it had penetrated the torpedo bulkhead, and caused internal flooding in the battleship's engine spaces. Eventually No. 2 boiler room had to be shut down, meaning *Bismarck* lost power to her port propeller, causing a diversion of steam from her other boiler rooms, and a consequent reduction in propulsive power. To deal with this Lindemann planned to slow down the ship, and to temporarily flood empty tanks on her starboard side to raise the holes above the level of the sea. Then teams would pump out the compartments, and weld temporary steel plates over the inner side of the holes. This proved too difficult to undertake. So, attempts were made to 'fother' or stuff the holes using a combination of collision mats and hammocks.

This was a technique that mariners had used for centuries, but somehow it seemed anachronistic when used on *Bismarck*. In any event this was a very temporary solution, and it was soon clear that if *Bismarck* was to be repaired properly, then she needed to return to port. While Captain Lindemann favoured a return to Bergen, and then to the Baltic, Admiral Lütjens rejected this in favour of a more face-saving solution – a voyage south and east to Saint-Nazaire. So, while the Battle of the Denmark Strait may have been an unmitigated disaster for the Royal Navy, two of the three hits scored by *Prince of Wales* during the engagement caused sufficient damage to *Bismarck* that Operation *Rheinübung* was abandoned. Thanks to those two 14in shell hits, a train of events would begin which would end in the loss of Germany's greatest battleship.

ABOVE The critical torpedo hit on *Bismarck* occurred at 21:05, after the Swordfish launched its Mark XII torpedo from a range of 1,000yd, off *Bismarck*'s starboard beam. Ironically, if *Bismarck* had maintained her course, the torpedo would have hit her armoured belt and caused minimal damage. Instead, *Bismarck* was turning to port, and the torpedo therefore struck the battleship below her stern, where the rudder emerges from the hull. The resulting detonation was sufficiently powerful to jam the rudder in place.

LEFT Survivors from *Bismarck* are put ashore in Leith, near Edinburgh, after being rescued by the destroyer HMS *Maori*. She picked up 25 survivors from the water. Once put ashore the prisoners were transferred into the care of the British Army, who reportedly lacked the empathy shown by the British sailors on board *Maori*. This is probably because seamen shared a common bond, and realised that it could just as easily have been them who were rescued and taken prisoner.

251 shells in each one. Approximately 80 of these shells would have been AP and HE (base-fused), and the rest HE (nose-fused). During the engagement against *Hood* and *Prince of Wales*, *Bismarck* fired 11 full or partial salvos, using just over 30 per cent of her AP ordnance.

'Anton' and 'Dora' turrets consisted of six working levels, four of which rotated with the turret (gun house, gun training, turret machinery and an intermediate mezzanine platform), while two remained stationary beneath the armoured deck (magazine and shell-loading area), which were connected to the turret by means of a shell hoist housed within the barbette. The two superimposed turrets 'Bruno' and 'Caesar' had an additional mezzanine level due to the additional height of the upper barbette.

Secondary guns

Bismarck's secondary armament consisted of twelve 15cm (6in) guns, mounted in six twin turrets. These weapons were designated 15cm SK-C/28, as the weapons were first designed in 1928. The six turrets were officially known as Drh L C/34 turrets – the same designation as those used for the main armament, but distinguished by the different calibre of guns carried in them.

BELOW An ice-bound *Bismarck*, photographed during the harsh winter of 1939/40 as she lay alongside the shipyard in Hamburg where her fitting-out was nearing completion. That winter, the Kuhwerder Basin where she lay was covered in ice for much of January and February.

15cm SK-C/28	
Gun weight	9.08 tonnes (8.94 tons)
Bore	15cm (6in)
Calibre	55
Length (overall)	8.2m (27ft)
Length of bore	7.8m (25ft 7in)
Length of rifling	6.6m (21ft 8in)
Rate of fire	6–8 rounds per minute (1 round every 7.5–10 seconds)

Three turrets were mounted on each side of *Bismarck*'s superstructure, and were designated 'P' or 'S' for port or starboard, and then turrets I, II and III. These were located at frames 150.1, 131.4 and 97.85 respectively, the first two pairs sited on either side of the forward superstructure, while PIII and SIII were located on either side of the after superstructure, beside the ship's double hangar. These guns were carried to protect *Bismarck* from attack by enemy cruisers, destroyers or torpedo boats, and were primarily designed to be directed through secondary battery fire control to engage targets as a combined battery, one firing on each beam of the battleship.

Electrical power was used to operate the gun-training motor, as well as its auxiliary, and elevation was achieved hydraulically. The turrets could be trained manually if electrical power failed. Unlike the main turrets, loading of both shells and cartridges in the handling rooms was carried out by hand. Internally the turrets were designed in a similar manner to those serving *Bismarck*'s main guns. Each secondary turret consisted of five working levels, three of which (gun house, gun training and intermediate machinery platform) all rotated with the turret. The shell- and cartridge-loading rooms were protected below the armoured deck, and were linked to the turrets by shell hoists located inside the secondary turret barbettes. Ammunition was supplied to the turrets by means of the ammunition hoists, and then loaded into the guns.

No AP shells were provided for these 15cm guns, but *Bismarck* carried two different types of HE shell. These were referred to in a similar way as their larger 38cm counterparts, so the 15cm Spgr. L/4,5

Bdz (m.Hb) was a base-fused HE shell with cap, used against lightly armoured targets, while the 15cm Spgr. L/4,6 Kz (m.Hb) was its nose-fused counterpart. In addition a 15cm Lg L/4,6 was carried – the Lg standing for *Leucht geshoss* (illumination projectile), more commonly known as a starshell. Each gun carried 130 rounds, a mixture of all three shell types. Therefore a total of 1,560 rounds were carried, 622 and 666 of these shells being base-fused and nose-fused HE rounds, and the rest starshells.

ABOVE This photograph of the port side of *Bismarck*'s after superstructure provides us with a clear view of secondary turret PIII, sitting beside the hangar and beneath the after boat deck. Unlike the central 15cm turrets PII and SII, the four end 15cm turrets lacked a dedicated 6.5m rangefinder. Instead they were fitted with a simpler periscope rangefinder.

BELOW In this view of secondary turret PIII, viewed from the after port side of the searchlight platform beside the funnel, the scalloped recess in the deck to permit the turret to train can be clearly seen. PII and SII and PIII and SIII turrets had this recess. PI and SI turrets were sited further forward in the waist where the superstructure was narrower, and so there was no need for this recess.

Heavy anti-aircraft guns

Bismarck carried a total of 16 10.5cm SK-C/33 heavy anti-aircraft guns, accommodated in eight two-gun mountings. Two of these mountings were sited on either side of the forward superstructure, above and slightly behind the secondary gun turrets, while the remaining four 10.5cm mountings were in a similar position on the after superstructure, close to the aftermost pair of secondary turrets. The four forward mounts were officially designated Dopp L C/33 mountings, while the four further aft were Dopp L C/37 mounts. Dopp L stood for *Doppellafette* (twin mounting).

ABOVE **This photograph shows one of the eight twin 10.5cm anti-aircraft mountings carried on *Bismarck*. This one is the aftermost of the two 10.5cm mountings fitted to the starboard side of the battleship's forward superstructure, directly above secondary turret SII.**

RIGHT ***Bismarck*'s anti-aircraft guns were grouped around the forward and after superstructure. In the foreground can be seen two of her twin 10.5cm anti-aircraft mountings (10.5cm L6 SK-C/33) on her starboard side, while beneath them is the second twin 15cm turret, designated SII.**

10.5cm SK-C/33	
Gun weight	4.56 tonnes (5.03 tons)
Bore	10.5cm (4.1in)
Shell weight	15.1kg (33lb 4oz)
Length (overall)	6.82m (22ft 4in)
Maximum elevation	80°
Maximum range	17,700m (19,357yd)
Muzzle velocity	900m (2,953ft) per second
Maximum horizontal range	17,700m (19,360yd)
Maximum vertical range	12,500m (41,000ft)
Rate of fire	18 rounds per minute (1 round every 3.3 seconds)

The forward mounts were fitted before *Bismarck* was commissioned, but the more advanced after mountings replaced four earlier mounts in November 1940, when *Bismarck* was in Gotenhafen. The shell fired was of a fixed type, with a 27.35kg explosive charge. However, a mixture of AP, nose-fused HE, incendiary HE and starshells were carried. Both types of mountings were stabilised to enhance their firing performance, and were electrically trained and elevated. A hand-operated training and elevating system was used in case of electrical failure. Ammunition was supplied to the mounts by way of ammunition hoists running up from gun ready rooms, and once beside the mounting they were loaded by hand. A fuse-setting device was located on either side of the gun mounting, one for each barrel, and was used to alter manually the fuse settings on the shells before they were fired. Each gun was supplied with 425 rounds of assorted types, for a total of 6,800 rounds embarked.

Medium anti-aircraft guns

For close-range anti-aircraft protection *Bismarck* carried an array of smaller flak guns. The largest of these were her 16 3.7cm guns, carried in eight twin mounts. Four of these were grouped forward, and the rest aft. Two mounts were sited at the rear of 'Bruno' turret, one on each beam, while two more sat on either side of her foretop, on the upper mast deck. Further aft another pair of guns was mounted on the after superstructure, on either side of the lower bridge deck, while the last pair sat behind 'Caesar' turret. These 3.7cm SK-C/30 guns were carried on Dopp L C/30 mountings, which were trained and elevated by hand.

3.7cm SK-C/30	
Gun weight	243kg (536lb)
Bore	3.7cm (4.1in)
Shell weight	0.748kg
Length (overall)	3.07m (10ft)
Maximum elevation	85°
Muzzle velocity	1,000m (3,281ft) per second
Maximum range	8,500m (9,296yd)
Maximum vertical range	6,800m (22,310ft)
Rate of fire	30 rounds per minute (1 round every 2 seconds)

A simple gyroscopic guide for the cross-levelling of the barrel helped the gunners to determine the correct aiming point for enemy aircraft approaching the ship at an angle. Like *Bismarck*'s heavier anti-aircraft guns, these weapons were single-shot guns, but reloading them using a vertical sliding block breech mechanism took seconds. While in theory they could attain a higher rate of fire, the practicalities of ammunition supply and loading meant that a rate of fire of 30 rounds per minute was only practical with a well-trained crew, and only for a brief period. The 3.7cm gun fired a round weighing 0.748kg, but with the casing the complete round weighed 2.1kg (4.63lb). The usual projectile was an HE *leu* round, the abbreviation standing for *Leuchtspur* (tracer). Up to 2,000 rounds per gun were carried, for a ship-borne total of 32,000 rounds.

Light anti-aircraft guns

To complete her suite of anti-aircraft ordnance, *Bismarck* carried eighteen 2cm light flak guns, in two different types of mounting. Her ten 2cm C/30 guns were fitted to single pedestal mounts, while her eight 2cm C/38 guns were grouped together in two 2cm Flak 35 Vierling L38 mounts, each of which had four barrels. These *flakvierling* mountings were sited beside the 3.7cm guns on the forward superstructure on the main mast deck. The ten single 2cm

ABOVE The crew of a twin 3.7cm anti-aircraft mounting on the starboard side of *Bismarck*'s after superstructure. Below it the barrels of a twin 10.5cm mounting are also trained outboard. This photograph was taken during *Bismarck*'s gunnery exercises conducted in the Baltic during the spring of 1941.

BELOW A twin 3.7cm anti-aircraft mounting, one of eight such mounts located in *Bismarck*'s superstructure. These weapons had a range of approximately 8,500m (4.6 nautical miles), and could maintain a high rate of fire against approaching aircraft. This weapon was mounted on the port side of *Bismarck*'s foretop superstructure.

ABOVE The two 2cm *flakvierling* (quadruple flak) mountings carried by *Bismarck* were added to the ship in April 1941, while she was in Gotenhafen. Experience during the invasion of Poland and France showed that these flak weapons laid down an impressive and concentrated volume of fire, and were collectively more effective than four single-mounted weapons. They were mounted on either side of *Bismarck*'s foretop superstructure.

mountings were scattered around the ship. Two were mounted on the upper deck at the rear of and on either side of 'Bruno' and 'Dora' turrets, another pair completed the anti-aircraft battery on either side of the main mast deck, two more sat on either side of the funnel, and the final pair were fitted to the after superstructure, on either side of the mainmast.

This flak gun was one of the most widely used German weapons of the war, and was recoil-operated, air-cooled and automatic. It was magazine-fed, and on *Bismarck* a 75-round saddle drum was used. Therefore, the stated rate of fire of 280–300 rounds per minute was subject to delays when the empty drum was ejected and replaced by a full one. In practical terms a sustained average of 120 rounds per minute was usual. A stock of 2,000 rounds per gun was provided, so *Bismarck* carried approximately 36,000 of these 2cm rounds on board, many of which were preloaded into drums and magazines.

2cm SK-C/30 and C/38	
Gun weight	C/30: 64kg (141lb) C/38: 57.5kg (127lb)
Bore	2cm (0.79in)
Shell weight	0.132kg (0.29lb)
Length (overall)	1.3m (4ft 3in)
Maximum elevation	90°
Muzzle velocity	900m (2,953ft) per second
Maximum range	4,800m (5,249yd)
Maximum vertical range	3,700m (12,139ft)
Rate of fire	120 rounds per minute

BELOW Two seamen guard the inboard end of the after gangway, while behind them stands a single 2cm anti-aircraft mounting, one of two placed on either side of the quarterdeck, just abaft of 'Dora' turret. A dozen such mountings were emplaced around the ship.

The shells fired from these guns were too light to stop an oncoming aircraft on their own – multiple hits were required for that. This led to the development of the Flak 38 *flakvierling*, which had a higher rate of fire (450–500 rounds per minute), and the shells were grouped together in close proximity, as all four barrels were trained and elevated together. However, it used a magazine of either 20 or 40 rounds, and so delays in reloading meant that its average rate of fire was similar to that of the 2cm C/30. When *Bismarck* was first commissioned she carried 12 2cm C/30 guns on single mounts, but shortly before Operation *Rheinübung* began two of these were landed in Gotenhafen, and replaced by the two C/38 *flakvierling* mounts. These weapons fired HE tracer rounds – while AP rounds were produced, there is no record that any were carried on board *Bismarck*. The complete round weighed 0.312kg. (0.69lb), and was 203mm (8in) long.

Fire control

While *Bismarck* carried an extremely powerful array of main and secondary batteries, these guns were virtually useless unless their fire was accurately directed on to their target. While each 38cm and 15cm turret could be fired under manual control if necessary, the turret gun captains lacked the sophisticated fire-control equipment that would dramatically increase their chance of scoring a hit. A fire-control system involves the collection of information from a number of sources, such as rangefinders, radar bearings and visual sightings. These devices all calculate the distance to a target, as well as its range and bearing. Additional gunnery information such as weather conditions, atmospheric conditions and the relative movement of both ships is fed into a mechanical computer, which then produces the information required by the gunners to hit their target.

The fire-control system used on *Bismarck* was similar to that established for earlier German warships such as the Deutschland and Scharnhorst classes. These in turn were based on the fire-control layout developed for the Königsberg class cruisers built during the late 1920s. The system centred around three fire-control positions located in the forward superstructure, the foretop and the after superstructure. This ensured good all-round visibility, while also permitting fore and aft directors to operate independently from each other to process information on the fore and aft main armament. These three locations, incidentally, were also where the *Bismarck*'s three FuMG40G (gO) radars were sited. This was not a coincidence – these radars also needed good all-round visibility, and they were also able to process target data such as range and bearing, which was then fed into the fire-control system.

The principal element in this information gathering was the rangefinder. *Bismarck* carried 12 of them in various parts of the ship, in 4 different sizes. The largest of these was the two stereoscopic 10.5m rangefinders she carried, one mounted in a rotating dome on her foretop, and the other in a similar rotating dome above her aft fire-control position on the after end of the battleship's after superstructure. These provided range and bearing information for both the main and the secondary armament. A smaller 7m rangefinder was mounted in another rotating dome on top of the forward fire-control position. Like its larger partners it also provided information for both the 38cm and 15cm guns.

ABOVE In front of the heavily armoured conning tower and bridge structure, this small open control position was used to direct the battleship's anti-aircraft guns. From here information on enemy course, speed and altitude was fed to the anti-aircraft control centre, which in turn sent the relevant gunnery information to *Bismarck*'s anti-aircraft batteries.

Information gathered by these rangefinders, together with any radar targeting information, was passed electronically to the main gun target solution room, where the data was fed into a mechanical computer. It was located on the middle platform deck, in compartment XV. There the relevant information was processed, analysed and passed on to both the fire-control positions and the gun turrets. During an engagement a constant stream of information was being passed through this system, and calculations were continually being updated. As a result, *Bismarck*'s main gun battery could react to course changes very rapidly, and information could be processed in the time it took to reload the guns. A reserve target solution room was located further aft in compartment VII. This was similar in function to the main room, but was smaller, and omitted certain functions such as the mechanical computer designed to be used during shore bombardment missions.

To provide the individual turrets with their own independent source of targeting information, each of *Bismarck*'s four main turrets was originally fitted with another 10.5m rangefinder. However, the one fitted to 'Anton' turret was rendered largely unusable by spray thrown up over the bow, so it was removed in December 1940, when *Bismarck* had returned to the

ABOVE This view of the forward superstructure of *Bismarck* is dominated by the foretop, which housed various command spaces including the admiral's bridge, and was surmounted by the foretop fire-control position and radar. Astern of it the domed cupola of the port anti-aircraft SL-8 rangefinder can be seen.

RIGHT *Bismarck*'s after fire-control position, with the starboard arm of its 10.5m rangefinder protruding from the structure beneath the after FuMG40G (gO) radar set. In the foreground is a communications box, providing a reserve telephone link between the fire-control position and the gunnery control team located inside *Bismarck*'s armoured citadel.

Blohm & Voss shipyard in Hamburg. These were purely local rangefinders, designed to be used in the event of the main fire-control system breaking down. This is exactly what happened during *Bismarck*'s final battle on 27 May. The comparative lack of accuracy of local rather than centralised fire guidance was demonstrated by *Bismarck*'s subsequent inability to score any hits against her British opponents.

Similarly, secondary 15cm turrets PII and SII (located on either beam near the mainmast) were both fitted with 6.5m rangefinders to provide some form of local fire guidance for each group of three secondary battery gun turrets. The remaining 15cm gun turrets had simpler periscope rangefinders, in case even this reserve method of gun direction should cease to function. These had a limited rotation of 90° from the front face of the turret.

In addition to her three fire-control positions, *Bismarck* also had four anti-aircraft fire-control stations, labelled A to D. Fire-control stations A and B were housed in towers with large Wackeltopf cupola domes, situated on either side of the foretop superstructure. A was the starboard station, while B was the port one. Each of these contained a Type SL-8 high-angle 4m rangefinder, which was primarily used to gather fire-control data for the ship's anti-aircraft batteries. SL stood for *Stabilisierter Leitstand* (stabilised fire control). These rangefinders were triaxially stabilised to allow operators to smoothly track aircraft approaching the ship from either its port or starboard sides.

Fire-control stations C and D were situated on the centreline of the after superstructure, with C just abaft the mainmast and D immediately forward of 'Caesar' turret. Each of these had a 4m SL-8 rangefinder in them, but they were open to the elements, lacking the additional protection of a Wackeltopf cupola. These last two stations were not operational when *Bismarck* began Operation *Rheinübung*. The targeting information gathered by these rangefinders was sent to the flak work station located below the upper deck, in watertight compartment X. It was from there that the information was sent to the heavy and medium anti-aircraft batteries. The smaller 2cm guns were unguided, and were fired

LEFT This photograph, taken during the fitting-out process, provides a clear view of *Bismarck*'s forward superstructure, which was dominated by the foretop superstructure, surmounted by the foretop fire-control position. Below it was the admiral's bridge. In front of this was the open bridge of the battleship, running around the armoured conning tower, which included the wheelhouse and the forward fire-control position.

under purely local control. In the foretop was a flak fire-control position, equipped with four *Zeilanweisergerate* (target information sights), abbreviated to ZAG. This was used to provide additional visual data to the flak work station.

Bismarck also had fire-control facilities for night fighting. A pair of 3m night vision rangefinders was located on either side of the admiral's bridge at the base of the foretop. There were also two night control stations, from which *Bismarck*'s battery of searchlights could be controlled, aided by a pair of Zielsaule C/38 night vision searchlight directors.

Aircraft

Bismarck carried four Arado Ar-196 float planes, which were used for reconnaissance duties. They formed part of 1/Bordfliegerstaffel 196 (Shipboard Squadron 196). Pilots and aircraft technicians or armourers were provided by the Luftwaffe, on secondment to *Bismarck*, while the observers were supplied by the Kriegsmarine. If the ship had managed to operate as a surface raider, then these little float planes could – if weather conditions were favourable – scout the North Atlantic in search of enemy convoys.

Ar-196A details	
Type	Monoplane float plane
Length	11m (36ft 1in)
Wingspan	12.4m (40ft)
Weight (empty)	2,990kg (6,592lb)
Crew	2 (pilot and observer)
Maximum speed	311kph (193mph)
Ceiling	7,011m (23,000ft)
Range	1,080km (670 miles)
Armament	2 × 20mm, 2 × 7.92mm machine guns

Their range of approximately 1,080km (583 nautical miles) could be increased by 50 per cent if an additional drop tank was fitted. In theory this gave them a search range of up to 450 miles from *Bismarck*, and in good visibility each aircraft could be expected to search a lane up to 25 nautical miles on either side of the aircraft when operating at an altitude of 2,500m. In theory these float planes could also carry up to two 50kg (110lb) bombs apiece, which were mounted under the wings. *Bismarck* carried a stock of 104 pieces of ordnance of this size – a mixture of 40 SC 50 (general-purpose) or SD 50 (semi-armour-piercing) bombs, as well as 54 LC 50 parachute flares.

RIGHT ***Bismarck*** **was provided with four of these Arado Ar-196 float planes. They were carried in order to conduct reconnaissance patrols, and when hunting for convoys in the North Atlantic they would have proved invaluable. Two of the four planes were stowed in the central hangar abaft the catapult, while two more were fitted into smaller one-plane hangars located on either side of the funnel.**

These bombs were stored in three locations. The main bomb store was below decks, but two ready-use stores were located on the upper deck near the hangar – one on the port side of the upper platform deck, the other on the middle platform deck. The aircraft themselves were stored in the ship's double hangar, located beneath the mainmast, behind the catapult. There were also two single hangars further forward, one on each side of the funnel. Space was at a premium, so these aircraft were designed to be stowed on board with their wings folded. The wings were deployed when the aircraft was on the catapult, ready to launch.

There were two catapults, allowing an aircraft to be launched from either the port or the starboard side, depending on wind conditions and the ship's heading. These could be extended from 16 to 24m long by mechanical means, so that the catapult projected over the side of the ship, approximately 2.5m above the upper deck. These catapults were hydraulically powered, and allowed the Arado float plane to attain its launching speed of 110kph (68.4mph) within seconds. On its return the aircraft was recovered by means of a crane.

RIGHT An Arado Ar-196 float plane is pictured being launched from ***Bismarck*****'s catapult, flying off the port side of the ship. The catapult was capable of extending over the side of the ship, thereby increasing the length of the catapult before the launch, and ensuring that the aircraft safely cleared the side of the ship. The launching trolley can be seen at the outboard end of the catapult.**

LEFT The cluttered after starboard boat deck of *Bismarck*, viewed from the starboard side of her upper deck, just abaft of SIII turret. The boats sat on top of the hangar, at the forward end of the after superstructure. In the upper left of the photograph the base of the mainmast can be seen, behind the after starboard searchlight mounting.

Sensors

Bismarck carried three Seetakt radars, one above the bridge and forward fire-control position, one on her forward superstructure above the foremast fire-control position, and a third behind her mainmast on the after superstructure, on top of the after fire-control position. Officially these radar systems were designated as FuMG40G (gO), but in 1944 these systems were reclassified by assigning them a FuMO designation. Therefore they became known as FuMO27 radars. The abbreviation FuMG (sometimes written as FMG) stands for *Funkmessgerrät* (radar device), while 40G refers to the year of production (in this case 1940), and the manufacturer – G standing for the German electronics company GEMA. The final part of the designation (gO) refers to frequency code 'g' (sets working on a 335–430MHz waveband) while 'O' refers to sets carried on battleships, either in a radar tower or on top of a rangefinder.

These sets were developed during the late 1930s by the German electronics engineer Hans Hollmann, while acting as a consultant for the electronics company Gesellschaft für Elektroakustische und Mechanische Apparate (GEMA). Using a pulse modulation system he developed a device which could estimate the range and bearing of a target. At first this only had a detection range of around 10km, using a 50cm (600MHz) wavelength, but Hollmann was encouraged to persevere, and eventually developed a more powerful radar prototype for naval use, using a 60cm (500MHz) wavelength and a larger land-based system, which was eventually code named Freya. Hollmann's naval radar soon developed into his Seetakt system, which could be used for gun direction, as it had a range accuracy of 50m (i.e. it could direct gunfire to within 50m of an unseen target).

What let the system down was its short range. So, in 1939 Hollmann and his team at GEMA developed a more powerful version of their radar, operating at a wavelength between 71 and 81.5cm (368–390MHz). This became the FuMG40G radar. In theory this system could detect targets as far as 220km away, but in usage performance was limited by atmosphere, sea conditions and the radar horizon, which was dictated by the curvature of the earth. In practice, targets could usually be detected at a much shorter range – usually around 20–25km (10.8–13.5 nautical miles), although very large targets such as battleships could be detected at ranges of up to 30km (16.5 nautical miles). Even then performance was erratic, and Seetakt was never as good as its British counterpart.

The FuMG40G (gO) radar sets were of the 'bedstead' type, so called because they resembled a large bed frame, measuring 4 × 2m. It had a wavelength of 80cm (368MHz),

ABOVE *Bismarck* carried three of these 'bedstead'-style aerials for its three FuMG40G (gO) radar sets – one on top of each of its three fire-control positions. This was the set mounted over its after fire-control position, located high above the battleship's after superstructure.

and a pulse repetition frequency (PRF) of around 500Hz, but this could be altered slightly so that the signals from the battleship's three sets did not interfere with each other. Its power output was 8kW, and it had an accuracy of within 50m, making it accurate enough to use for gunnery direction as well as for surface search functions. What it did not have was an air search capability. For that *Bismarck* had to rely on her lookouts.

One criticism of these radars was that as they were mounted on top of *Bismarck*'s three fire-control positions (forward, aft and a subsidiary position in the foretop), and were coupled with the rotating rangefinders mounted on these positions, then their weight put added strain on the turning motors on these towers, which made them operate more slowly than they would ideally. This said, the towers themselves were large enough to accommodate the FuMG radars, and there is no account of them having curtailed the operation of the rangefinders themselves. What was more problematic was their exposed position. The damage to her forward radar on 25 May limited *Bismarck*'s ability to detect targets in her path, so the assumption is that the second radar in her foretop was also malfunctioning by this stage of Operation *Rheinübung*.

The other sensor that had an impact on *Bismarck*'s performance during the Battle of the Denmark Strait was her sound locator system. Its German name was the *Gruppenhorchgerät* (or GHG), and was located in the lower hull of *Bismarck*, on both her port and starboard sides below the breakwater on her forecastle. Produced by Atlas-Werke of Bremen, this device was designed to pick up the sound of approaching submarines, surface ships and even torpedoes. A trained GHG operator could identify the size of a vessel, its approximate speed, its propulsion system and possibly even its course. The version fitted to *Bismarck* was known as the GHG AN 302m, and on either side of her bow it consisted of 64 crystal microphones, formed in three curved lines, arranged in the shape of an upside-down horseshoe. It was this device which first detected the approach of *Hood* and *Prince of Wales*. At 05:25 on 24 May the GHC team contacted *Bismarck*'s bridge to report: 'Noise of two fast-moving turbine ships at 280° relative bearing – range 20 miles.'

Other equipment

Various other groups of equipment contributed to *Bismarck*'s operational efficiency, from searchlights and ship's boats to rarely used defensive equipment. These were all located around the ship's superstructure, and therefore were exposed to potential damage and the shock waves of the main guns if the ship went into action. This is why the more vulnerable elements such as boats and searchlights were located away from the main guns.

Searchlights

Bismarck carried seven searchlights (*scheinwerfer*), all of which were designed to operate together using central direction. One was located on the foremast searchlight platform below the fire-control position, while four more were grouped together on a searchlight platform built around the funnel – two on the port side, and two to starboard. The final two searchlights were sited behind the mainmast, one on each side of the ship. All of these searchlights were 1.5m (4ft 11in)

LEFT This view of the underside of the searchlight platform at the rear of *Bismarck*'s funnel shows the mechanism used to rotate the 4-ton port crane into position and the underside of the after searchlights. Above them the jib of one of the battleship's two 12-ton cranes can be seen.

in diameter, and were manufactured by Siemens-Schuckert.

Ship's boats

Officially, *Bismarck* was designed to carry 18 ship's boats of various sizes. However, only 9 of these were carried on board her during Operation *Rheinübung*. These 18 craft were all located amidships, with most boat positions sited either around the funnel or above the hangar. Three boat positions existed on each side of the funnel. To port these consisted of the commander's boat (11.52m long), and two 8.5m-long sailing cutters, with the captain's boat (*Chefboot*) housed outboard of the other two. The two cutters were also designed to house two 6m sailing yawls, one housed inside each of the cutters. Of these five craft only the commander's boat was embarked during Operation *Rheinübung*. However, before she sailed, two 9.2m-long motor yawls without cabins were winched on board, to occupy the spaces vacated by the two cutters.

On the starboard side of the funnel were housings for three larger craft. From inboard to outboard these consisted of a 9.2m-long motor yawl with a cabin structure, another 11.52m-*Chefboot* of a slightly newer model, and a 13m-long admiral's barge, which was not carried since *Bismarck* finished fitting-out. Two more 8.5m-long sailing cutters were normally carried on the upper deck, immediately in front of PII and SII secondary turrets, but these were not embarked during Operation *Rheinübung*. Two similar cutters with smaller craft inside them (a 3.84m-long sailing dinghy and a 5.5m sailing yawl) were also left behind when the battleship sailed. Their normal position was on the upper deck immediately in front of PIII and SIII secondary turrets.

Finally, four larger boats were carried on top of the hangar. These were all 11.52m-long

BELOW The forward port boat deck of *Bismarck* on her forward superstructure, where she carried three boats – a commander's launch and two motor yawls.

RIGHT The outboard boat on the port side of *Bismarck*'s forward boat deck was the captain's barge (the 11.52m commander boat – new model), while inboard of it lay two 9.2m motor yawls. Two boats – another commander boat and a motor yawl were carried on the starboard side of the funnel.

picket boats, designed to carry up to 85 passengers apiece. So, in the spring of 1941, the five sailing cutters, three sailing yawls and the sailing dinghy were left behind. There would be no scope for recreational sailing where *Bismarck* was going. Similarly, the prestigious admiral's barge was left in Hamburg, and never re-embarked when Admiral Lütjens raised his flag in *Bismarck* shortly before she sailed on her last voyage. In addition to her 9 ship's boats, *Bismarck* also carried 16 life rafts. These were barely large enough to accommodate more than a dozen survivors, being approximately 1.5m long and 1.4m wide. These were located in life raft stations at various places around the superstructure and upper deck, secured against the superstructure and housed in metal troughs.

Cranes

Bismarck was fitted with four cranes. Her two larger ones were located on the upper deck on either side of the funnel, just forward of the catapults, and her two smaller cranes were sited beneath the funnel searchlight platforms, one on each side of the funnel. Her larger 12-ton cranes were used to service the ship's boats, to recover the aircraft after they landed in the sea and to winch stores and ammunition on board. Her smaller 4-ton cranes were primarily used to move the aircraft from the hangars to the catapult. In mid-May 1941 problems with *Bismarck*'s port 12-ton crane led to the temporary postponement of Operation *Rheinübung*.

RIGHT *Bismarck* was fitted with two of these 12-ton cranes – one sited on each side of her catapult deck. They were used to move the aircraft around, to launch and recover her boats and to take on board supplies.

Defensive equipment

In the stern of *Bismarck* was a chemical smoke generator, designed to put up a smokescreen to hide her withdrawal, if the need arose. This relied on *Nebelkannen* (smoke-generating canisters), which were filled with 500 litres (110 gallons) of chlorosulphuric acid. Two circular hatches in the stern of *Bismarck*'s upper deck led to the smoke generator room at the after end of the battery deck. The canisters were lowered into this compartment, where they were connected to the base of an oval chimney which also emerged on to the upper deck, immediately forward of the two loading hatches. The canister was then opened and compressed air was used to project the acid upwards through an atomising jet and into the funnel. As it met the open air the acid condensed into minute particles, which, when it came into contact with the moisture in the air, produced a dense cloud of white smoke. Each canister could emit a continuous stream of smoke lasting for up to 10 minutes. The acid and the smoke were both extremely toxic.

Even more surprisingly, *Bismarck* carried six minesweeping paravanes. These *Ottergerät* (otter boards or paravanes) were stored around the upper deck in three locations – one pair below 'Bruno' turret, another pair a little further aft near secondary turrets PI and SI, and the final pair beneath 'Caesar' turret. Their function was to help protect *Bismarck* from tethered mines. A paravane tube ran from the forecastle down through the bow to emerge at its base. The leading paravane pair was streamed from this location, while others were rigged further aft.

There was never any suggestion that *Bismarck* would be put at risk conducting minesweeping duties on her own unless there was no other choice. In fact, when she sailed through a minefield between Denmark and Norway she passed along a lane freshly cleared by German minesweepers. Her paravanes were fitted so that in the unlikely event she would find herself trapped on the wrong side of a minefield, then she could at least attempt to pass through it without assistance. The paravanes were essentially submerged floats, and wires strung between these and the ship would – in theory – sever the anchor cables of the mines, which would then float to the surface. They would then be detonated by small-calibre weapons, such as *Bismarck*'s 20mm anti-aircraft guns.

ABOVE The after end of *Bismarck*'s forecastle, abreast of 'Bruno' turret, showing the sweep of deck running along the battleship's starboard waist, towards SI turret. To the right, behind the upper turret barbette, can be seen a minesweeping paravane, with its attendant cable drum. Above it the telescopic starboard bridge wing is shown fully extended.

BELOW This minesweeping paravane was fitted to the starboard side of *Bismarck*'s after superstructure, and was mirrored by a second paravane on her port side. This pair was one of three such sets carried on board *Bismarck*. They were towed by the ship, and were designed to cut the cables of tethered mines, which could then be disposed of once they broke the surface.

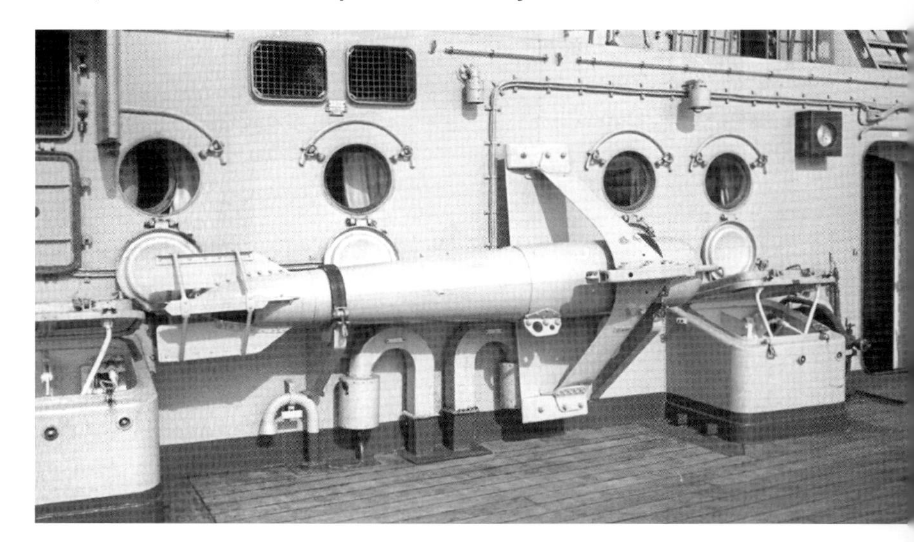

Chapter Four

Life on board

Bismarck was a floating city and home to over 2,000 sailors who were accommodated in a range of cabins and mess decks. The battleship contained all the facilities they would need, from tailors and shoe repairers to cooks, doctors and dentists. Each man had his assigned workplace and action station onboard. Shipboard organisation and routine ensured that they all had a part to play in the efficient operation of the ship.

OPPOSITE This photograph from the German Bundesarchiv shows two senior Kriegsmarine officers watching from the starboard side of the catapult deck as *Bismarck*'s crew go about their duties. The officers have tentatively been identified as Generaladmiral Alfred Saalwächter (Commanding Officer of Group West) and Kapitän zur See Netzband (Chief of Staff to Admiral Lüjens). Saalwächter visited *Bismarck* on the morning of 18 May 1941, hours before the commencement of Operation *Rheinübung*. *(Bundesarchiv)*

RIGHT A working party is photographed bringing provisions on board, carrying what appears to be a large cheese, while behind them another working party is busy repainting the forward hull of the ship. The two groups are dressed differently – one in all-white working dress, the other in a mixture of overalls, or blue shirts and white trousers.

Crew numbers

Before Operation *Rheinübung* began, *Bismarck* had a complement of 2,065 men. This included 103 officers, ranging in rank from Captain Lindemann to the midshipmen. The remaining total of 1,962 men included both non-commissioned officers and enlisted men. Additional personnel were embarked shortly before the operation began. The majority of these extra men formed the staff of Admiral Lütjens, many of whom had already conducted an Atlantic sortie on board the *Gneisenau*, as part of Operation *Berlin*. This staff numbered 75 men, from the admiral to his own assigned cooks and stewards. Some were officers, but many were non-commissioned officers who were responsible for gathering information, running a signals intelligence section, maintaining communication links and updating the admiral's strategic plot information and charts. This provided Lütjens with the information he required to make his strategic and operational decisions.

Shortly before sailing, two other groups were embarked on *Bismarck*. The first was what was officially claimed to be a boarding party of 1 officer and 80 men, whose official role was to gather information from any merchant ships encountered by *Bismarck* during her sortie. However, it appears that this unit may have been made up of soldiers rather than naval personnel. This in itself is unusual, as a boarding party would require men trained in a range of naval skills, including technicians and seamen. However, a claim by one of *Bismarck*'s survivors, a *maschinengefreiter*, sheds more light on this unit. He claims the men were from the Allgemeine Schutzstaffel – the SS. Their task was to guard captured merchant seamen and to safeguard order on board. However, this claim remains unverified.

Finally *Bismarck* was joined by a large party sent from the German Ministry of Propaganda. These included a full film team, accredited newspaper journalists, radio reporters and

BELOW *Hauptgefreiter* (leading seamen) in a forward mess deck on board *Bismarck*, enjoying a meal. Conditions were cramped on board, but the layout of these mess decks was well planned and served multiple functions – for eating and sleeping in, as well as for recreation.

finally a small team of writers, who had orders to produce a morale-boosting record of *Bismarck*'s exploits. The exact number of media people in this all-male party is not fully established, but has been estimated at approximately 120. Ironically, none of the party sent to join *Bismarck* by Josef Goebbels's Ministry of Propaganda survived the sinking of the battleship, and so not only did they fail to generate the propaganda Goebbels wanted, but their work was lost. It would have been fascinating if even a little of their film, voice and written records had survived.

For Operation *Rheinübung*, *Bismarck* embarked approximately 2,229 men, excluding the media party, which would probably have brought the total number of men embarked to 2,349. Of these, 106 were officers, and the rest both non-commissioned officers and men. Of this number only 116 crew survived the sinking – a total reduced by one when a *machinengefreiter* (machinist) rescued by HMS *Devonshire* died of his wounds. That meant that approximately 95 per cent of the crew of *Bismarck* were lost during her final battle and sinking.

Command structure

Initial planning for Operation *Rheinübung* was carried out by Großadmiral Raeder and his staff, who were based in Berlin. Much of this was done by the *Seekriegsleitung*, supervised by Generaladmiral Schniewind. However, during the operation Raeder maintained strategic operational control. This meant that while operational control rested with Admiral Lütjens, the großadmiral could intervene if he felt it necessary, and issue Lütjens with direct orders. However, he had faith in his commander and chose not to intervene, apart from attempting to do what he could to send aid to *Bismarck* during the final phase of the campaign.

During the operation Lütjens also answered to two regional commanders. The first was Generaladmiral Rolf Carls, the commander of Kriegsmarine Group North, which was based in Wilhelmshaven. It had operational control of *Bismarck* and *Prinz Eugen* until the ships had passed a line running from Cape Farvel on the southern tip of Greenland to Cape Wrath, on the north-western corner of the

GERMAN NAVAL RANKS AND THEIR ROYAL NAVY EQUIVALENTS

Kriegsmarine	Royal Navy
Großadmiral	Admiral of the Fleet
Generaladmiral	—
Admiral	Admiral
Vize-Admiral	Vice Admiral
Konter-Admiral	Rear Admiral
Kommodore	Commodore
Kapitän zur See	Captain
Fregattenkapitän	Commander
Korvettenkapitän	Lieutenant Commander
Kapitänleutnant	Lieutenant
Oberleutnant zur See	Sub-Lieutenant
Leutnant zur See	Midshipman
Oberfähnrich zur See	
Fähnrich zur See	

Note: US Navy ranks were identical to Royal Navy ones, with the exception of the rank of midshipman. There – as in the Kriegsmarine – senior midshipmen were given the rank of ensign (or leutnant zur see). For the sake of clarity Royal Navy ranks are given throughout this manual.

BELOW On 24 August Captain Lindemann arrived on board to lead the commissioning ceremony. Here his captain's barge can be seen below the main starboard side gangway, while Lindemann himself is returning the salute of his welcoming party.

ABOVE On 5 May 1941, Adolf Hitler conducted a brief inspection of ***Bismarck*** **and** ***Prinz Eugen*** **in Gotenhafen. Behind him is Generalfeldmarschall Keitel.**

RIGHT Captain Lindemann was a gunnery expert who had seen action during the First World War. Before his appointment to ***Bismarck*** **he had served as the Director of the Kriegsmarine's Gunnery School at Kiel, and so he was well versed in gunnery theory and tactics.**

Scottish mainland. Once Lütjens passed this operational border his force passed into the hands of Kriegsmarine Group West, based in Paris. Its commander was Generaladmiral Saalwächter, who supervised all Kriegsmarine operations in the North Atlantic. Once again, these regional commanders were there to support Lütjens, rather than to interfere in his operation. Therefore Admiral Lütjens retained full operational and tactical control of *Bismarck* throughout Operation *Rheinübung*.

While Lütjens decided the operational fate of the battleship, as *Bismarck*'s commanding officer (*Kommandant*) Captain Lindemann retained complete command of his own ship. Lütjens was unable to interfere in the running of the vessel, and in the way it fought. While he could issue Lindemann with operational orders, tactical matters were – in theory – the strict preserve of the battleship's captain. However, for all practical purposes the two men worked as a team. Given their performance during the Battle of the Denmark Strait they made a particularly effective one. During the battle Lütjens told Lindemann what course to steer, when to open fire and what target to select. It was Captain Lindemann's job to make sure this happened quickly and efficiently.

As fleet commander (*Flotenchef*), Admiral Lütjens was accompanied by an experienced chief of staff (*Chef des Stabes*), Captain Harald Netzbandt. He had recently commanded Lütjens's previous flagship *Gneisenau*. In addition he had a small team of three staff officers, a fleet engineer and a Luftwaffe liaison officer. Like Lütjens they had no say in the running of the ship – their role was to assist their admiral. While Captain Lindemann maintained full control of *Bismarck*, the day-to-day running of the battleship was left in the hands of his First Lieutenant (*I. Offizier* – first officer) Commander Hans Oels. He was responsible for the carrying out of evolutions ordered by the captain, and for the maintenance of order and discipline on board. This devolvement of duty freed Captain Lindemann from having to deal with most routine matters on board *Bismarck*, except when necessary. Fortunately Oels was an experienced officer, and so the day-to-day running of the battleship was in safe hands.

RIGHT ***Bismarck*** **had a small naval tailor's shop, where uniforms could be repaired or altered. In addition there was a larger ship's laundry, where the washing and pressing of clothes took place.**

Shipboard organisation

The ship's company were divided into 12 divisions of approximately equal size, so that each consisted of between 150 and 200 men. Each of these was based around the specialism of the crew (gunnery, engineering, etc.), and was administered by an officer from that speciality. Approximately half of *Bismarck*'s crew were from the seamanship speciality, which provided the crew for the battleship's main and secondary armament. The rest were from the other assorted specialities, the largest of which was the technical speciality – the engineers. Within each division there were two watches – red and green (the equivalent of the port and starboard watches in the Royal Navy), although these were further divided into two or sometimes three smaller groups, which were assigned numeric designations (Red II, Green I, etc.). These sub-groups were further divided into sections (*Korporalschaften*), administered by a petty officer. Each of these consisted of 10–12 men.

The division served two functions. First it was an administrative unit, and the officer in charge of it, supported by other more junior officers and non-commissioned officers, were there to look after the men who made up their division. It was also used as a first level of adjudication for grievances, and for matters of shipboard discipline. When the ship's company were inspected they also mustered by divisions, and their divisional officer was held accountable for their appearance and conduct. However, as the divisions were based

RIGHT These three men represented ***Bismarck*****'s team of cobblers who had their own shoe repair shop. These men had all learned their skills as civilians and were allowed to specialise in their old trade once they enlisted in the Kriegsmarine, after their basic training was completed.**

BISMARCK'S DIVISIONAL STRUCTURE

Division	Speciality	Task	Officer in charge
Div. I	Seaman	Seamen and crews for main and secondary guns	KptLt Schaaf
Div. II	Seaman		KptLt Tils (second navigation officer)
Div. III	Seaman		KptLt Knappe (gunnery officer, 'Caesar' turret)
Div. IV	Seaman		KptLt Kühn (gunnery officer, 'Caesar' turret)
Div. V	Flak	Light anti-aircraft crews	Oblt Brandes (light A-A control officer)
Div. VI	Flak	Heavy anti-aircraft crews	KptLt Troll (heavy A-A control officer)
Div. VII	Functionaries	Cooks, stewards, bandsmen, specialist trades (e.g. tailor, carpenter, shoemaker, etc.)	KptLt Mihatsch (divisions officer)
Div. VIII	Seaman	Gunnery artificers, gunner's mates, etc.	Oblt Hins (technical officer)
Div. IX	Navigation	Signalmen, telegraphists, radio operators, helmsmen, sound detection operators, etc.	KptLt Krüger (gunnery calculation officer)
Div. X	Technical	Engineers, technicians and machinists	KptLt Hasselmeyer (machinery officer)
Div. XI	Technical		KptLt Junack (turbine officer)
Div. XII	Technical		KptLt Schock (damage-control officer)

BELOW A group of sailors from *Bismarck* dressed in their summer uniform of whites and naval cap. The white *arbeitsbluse* (work shirt) was worn with white linen trousers. The captain and first officer could choose the crew's dress for the day, and so the *dunkelblaues hemd* (dark blue shirt) could also be worn with white trousers, while working parties could be issued with overalls or greatcoats as appropriate.

on branches of the service or a specialism, then they were also used as a vehicle for crew training in the various branches, and for considering promotion and advancement among enlisted men and petty officers.

Berthing arrangements

Bismarck's crew were accommodated and fed according to their rank. The admiral and captain usually ate alone, or with their guests in the solitude of their own day cabins. They also had night cabins, and both were close to the admiral's bridge and ship's bridge respectively. There was actually an admiral's mess in the after superstructure, which was used by the admiral's staff, and sometimes by Lütjens himself. Both flag staff and ship's officers had cabins in the forward and after superstructure, with the most junior officers housed immediately below the upper deck in the aftermost part – Section I – of the battery deck. The wardroom, where meals were served, was in the after superstructure in Sections X and XI, beneath the mainmast. Immediately forward of this was the officers' pantry, where cooks and stewards prepared food for serving. The actual cooking was done elsewhere, and brought to the wardroom before mealtimes.

Non-commissioned officers had their own messes, and the more senior of them also had twin cabins, located in the stern above the rudder, either on the battery deck or the main armour deck below it. Their mess decks were located on the main armour deck, around and between the barbettes of 'Caesar' and 'Dora' turrets. Washrooms and toilets were in the battery deck. Engineers also had their messes on the battery deck, mainly on the outboard compartments of the ship. A suitably large washroom was provided between the two after turret barbettes. This was also the site of one of the two ship's galleys. Although dubbed the engineer's galley, it also prepared food for other messes, including the wardroom.

Working forward along the battery deck were several mess decks for seamen, running from compartments IX all the way forward to XXI. Like the mess decks for the engineers, most of these were outboard – the central space taken up with funnel intakes and communal areas such as the seamen's main washroom, the bakery and the laundry room. The exception were the forward seamen's mess decks, which lay forward of 'Anton' turret, around which were two large outboard mess decks for the seaman branch petty officers.

On the deck below – the main armour deck – berths were arranged in a similar way. A cluster of cabins for senior NCOs lay aft, flanking their mess. Forward of this were another row of six large outboard mess decks for engineers, while inboard of them in compartments VI to XI were seamen's mess decks and washing facilities. From compartment X forward to the forward end of the armoured citadel ran another long line of seamen's mess decks, six on each side of the hull. Between 'Anton' and 'Bruno' turrets were more inboard messes for petty officers, while right the way forward in the bow was another large petty officers' mess, with two smaller seamen's mess decks which extended forward to the bow. That meant that in these two decks were 42 large mess decks for seamen, 14 for engineers and several smaller messes for various specialists. Petty officers tended to be housed forward, clustered around the turret barbettes of 'Anton' and 'Bruno', while more senior NCOs were berthed aft, as were the more junior officers. Each of the mess decks accommodated a varying number of enlisted men or petty officers, depending on their location, size and shape. Most, though, accommodated up to 30 men.

In the forward superstructure was a small officers' kitchen and bathrooms, more cabin space for senior NCOs, midshipmen and watch officers, while further forward, behind 'Bruno' turret's upper barbette was the

ABOVE Attached to the sick bay was the ship's dispensary. Here a medical orderly can be seen measuring out a powder, ready for it to be issued to a sick crewman. Note the bars across each alcove, to prevent the jars from falling from the shelves in rough weather.

LEFT This Kriegsmarine boatswain is shown wearing one of the most commonly found uniform variants on board *Bismarck* – a *dunkelblaues hemd* worn with white linen trousers. The badge on his left arm indicates that he is an *Oberbootsmannsmaat* (chief petty officer, seaman branch), while below it he wears the trade badge of a *Luftgeschutz II* (anti-aircraft gun commander).

ABOVE **In April 1941 *Bismarck* was conducting trials and exercises in the Baltic, operating alone as well as in company with *Prinz Eugen*. In this photograph taken from the deck of an unidentified German warship or supply vessel, the battleship can be seen in her Baltic camouflage scheme, which is dominated by the diagonal chevrons that cover both her hull and her superstructure.**

main sick bay. In the more substantial after superstructure were most of the officers' cabins and washrooms, running forward from 'Caesar' turret's upper barbette. These included the office and cabin of the first lieutenant. Forward of this, in between secondary turrets PIII and SIII, was the wardroom. Above this on the first deck was the suite of cabins used by the admiral and the captain, as well as the admiral's mess. Above this, on the lower bridge deck was the cabin of the admiral's chief of staff.

Effectively *Bismarck* was a floating town, with many of the facilities one would expect of a large conurbation. If the cabins and mess decks were the housing of the town, on the battery deck, the main armour deck and in a few other locations were many of the vital compartments that helped the ship function. These included a large laundry, equipped with steam-powered presses. There was a complete cobbler's shop, a pharmacy, canteens, a band practice room, a place where sailors could write letters, administrative offices, clothing stores, a post office, a bakery, a potato preparation room and even detention cells.

Just as importantly there was a modern and fully equipped sick bay, which included dental facilities, as well as two casualty dressing stations. *Bismarck* carried three doctors, the most senior of whom was Dr Busch, a highly trained naval surgeon. While these medical facilities were more than adequate for the day-to-day operation of the ship, and even for coping with the aftermath of actions where little damage was suffered, they were wholly inadequate to cope with the aftermath of major damage to the ship. While survivors testify to the courageous actions of medical staff, assisted by bandsmen in evacuating casualties from their action stations, the sheer scale of the casualties inflicted on *Bismarck*'s crew during her final battle proved too much for this small medical team to handle.

Catering

Bismarck had two main galleys, both located on the battery deck. The forward galley was in compartment XV, just aft of the 'Bruno' turret barbette, and was the larger of the two, designed to provide food for the majority of the ship's seamen and petty officers. A second galley could be foiund further aft, amidships in compartment VI. For the most part it provided food for the engineers. A separate galley for the senior NCOs was located forward of this, on the port side of compartment VII. Officers had their own galley in the forward superstructure, but at sea the tendency was for meals to be sent there and to the wardroom pantry, where the dishes were prepared and garnished before being served.

On *Bismarck* two kinds of messing arrangements were in operation. For junior NCOs and enlisted men a general messing system was used, where cooking was centralised. Food was prepared in a galley, and once ready it was sent to a serving area. There a duty cook would serve the food to the crew from a large cauldron. Rather than serving everybody, a duty messman from each *Korporalschaften* or part of a mess deck would collect the food for the group, usually in a large pot. It would then be taken back to the mess deck where it was dished up and eaten. The men ate at their mess tables and after the meal the plates, trays and serving pot would be cleaned in a scullery by the duty messman.

For senior NCOs and officers the food was served to the mess or the wardroom, after having been collected on their behalf. In the wardroom, as well as the captain and admiral's quarters, food was served by stewards, who also waited at the table. There were also pantries for the engineers in compartment III, and two for seamen in compartments VI and XIV. This was where simpler meals were served to the men on watch, who were unable to leave their posts at mealtimes.

While the meals served on board *Bismarck* were better and more varied than those served on smaller German warships, they were still somewhat monotonous. Snacks such as chocolate and biscuits were served from one of two canteens on board, which also served Pilsner beer, although these had to be paid for by the men. After the interrogation of survivors, a British intelligence report on *Bismarck* produced in August 1941 had this to say about messing arrangements:

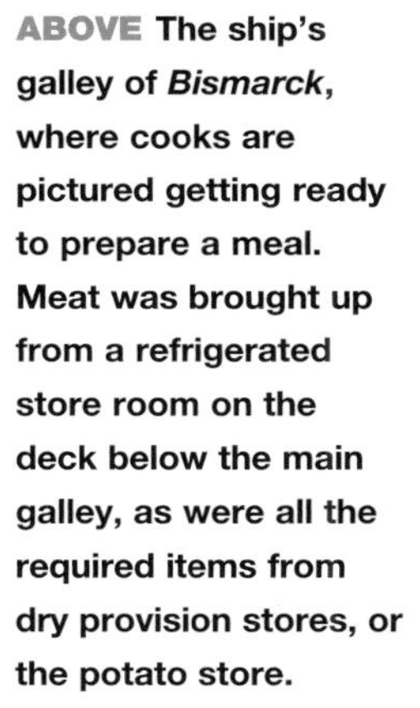

ABOVE The ship's galley of *Bismarck*, where cooks are pictured getting ready to prepare a meal. Meat was brought up from a refrigerated store room on the deck below the main galley, as were all the required items from dry provision stores, or the potato store.

LEFT Cooks at work in the *Bismarck*'s pantry, where potatoes were prepared for meals, and other preparatory work was done to food before it was taken to the main galley. In this photograph one cook appears to be sorting through a crate of potatoes, while another is weighing provisions. Note the cartoon-like images decorating the bulkhead.

Messing

Canteens, galleys and refrigeration

'Two canteens were provided, one to serve the ship's company forward, situated on the battery deck in Section XV, one aft in Section VIII, also on the battery deck. A staff of six to eight men manned each canteen.

ABOVE On board *Bismarck* the sailors ate on their mess decks, but representatives of each mess took turns to collect food from the central galley's serving area. Here a mess cook ladles out soup into pots, which were then taken back to the mess decks. Another cook stirs the soup cauldron.

BELOW Sailors on board *Bismarck* are pictured eating what looks like *suppenfleisch* (meat soup) at their mess table. Behind them can be seen their bunks and lockers. The large pot was used to transport the food from the serving area.

'Beer, cigarettes, chocolate, biscuits, writing materials etc. were sold there. A substantial quantity of beer was consumed; this was sold in ½ litre (0.9 pint) glasses at 30 pf. (about 4d.) Beer was stowed in 50 litre casks in special compartments in Sections XVII and VIII, and it was indicated that some 500–1,000 casks could be stowed in the ship. Beer was specially oxygenated before consumption.

'A portion of each canteen was reserved for petty officers' use.

'Two galleys (*combüse*) were provided for the ship's company, and one for petty officer, in the same section as the canteens, and an officers' galley was located in the superstructure.

'It was stated that 500 pig and 300 ox [actually beef] carcases were carried on board, and it was calculated that sufficient provisions were on board to feed for one day a city of 250,000 inhabitants.

'The ship's refrigerating plant was located in Section XV on the upper platform deck; this was operated electrically with CO_2 gas. The refrigerating rooms were amidships in Section XVI on the lower platform deck, under turret 'B'; an 'Aka' thermostatic system was used for controlling the temperature in the various compartments.

'All prisoners agreed that the food on board was a great improvement on the landlubber's diet; the actual bill of fare in the *Bismarck* for the last two days of her voyage, committed to paper by the writer who was responsible for typing them, was as follows:

25.5.41
Breakfast: Coffee, butter, jam
Lunch: Potatoes with dumpling pudding
Dinner: Tea, butter, egg, sausage

26.5.41
Breakfast: Coffee, dripping
Lunch: Soup, potatoes, sauce, meat, lemon
Dinner: Coffee, butter, cheese, sausage

'It will be noted that the actual food is chiefly bulk (soup and potatoes), and therefore, as accounts of most German prisoners of war describe the excellent and plentiful food in Germany, this statement is significant.'

ABOVE This steam pressing machine dominated *Bismarck*'s laundry, where dozens of shirts, trousers and other garments could be pressed simultaneously. With a crew of around 2,000 men on board, the laundry was kept in near-constant operation.

Watch system

On board *Bismarck* the majority of the ship's company maintained a watch system. This governed their lives when they were at sea. For the lucky few 'functionaries' in Division VII the watch system didn't apply – they were on duty between 08:00 and 16:00, almost as if they held a job on shore. These functionaries were specialist crewmen, such as barbers, tailors, canteen staff, bandsmen, laundrymen, shoemakers and carpenters on board. Some functionaries, such as canteen staff, had different hours, as their duties effectively began at 12:00 and continued until 20:00. Other functionaries like medical staff, bandsmen, cooks and stewards had their own watch or rota system, which was separate from that adhered to by the watchkeepers on board, who were primarily the seamen and technicians. Many of them stood watches of either eight or twelve hours.

With one exception the watch system divided the 24-hour day into watches of 4 hours each. The exception were the two 'dog watches' between 16:00 and 20:00, which lasted for two hours each. The watches were as follows:

00:00 to 04:00	Middle Watch
04:00 to 08:00	Morning Watch
08:00 to 12:00	Forenoon Watch
12:00 to 16:00	Afternoon Watch
16:00 to 18:00	First Dog Watch
18:00 to 20:00	Last Dog Watch
20:00 to 24:00	Evening Watch

As most watchkeepers were on duty for one watch in every four, the introduction of the two shorter dog watches meant that the men would not repeat the same watches every day. This arrangement allowed them some chance of snatching a decent night of sleep while they were at sea. The whole crew was woken at 08:00 every day, regardless of what watch they kept, and were considered on duty until 16:00 every evening, when their time was their own, unless they had to stand a nocturnal watch. The exception was the group of men who had just served on the Middle Watch, who were allowed to remain off duty until 12:00. Traditionally the two dog

LEFT *Bismarck*'s crew are shown here taking on stores, while the battleship lay alongside the Scheerhafen in Kiel. The ship's officer in the foreground is Korvettenkapitän (Lieutenant Commander) Hartkopf, who was *Bismarck*'s supply officer.

watches were also the time when meals would be served, so they overlapped the end of one dog watch and the start of the other.

Each division was divided into two watches – red and green. This was used during the normal working day (08:00 to 16:00) on board the ship – both in harbour and at sea – to allocate duties and training routines. For instance, at sea although the entire watch might be on duty, only one – red or green – would be 'closed up' at their weapons stations, while the other watch either had free time, or were allocated other duties. Similarly this system allowed the technicians or seamen of a division to be divided into smaller groups for training

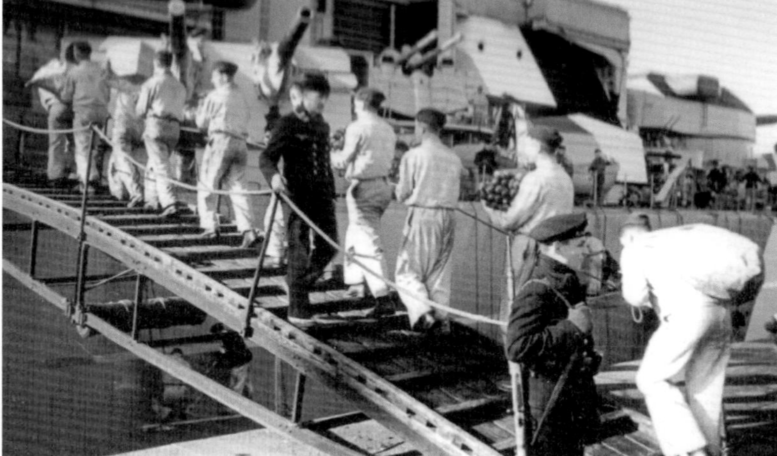

LEFT A working party from *Bismarck* is pictured loading supplies on board, while the battleship lay alongside the Scheerhafen in Kiel, March 1941. Note the presence of the armed sentry at the foot of the gangway.

RIGHT *Bismarck* pictured lying alongside the Scheerhafen quayside in Kiel, March 1941. When the ship was alongside, the quayside would be a busy place, with supplies being loaded on board, men moving on and off the ship and working parties busying themselves with repairs and maintenance. In this photograph two vans from a Kiel bakery are being unloaded, while in the background men carry large boxes and sacks on board.

purposes, or to perform housekeeping tasks such as scrubbing the decks, cleaning their allocated part of the ship, maintaining equipment or painting sections of the vessel.

When 'Action Stations' was sounded, men would run to their allocated battle stations, whether that was at their weapons or machinery spaces, or forming specialist damage control, casualty handling or emergency communication teams. *Bismarck*'s crew were well drilled in the quick and efficient transition from their normal sailing routine to one where they and their ship were fully prepared for battle. As in any warship, *Bismarck* relied heavily on the expertise of her officers and non-commissioned officers to maintain her combat efficiency in these conditions, and to ensure the crew were ready for battle.

In harbour a completely different watch system was in force. In harbour watch, the red and green divisions allowed part of the crew to remain off duty, rather than be required for duties on board ship. Usually, only one watch – red or green – would be on duty, allowing the rest of the ship's company to enjoy shore leave (if applicable) or to relax. However, if it was felt the ship was under potential threat, say from air attack, then a less relaxed state of readiness would be enforced. If the ship was at anchor, an anchor watch kept watch over the anchor and the movement of the ship, but otherwise the routine was similar to that if the ship was berthed alongside a quay. The following harbour routine was provided by the senior-ranking *Bismarck* survivor, Burkhard Baron von Müllenheim-Rechberg:

06:00	Reveille
06:30	Breakfast
07:15	Sweep decks and clean ship
08:00	Muster, followed by assignment of duties
11:30–13:30	Noon break
17:00	Evening meal served
18:30	Clean decks
22:00	Sling hammocks

Above all, the division and watch systems were there to regulate life on board and to ensure that every sailor – from the captain to the ship's tailor – knew what was expected of them, and where they had to report for duty at any particular time. At sea *Bismarck* had to maintain a high state of readiness at all times, and so her young sailors (the average age of a seaman on board was just 21) would have to learn to function as part of a large and highly efficient team. As Müllenheim-Rechberg put it:

> *In many ways, it must have seemed to the greenhorns in the crew that their ship belonged less to the world of war than to the world of modern industry. Many of them worked in confined spaces, far from the light of day, their eyes on pressure gauges and indicators, their hands on valves and levers, as they struggled to keep a wandering pointer at the proper place on the dial. Bound to their stations, they would have to manipulate their precision instruments with cool deliberation, even in the heat of battle. Their world was not that of the infantryman, who can release tension during an attack by such satisfying means as firing his rifle; it was a stationary world of highly specialised technology. The hardest test of their physical and psychological endurance, of course, would come in actual combat.*

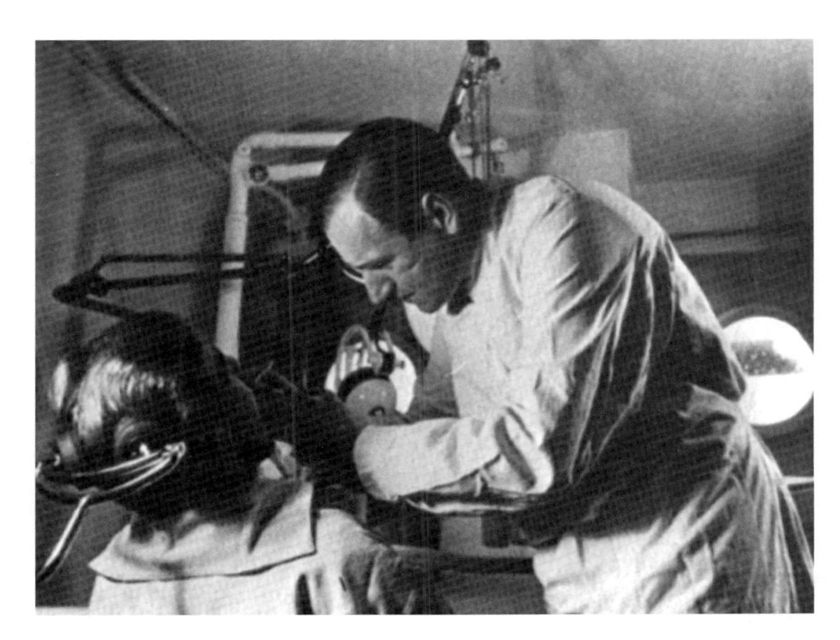

ABOVE As well as having a large and fully equipped surgery and sick bay, *Bismarck* also boasted a dentist's surgery. Here the ship's dentist Dr Hinrichsen is seen examining a patient.

Vorsicht !

Chapter Five

Combat potential

Bismarck was a battleship – the largest operational vessel in the Kriegsmarine – and one of the most modern and powerful warships afloat at the time. That means that for all her other virtues, her main *raison d'être* was to act as a floating gun battery, capable of unleashing a deadly salvo at enemy warships at ranges in excess of 15 nautical miles.

OPPOSITE The roof of *Bismarck*'s conning tower, pictured during the fitting-out of the battleship during the winter of 1939/40. The rangefinder, radar and fire-control position have yet to be added, but this provides us with a clearer view of the small deck area above the open bridge, which served as the anti-aircraft control deck.

ABOVE In this view of *Bismarck*, the FuMG40G (gO) radar on top of her forward fire-control position is clearly visible.

Her firepower was awe-inspiring, but shell-for-shell it was no more so than that of many of her contemporaries. Even ageing British battleships and battlecruisers such as *Hood*, *Repulse*, *Warspite* and *Ramillies* had guns of a similar calibre, and while the 14in guns of the new King George V class of battleship might have been of a slightly smaller calibre, this was offset by the fact these ships mounted ten guns. Even more deadly in terms of weight of broadside was *Rodney*, with her nine 16in guns.

The difference, though, was that compared to, say, *Hood*, *Bismarck*'s 38cm (14.97in) guns were modern weapons, supported by equally modern fire-control systems. By contrast *Hood* had received a number of upgrades during her long service life, but essentially she remained a capital ship from the First World War, and did not reflect recent advances in both gun accuracy and fire-control technology. Essentially *Bismarck* represented the cutting edge in terms of these key factors, and this gave her a distinct advantage when it came to fighting a gunnery duel.

Main guns

While *Bismarck*'s guns were described earlier, this omitted any account of their range and effectiveness. The 38cm SK-C/34 guns mounted in *Bismarck*'s four turrets fired an 800kg (1,764lb) projectile, and used a propellant charge weighing 212kg (467lb). This propellant came in two parts – a 112.5kg (248lb) main charge, inside a 70kg (154lb) brass case, and a fore charge weighing 99.5kg (219lb).

This charge gave this large shell an impressive range (see table below).

Loading process

The twin Drh L C/34 gun turrets used on *Bismarck* were hydraulically powered, using two electrically driven hydraulic pumps fitted to the base of each turret. These used a mixture of water and glycerine as their pressure medium, and the system could traverse the turret at a speed of 5.4° per second. In addition to hydraulic power, the turrets had an electrical training system in place in case of hydraulic failure.

Range (m)	Range (yd)	Elevation	Descent	Time of flight (seconds)	Striking velocity (m/s)	Striking velocity (ft/s)
5,000	5,470	2.2°	2.4°	6.5	727	2,385
10,000	10,940	4.9°	5.8°	13.9	641	2,103
15,000	16,400	8.1°	10.4°	22.3	568	1,864
20,000	21,870	12.1°	16.4°	32.0	511	1,677
25,000	27,340	16.8°	23.8°	43.0	473	1,552
30,000	32,810	22.4°	31.9°	55.5	457	1,499
35,000	38,280	29.1°	40.3°	69.9	462	1,516

There were also auxiliary systems in place for gun elevation, for operating the shell hoists and also to power some elements of the loading assembly. Both of the two barrels were mounted in their own cylindrical cradle, which meant that they could be loaded, elevated and fired independently. However, the guns were almost always coupled together for firing, and so were aimed and fired together as part of a combined salvo, not just within the turrets but in concert with the other three main gun turrets on board.

A hydropneumatic running-out system was used, with one recuperator and four pneumatic recoil cylinders per barrel. Hydraulics were also used to power the elevation mechanism, using a hydraulic cylinder to operate a mechanical rack-and-pinion elevating arc. Using this elegant system the guns could train at up to 6° per second. The maximum elevation possible for the guns using this system was 30°, and in theory the barrels could also be depressed to 5.5° below the horizontal. An auxiliary elevating system was provided, using an electric motor, which powered a screw-thread or worm-drive ratchet. There was also an emergency back-up system which involved a portable electrical motor fitted with a chain hoist.

When *Bismarck* was first designed, an electrohydraulic remote power control system (RPC) was tried, where elevation and training could be operated from outside the turret in the forward and after fire-control positions. However, this proved difficult to operate effectively, and attempts to use this RPC system were abandoned. Instead, gun-aiming directions were sent to the turret electronically, and the gun crews themselves moved the turret and barrels into position. According to the gun turret training manual for *Bismarck*, if the guns were at their optimal elevation of 4° – their normal 'at rest' position when not in use – then the complete firing cycle, including the loading, training and elevating of the guns – could be completed in 26 seconds.

Just as the turrets relied on hydraulic power for their training and elevation, so too did the complex mechanism which brought the shells and cartridges up from the magazines to the guns. The 38cm shell rooms were on the middle platform deck, flanking the turret's shell-handling room at the base of the barbette. Passageways to the side of the magazines separated them from the torpedo bulkhead, thereby providing another layer of protection to the shell stores and magazines. A ring car was used to move the shells to the bottom of the main hoist, which was powered hydraulically using hydraulic cylinders and a rack-and-pinion system. These hoists ran from the shell room up the barbette to the gun platform inside the gun turret. There was also an auxiliary hoist for each barrel, to be used in the event of a serious malfunction with the main hoist mechanism.

Cages carried the shells up the hoist, pausing on the way at the deck above the shell room – the upper platform deck – to collect the cartridges from the magazine (or 38cm powder/cartridge room). There the main charge and the fore charge were loaded into a tray fitted to the cage, having been moved to the hoist by means of another ring car trolley system. One side of the hoist served each gun, and it emerged into the gun platform between the two barrels. From there rammers moved the shells on to a pivoted loading tray, which was moved into position, one behind each barrel. Meanwhile, the charges were moved mechanically on to a waiting cage, which was hoisted up out of the way.

LEFT German 38cm (15in) shells being loaded on board *Bismarck*'s sister ship *Tirpitz*. Each of these projectiles weighed 800kg (1,764lb), and so mechanical and hydraulic loading systems were essential – they were simply too heavy to move by hand. The armourer in the background is busy checking the cap, before the shells are sent down to the shell room.

The shell on its tray was slid forward towards the open gun breech, whereupon the hydraulic chain-operated telescopic rammer slid the shell forward into the breech. Once this was done the cages containing the charges were lowered down to the same level as the now empty loading tray, and they were rolled on to it. The rammer then rammed the fore and main charges forward inside the breech. The guns were then fired, the recoil being absorbed by the pneumatic recoil cylinders. The spent cartridge was ejected from the breech and collected on the loading tray. From there it was slid down a cartridge ejector – essentially a chute in the back corners of the turret – which ejected the cartridge case out on to the upper deck.

In the event of a power failure to the main hoist, the shells could still be transported up the auxiliary hoist (which used a secondary power supply) to emerge at the rear of the guns, standing upright. The ammunition was moved on to a cage which would tilt the shell and then deposit it on the pivoted loading tray. Then the rammer would take over. The process was repeated for both the fore and main charges, which arrived separately up the hoist. If the hydraulic rammer was put out of action, then an auxiliary loading rammer could be used to load the shells and charges into the guns. This, however, was powered by hand, and required between 10 and 14 men to operate it.

Gun operation

It is worth recounting what the survivors of the *Bismarck* had to say about the way the main gun turrets operated, based on the account they gave to British naval intelligence. While some of the information merely repeats the information given above, it also contains a few interesting nuggets of fresh information:

> Each of the 38cm turrets contained their own electrically driven hydraulic pump. It was possible for either of the fore pumps to operate both the fore turrets, and similarly either of the after pumps could operate both the after turrets, but fore turrets could not operate after turrets, and *vice versa*.
>
> Both the training and elevation were hydraulic, and if required, by hand.
>
> The arc of fire was stated to be 300°, the maximum elevation 40–45°, and the maximum range 38 km. (41,1558 yards). The weight of the projectile was given as 1,760 lbs. The propellant was given as a mixture of Nitro Glycerine and Nitro Cellulose, the latter probably a Tetra Nitro body. It was not flashless.
>
> The charge was made up in two portions; the main charge (*hauptkartusche*), weighing approximately 176 lbs, was supplied in a brass cartridge case, which was protected when in the magazine by means of a sheet iron case. The front charge (*vorkartusche*) was made up in a linen bag and was stated to weigh 90 lbs. Both portions of the charge were rammed into the gun at the same time, a hydraulic rammer in five sections being employed.
>
> The recoil was stated to be 1.5 metres (4.92'), and the rate of fire [was] one round (both guns) in one minute.

BELOW In this picture, taken in mid-May 1941, *Bismarck* is seen alongside the main wharf at Gotenhafen, with the *Seebahnhof* (sea railway station) visible behind her. By this stage the crew of *Bismarck* were preparing for their sortie, although at that stage only Admiral Lütjens and Captain Lindemann knew exactly when and where this would take place.

> For each gun there was one hydraulic main hoist (*aufzug*), which transported, from below, both the projectile and the charges together. This loading cage was flash-proof, and there is no evidence of further anti-flash arrangements in these turrets. An electric auxiliary hoist (reserve *aufzug*) was fitted for each gun; the shell being hoisted first and then the charges. The main hoists were in the centre and to the rear of the two guns, the auxiliary hoists being further to the rear of the gunhouse.

There are problems with this account, particularly where it describes the maximum elevation of the guns within the turret and their rate of fire. It is clear from the accounts of *Bismarck*'s gun operation during the Battle of the Denmark Strait that the rate of fire was approximately half that claimed by the survivors during their interrogation. In all probability this was a problem with technical translation, rather than an attempt to deliberately mislead the British. The maximum range they stated – 38km – was actually greater than the German data provided for the gun, which listed a maximum range of 35.5km at a maximum elevation of 30°. The range quoted by the survivor was incorrect. In fact, due to the limitations of accurate rangefinding, maximum effective range was lower than this at around 30km – the equivalent of 16.4 nautical miles.

Turret and magazine organisation

The survivors then went on to provide a useful description of the way the gun turret crew was organised:

> The *Turmkommandant* [turret commander], usually a lieutenant or sub-lieutenant, was in command, and under him a *Turmführer* [turret leader], a Chief Petty Officer, who may have had the position of *Oberstuckmeister* [senior gun captain]. The gun-laying and training were normally carried out from the left gun position, and as a reserve from the right gun position. A telescopic sight was fitted to each gun.
>
> A No. 5 operated the lock mechanism, making the gun ready for firing (*ensichert*) or safe (*sichert*). No. 6 worked the loading cage, and also removed the spent cartridge cases, which came out of a chute and fell out of the bottom, to the rear of the gunhouse. No. 7, who had his station to the rear of the rammer (*ansetze*), operated both the breech (*bodenstück*) and rammer.
>
> Three rangefinder numbers stationed at the back of the turret operated a 10 metre stereoscopic rangefinder. There was telephone communication with the plotting room (*rechenstelle*), and the sight setters were also in telephone connection with the plotting room (control being exercised through either the fore or after plotting room, through changeover switches).
>
> The total number in the gunhouse was approximately one officer and 25 ratings.
>
> Signal lamps were fitted to indicate when guns were ready and fired, repeating in the plottings rooms, klaxons being used for firing. Turrets were fired locally (*trumabfeuerung*) or director fired (*zentralabfeuerung*). In the case of guns being fired locally, *mundabfeuerung* was employed; i.e. fired by the mouth, with a blowpipe system.

The same level of detail was provided by the survivors when describing the organisation at the other end of the hoist, in the shell rooms and magazines:

> In general the 38cm shell rooms (*granatkammer*) were on the middle platform deck, and the magazines (*pulverkammer*) were above them, on the upper platform

ABOVE This is the second of two photographs capturing the same scene – the painting of *Bismarck*'s bows as she lay alongside the quayside in Gotenhafen. It is likely that this took place in late April 1941, shortly before Adolf Hitler's visit to the battleship. This scene shows just how labour-intensive and arduous this process was.

ABOVE **Before Operation *Rheinübung* several of *Bismarck*'s boats were landed. These empty boat chocks on the starboard side, just aft of the catapult, were there to house two boats – one nested inside the other. The larger boat was an 8.5m cutter, while a 5.5m yawl lay inside it. Astern of the gun is the twin 15cm turret SIII, while above the boat deck is a 10.5cm twin anti-aircraft mounting.**

deck, the loading chamber (*beladeraum*) occupying both decks below the turret.

As an example, for turret 'D' there were two shell rooms, the after one in Section III, and the fore one in Section V, both on the middle platform deck. The main magazines for this turret were in Section III and Section V, abaft and before the loading chamber, on the upper platform deck. These were in use in action. In addition there were four reserve magazines in Section IV, in compartments outside the loading chamber, two each side, one on the upper and one on the middle platform deck.

The magazine crew consisted of some 15 men, in [the] charge of a Gunner's Mate [a petty officer] and a similar number, also under a Gunner's Mate, formed the shell room crew. It is probably that the entire turret's crew was about 70 men, as a number of artificers were required for the hydraulic and electrical equipment.

A prisoner stated that approximately 120–150 rounds per gun were carried. Both AP (*panzersprenggranaten*) and HE (*sprenggranaten*) were carried, the former being painted blue and the latter yellow (called *gefechtsmunition*). Practice shells were painted red. AP shells were fired at the heavier ships, and HE shells at the smaller targets. No tracer shells were carried. Some prisoners denied that gas shells were carried. Shells were fitted with nose fuses (*kopfzünder*) and base fuses (*bodenzünder*), the latter having a delay action, and were set by the Gunner's Mate in the shell room.

Secondary guns

The secondary armament of *Bismarck* consisted of twelve 15cm guns, mounted in six twin turrets, three on each side of her upper deck. The 15cm (6in) SK-C/28 had a maximum range of 23km at the gun's maximum elevation of 40°. It was a development of the C/25 guns designed for use in the Königsberg class of light cruiser – guns which were mounted in triple turrets. These earlier guns were also mounted in the Deutschland class of *panzerschiffe*. Unlike their predecessors, though, the guns designed in 1928 had a longer range, in exchange for a slightly lower muzzle velocity. On *Bismarck* these guns were mounted in the Drh L C/34 turret, and were in effect miniature versions of the battleship's main battery. Each turret had its own attendant barbette to protect its hoists, and was mounted to give as clear a field of fire as possible to the beam, and in the case of the fore and aft mountings into the bow and stern quarters.

The turrets had an arc of fire of 150° (up to 75° forward or aft of the beam), with the exception of turrets PII and PIII. Due to the location of the other turrets, their arc of fire was limited to 120°. These 15cm guns fired a shell weighing 45.3kg (99.87lb), which reached the turret by means of an electrically powered double hoist. This ran up through the barbette from the shell room on the middle platform deck and the magazine on the upper platform deck. The hoist served both guns and entered the gunhouse behind and between the guns. Due to their relatively small size, the shell and cartridge for both guns travelled together in the same cage. Because of the location of the gunhouse and hoist, these were just behind the torpedo bulkhead at the outer sides of the armoured citadel. An auxiliary hand-operated hoist also ran up the barbette in case of an electrical failure. Similarly the turret was trained and the guns elevated electrically, but a hand-operated auxiliary mechanism was also provided.

Unlike the main turrets, these secondary turrets had no rangefinders, apart from PII and SII, and so for the others a spotting periscope was used when firing under local control. Each turret had a crew of 1 officer, 2 petty officers and 18 men. This made them more cramped than the larger 38cm gun turrets. The two petty officers acted as gunlayer and gun trainer, while the rest of the crew loaded, operated the breech, worked the elevating mechanism and manned the telephone link to the fire-control positions. In the magazine and shell room another six ratings worked in each space, supervised by a gunner's mate.

Gunnery fire control

These main and secondary guns were controlled centrally – details of elevation and bearing were sent to the turrets from the fire-control position and plotting room, as did the order to fire. As a result *Bismarck* could fire coordinated salvos against a target, which ensured the greatest possible chance of scoring a hit. The senior gunnery officer on board *Bismarck* was Commander Schneider, who controlled the battleship's guns from the *Vormars* (foremast fire-control position). Lieutenant Commander Albrecht, the second gunnery officer controlled the 15cm guns from the *Vorderstand* (forward fire-control position). Lieutenant Commander von Müllenheim-Rechberg was stationed in the *Achter Stand* (after fire-control position), where he stood ready to take control of either or both the 38cm and 15cm batteries if either of the other fire-control positions were knocked out.

Information gathered from the rangefinders and radar was sent from the fire-control positions to the gunnery control centre or plotting office. There were two of these, both located on the upper platform deck, inside the armoured citadel. The forward gunnery plotting office was in compartment XV, while the after gunnery plotting office was in compartment VII. Lieutenant Cardinal was in command of the two plotting offices, assisted by midshipmen and NCOs. Next to these compartments were switchboards dedicated to maintaining communication links between the turrets, the fire-control positions and the plotting offices.

The fire control was simple in concept, but highly complex in execution. Once a target was spotted, stabilised rangefinders and binocular mounts in the fire-control positions would be used to gather information on a target's course, bearing, range and speed. This data would then be relayed to the plotting room. There a number of mechanical computers produced by Siemens, such as fire-control tables and rate solvers, would be used to convert this information into instructions that could be passed to the gun turrets. Other variables such as wind and sea conditions, plus the

ABOVE During April 1941 *Bismarck* conducted extensive exercises in the Baltic, and for much of this time the weather was pleasant, and the sea calm. Here the battleship is shown in transit from one exercise area to another, and is pictured overhauling a small Baltic schooner, while off-duty crewmen relax or sunbathe on the open deck. Note how the 10.5cm anti-aircraft guns have their barrels pointing upwards at a 45° angle, in readiness for any sudden air attack.

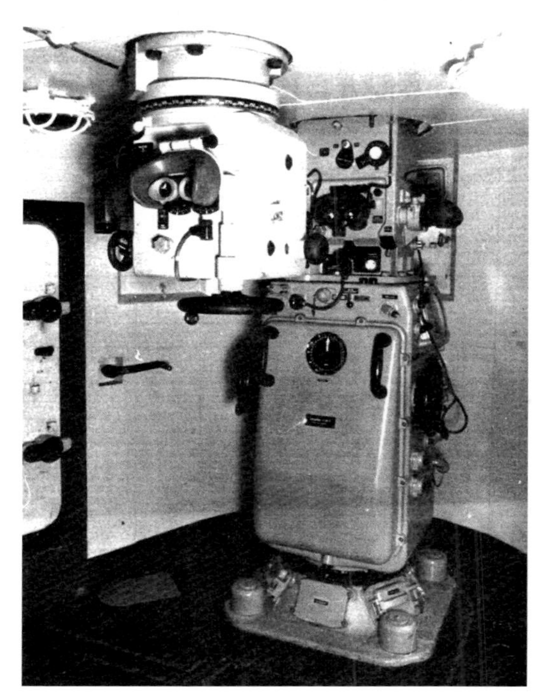

LEFT This photograph shows the inside of one of *Bismarck*'s three fire-control positions. The gun director stands on the central plinth, which provides a data link between the fire-control positions, the gun batteries and the fire-control centre, located inside the armoured citadel. In front of it is the optical telescope which serves the 10.5m rangefinder located on top of the fire-control position.

ABOVE **Inside the gunnery plotting room on the upper platform deck were the plotting machines that analysed the data sent in from the fire-control positions, translated these into gunnery bearings and angles and sent these to the gun turrets. This highly sophisticated mechanical computer was manufactured by Siemens, and was used to calculate the first half of this process – the analysis of the data. The results were then fed into a second machine, which turned this into the information required by the waiting gun crews.**

relative course and the speed of the two ships were added to the data being fed into the mechanical plotting table. The result would be a set of coordinates – range and deflection. This information was then passed back to the gunnery officer and the gun turrets, where it would be given as a simple elevation and bearing. Inside the turret, gunlayers and trainers would point the turret and the guns in the right direction. Lights in the turrets, the plotting rooms and the fire-control positions told the gunnery officer when the guns were loaded and ready. He would then give the order to fire.

The fall of shot would be observed from the fire-control positions and the results passed down to the plotting office, who would compensate for any overshoot or undershoot, while continuing to make all those other calculations necessary to keep the guns aimed at the target. Each turret had slightly different elevation and bearing instructions – this was to compensate for the distance between *Bismarck*'s turrets, and it meant that their fire was coordinated to land on the same spot of ocean. Corrections of shot would continue to be processed until the guns scored a hit. Throughout the engagement a constant stream of information would flow between the various positions. The result was that *Bismarck*'s fire would be as accurate – and as deadly – as possible.

The fire of *Bismarck*'s anti-aircraft batteries was coordinated in a similar way. In the foretop fire-control position Lieutenant Commander Gellert was the anti-aircraft gunnery officer in charge of all anti-aircraft fire. He was assisted by a control officer for the heavy (10.5cm) anti-aircraft guns. High-angle rangefinders in the armoured cupolas on either side of the forward superstructure were used to collect information on approaching aircraft, and this was passed on to the anti-aircraft gunnery officer. Two flak-plotting offices were located in compartment IX of the middle platform deck, and compartment XV of the upper platform deck. There the plotting teams performed the calculations needed to set up a flak barrage (*Zonenfeuer*), or to direct controlled fire (*Geleitsschiessen*) at approaching aircraft. This information was then relayed to the anti-aircraft gunnery officer and to the heavy and medium anti-aircraft batteries.

If aircraft attacked from different directions, the area around *Bismarck* could be divided into four 90° zones, each of which was controlled by its own *Flakleiter* (fire-control officer). When enemy planes came within 1,000m of the ship the light 3.7cm and 2cm anti-aircraft guns would open up. Their fire was unguided, but at that range targets were clearly visible, and would be fired at as and when the opportunity presented itself. Survivors from *Bismarck* expressed their amazement at the way the Swordfish attacks on the battleship, launched from *Victorious* and *Ark Royal*, were pressed home with such vigour – particularly as some of these biplanes came within 150m of the ship.

Damage control

For all its much-vaunted invulnerability, *Bismarck*'s crew expected their ship to sustain damage in action, and they were prepared for it. The ship's main damage-control centre (*Leckwehrzentrale*) was in compartment XIV of the upper platform deck, beside the lower conning tower. Commander Oels was responsible for damage control on *Bismarck*, and he coordinated the crew's response to enemy hits. He was assisted by an engineer, Lieutenant Jahreis. A reserve damage-control centre was located beside the turbine rooms in compartment X. During action stations there were 6 dedicated damage-control parties, each of 26 men led by a chief technician. Each was responsible for a number of watertight compartments within the ship. Their task was to contain flooding, pump out floodwater, combat fire and repair damage.

In damage-control operations the priorities are to float, move and fight – in other words the top priority was to prevent the ship from sinking. Keeping her moving and retaliation came next. Each damage-control team had a leak repair party, a flooding containment party, a firefighting party, a ventilation party to prevent smoke passing through the ship, a small anti-gas party and a communications group. Ten electrically operated pumps were sited at various key locations around the lower platform deck to cope with flooding. In addition powerful electrical bilge pumps were located in the propulsion spaces, to ensure these key compartments remained operational. As well as this, *Bismarck* carried a number of portable pumps to deal with flooding in otherwise inaccessible areas of the lower hull.

Similarly six electrically powered rotary fire pumps were sited throughout the ship to help combat fire. Hoses from these water pumps could reach anywhere in the ship. In addition numerous chemical and foam fire extinguishers were sited throughout *Bismarck* to allow an immediate response to any outbreak of fire on board. Electrically operated plants in compartments VI and XVI also produced foam and CO_2, designed to extinguish any fire in the magazine spaces without having to resort to flooding these areas. If this failed, water valves in each magazine allowed the compartment to be flooded within 2 minutes in the event of the risk of a catastrophic magazine fire.

During her last battle *Bismarck* faced almost all of these damage-control issues. Compartments had to be flooded – in the case of some of the 15cm magazines this had to be done while the men were still inside. Flooding on the port side had been compensated for by pumping water into the empty tanks on the starboard side to redress the trim of the ship. Even then water was still coming in. Fires had broken out below the upper deck, and when firefighting attempts failed yet more compartments had to be flooded. Above decks the fires were raging uncontrollably, virtually from stem to stern. Well coordinated though this damage-control organisation was, and however well trained the crew was in fighting flood and fire, the ship was ill prepared for the sheer scale of devastation wreaked upon it during her final battle. Seeing that nothing more could be done, and as the senior officer left alive, Commander Oels ordered the scuttling of *Bismarck*, and then ordered her crew to abandon ship. By then, though, *Bismarck* was already in her death throes.

ABOVE This view of *Bismarck*'s bow, taken during the final stages of her fitting-out in Hamburg, gives a clear view of the recess in her forecastle, which housed her port bow anchor. The photograph also provides a good view of her bow Plimsoll line.

BELOW This photograph of *Bismarck* was taken off Gotenhafen during early April 1941, and clearly shows the layout of her Baltic camouflage scheme, which consisted of three sets of chevrons. In addition, fake bow and stern waves were painted beneath the forecastle and quarterdeck, in an attempt to confuse enemy rangefinder operators into misjudging the length of the ship, and therefore the distance she was away from the observer.

Chapter Six

The wreck of the *Bismarck*

In June 1989, Dr Robert Ballard and his team discovered the wreck of the KMS *Bismarck*, lying 4,791m (15,719ft) below the surface of the Atlantic Ocean. *Bismarck* was no longer a vessel from the past – something to be read about in history books and archives. She was a tangible entity, whose remains, while treated with the utmost respect as a war grave, could now reveal vital new information. Above all, a study of the wreck could now help answer many of the long-unanswered questions surrounding her final moments.

OPPOSITE The hulk of the *Bismarck* lies upright on the ocean floor. In this port side view can be seen the empty turret barbettes for the main armament, the blasted remains of the bridge and the control station for the port side secondary armament, and the huge hole in the deck that was probably caused by the explosion of an ammunition magazine. *(Artwork by Richard Schlecht/National Geographic/Getty Images)*

Discovery of the wreck

Dr Robert D. Ballard (1942–) rose to international prominence in September 1985, when he discovered the wreck of the RMS *Titanic*. At the time he worked for the Woods Hole Oceanographic Institution based in Massachusetts, where he pioneered the use of remotely operated submersibles to explore the seabed. His discovery of the *Titanic* made Ballard a household name, and he was encouraged to repeat his success by searching for other important shipwrecks. While attending the Frankfurt International Book Fair he met Baron von Müllheim-Rechberg, who as a young lieutenant commander had served on the *Bismarck*, and survived the sinking. After talking to him, Ballard decided to make his next quest the search for the wreck of the German battleship.

Ballard had reservations when he began the search. He was worried he might be accused of glorifying the Nazi era, and of upsetting the sailors of both sides whose shipmates had lost their lives during Operation *Rheinübung*. However, there were also important questions to answer about how *Bismarck* had fared during her final battle, why she had sunk and exactly what remained of her after half a century on the seabed. The Woods Hole Institution allowed Ballard the time to conduct his quest and money was raised from financial backers. A team was assembled, a mother ship was found – the converted deep-sea hull trawler SS *Starella* – and the *Argo*, the remotely piloted submersible Ballard used to find the *Titanic*.

The starting point for any search for *Bismarck* was the location provided by the Royal Navy. The navigating officer on *Rodney* recorded that the position of *Bismarck* when she sank was 48° 10' North, 16° 12' West. This, though, was a very approximate latitude and longitude, because navigational accuracy was difficult that day, owing to rough seas and overcast skies. No satnav was available in 1941 – the navigator had to rely on his sextant and a clear view of the sun, moon or stars. Navigators on *King George V* and *Dorsetshire* simultaneously recorded slightly different positions. Ballard realised that not only could these positions be wrong, but that *Bismarck* might have travelled some considerable distance as she descended to the seabed. The ocean was almost 3 miles deep at that location, and so any number of factors could have influenced where *Bismarck* finally came to rest, including the way she sank, whether she broke up during her descent or how strong the underwater currents were at the time.

On 9 July 1988 *Starella* left La Coruña in Spain and began the voyage to this recorded location, 436 miles away to the north-west. The search began on 11 July, when the first of three sonar transponders were dropped to the seabed. These were used to send signals to a receiver suspended beneath the *Starella*, which allowed navigational data to be processed on board the mother ship. This information was used to guide *Argo* during the search. Two of the transponders landed on an underwater mountain range, which was less than ideal, as it created sonar 'shadows', making accurate navigation difficult. That in turn made it hard to accurately 'fly' *Argo* over the seabed.

Ballard began by exploring the western side of the underwater mountain range, where it rose from a flat seabed. He deduced that if *Bismarck* had landed on the high slopes, it would have slid down to the base of the mountain range. Nothing was found, despite combing the area surrounding the three navigational fixes from *Rodney*, *King George V* and *Dorsetshire*. Then they came upon an impact crater, which had been made by something heavy dropping on to the seabed. Any thoughts that it was made by all or part of *Bismarck* ended when the video footage revealed a wooden rudder – the remains of a 19th-century sailing schooner. The search ended on 21 July, and a disappointed Ballard returned home to raise funds for a second attempt the following year.

In May 1989 Ballard tried again. Fresh funding had been found, and this time the team would be using a larger and more suitable mother ship, the *Star Hercules*, a North Sea oil support vessel usually based in Aberdeen. Earlier that year Ballard had used her to search the seabed of the Mediterranean for ancient shipwrecks. She left Cádiz in southern Spain on 25 May, and arrived in the search area four days later. Once again transponders were dropped, and *Argo* was prepared. The previous year, Ballard had concentrated on the position given by *Rodney*. This time he planned to search further to the east, close to the underwater mountain range, and the positions recorded by *King George V* and *Dorsetshire*.

The plan was to move *Argo* across the seabed in an east–west line, then repeat the process a mile to the side. This way they hoped to cover a large area, but still be close enough to virtually guarantee coming across some sign of debris lying on the seabed. They could then follow the debris trail until they found the shipwreck. In the process they could get a better idea of the mountain range – which in fact turned out to be a single volcanic mountain some 10 miles in diameter. Eventually scattered pieces of debris were found, to the south of the position given by *Dorsetshire*. That, though, could have been dropped by a passing ship. By the evening of 4 June Ballard had searched 80 per cent of the planned search area, yet still nothing had been discovered. Shortly before midnight they were exploring the lower slopes of the underwater mountain when the video feed from *Argo* revealed small pieces of man-made debris on the seabed.

More were seen after midnight, and then signs of a seabed mudslide began to appear. The debris trail ended, so *Argo* changed direction to the north and picked up the trail again. Later they received a sonar contact and an impact crater appeared. It turned out to be a large piece of mangled wreckage – possibly a detached piece of the ship's superstructure. The search was widened to encompass the whole area. Several rubber boots were seen, and at noon on 5 June they found another large piece of wreckage. Ballard began to suspect that *Bismarck* had caused the landslide, but these were isolated pieces of debris. The wreck lay somewhere else. The search continued and just before 10.00pm they came upon one of *Bismarck*'s main gun turrets, lying upside down on the sea floor. After that they found nothing apart from scattered debris and another chunk of superstructure.

During the early morning of 8 June the team were exploring the eastern side of the area when they recorded a large sonar contact. *Argo* moved in to investigate and at 9.06am something rose out of the seabed ahead of them. The *Argo* pilot raised the submersible up

LEFT How *Bismarck* sank.

1. *Bismarck* slowly sinks by the stern.
2. She rolls over and the weakened stern breaks off.
3. The four heavy turrets and debris from the battle detach from the ship, which together begin their descent to the sea bottom.
4. With the hull fully flooded and purged of air *Bismarck* rights herself as she continues her descent.
5. The hull strikes an underwater sea mount and triggers a massive mudslide.
6. *Bismarck* and other heavy pieces of debris are carried down the slope by the avalanche and come to rest about two-thirds of the way down the mudslide, about 30 minutes after leaving the surface.

(Artwork by Richard Schlecht/National Geographic/Getty Images)

to pass over the top of the obstacle. At that moment a gun turret appeared on the video monitor. It was one of *Bismarck*'s secondary turrets. They had found the wreck. A glance at their chart showed that they had narrowly missed the wreck several times over the previous few days. Now the wreck of *Bismarck* was revealed to the human eye for the first time since her last terrible moments on the morning of 27 May 1941.

Examination of *Bismarck*

Finding *Bismarck* was only the first part of Ballard's mission. Now he wanted to explore her to see what he could learn about the great battleship's final moments. This had to wait, though. A storm passed through the area, forcing a temporary halt in the expedition. However, on 8 May the survey began. *Argo* was lowered back down to the wreck until the hull began to appear through the murk. Below the submersible was the starboard side of the ship, just behind the bridge superstructure, and the twin 15cm secondary gun turret, which was the first thing the team had spotted the previous day. Now the exploration could begin in earnest. The turret was well preserved and was pointing slightly outboard, as if it had jammed there during the battle. Next to it was a twin 10.5cm anti-aircraft gun, its barrels pointing towards the surface almost 4,800m above.

Argo continued her tour of the upper deck. During the voyage from Cádiz, the National Geographic film team on board built a plastic model of *Bismarck*. Now Ballard cut off gun turrets and bits of superstructure from the model to provide a clear visual reference to what they were now seeing. For instance, all four of *Bismarck*'s main gun turrets had fallen out of their barbettes as the ship sank, so Ballard removed these. He continued to pare off

BELOW The hull of the sunken *Bismarck* lies buried in 30ft of mud, 15,719ft below the surface of the Atlantic Ocean. *(Artwork by Richard Schlecht/ National Geographic/ Getty Images)*

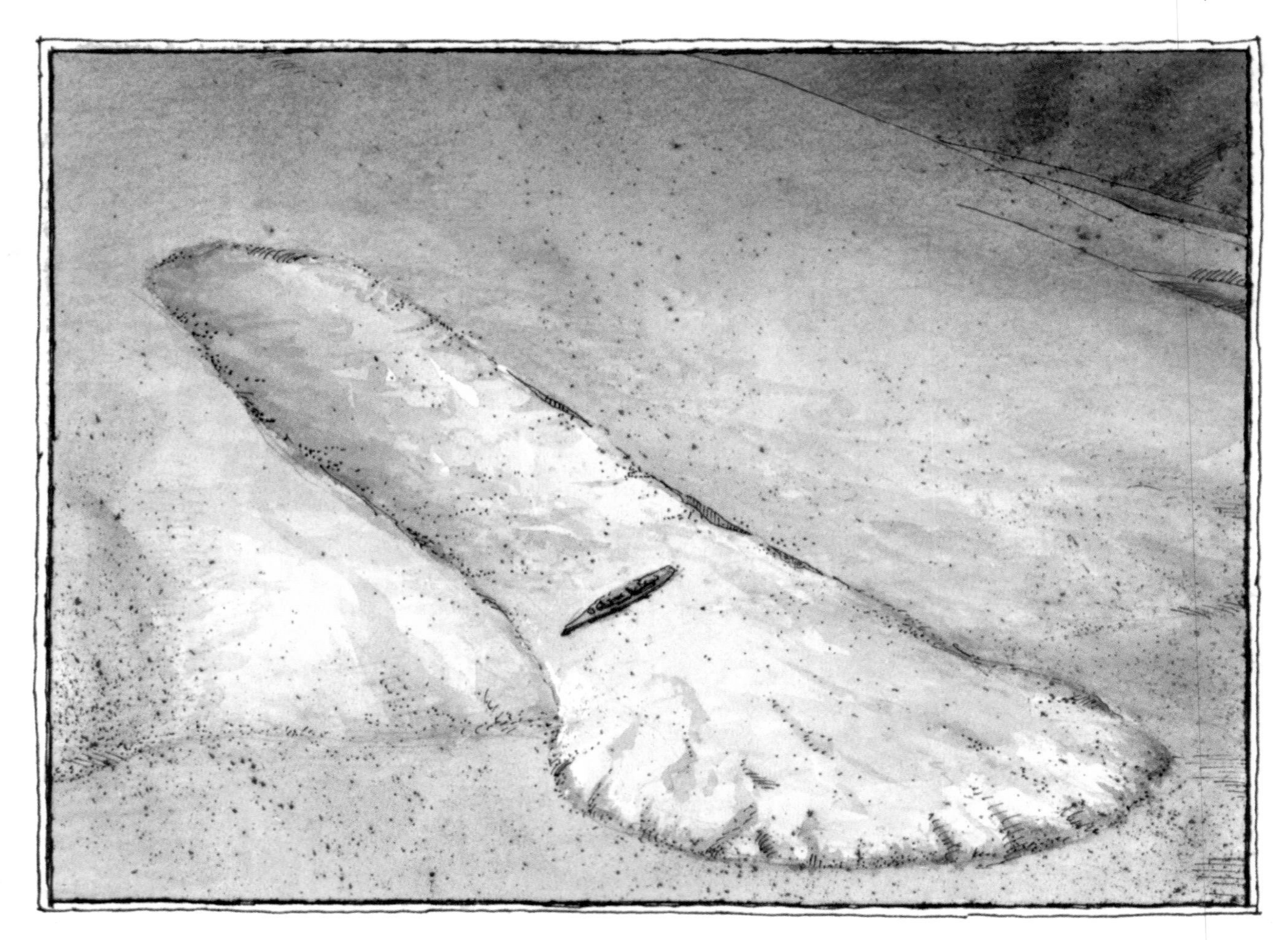

bits of superstructure and masts as the survey continued. Above the anti-aircraft gun was the starboard secondary gun director. It was now just an empty mount, the director blown away during the battle. So too was the main gun director on top of the forward superstructure, which looked as if it had been sheared off by a giant version of the knife Ballard was using on his plastic model. Behind it the upper superstructure was completely gone.

Beneath it was the forward conning tower and bridge, where Lütjens and Lindemann had directed operations, and where they died. The conning tower looked largely undamaged, but the open bridge around it had been badly hit. The team later counted 50 shell holes in that one area. The forward port 15cm turret had its after roof sliced off and was pointing aft, while in front of it were the empty round sockets formed by the main gun barbettes of 'Bruno' and 'Anton' turrets. Strangely the forecastle looked relatively undamaged, apart from a shell hole where the starboard anchor had once hung. Ballard surmised the hole there was made by a 16in shell from *Rodney*. The teak deck of *Bismarck* was still in good condition, and traces of the large swastika painted as an aerial recognition symbol could still be seen. In front of it a shell had chopped off the very tip of the battleship's bow.

Ballard moved aft again down the port side, continuing his underwater survey of the well-preserved shipwreck. Behind the place where the superstructure once stood, the remains of the port secondary gun control tower stood empty, above another pair of intact 10.5cm guns and a 15cm gun turret, this one pointing forward. Above and behind it *Argo*'s videos revealed a jagged hole in the deck where the funnel had once been. Behind it was the deck where the aircraft were housed and launched. There was no trace of their catapult, which once spanned the upper deck. Instead, on the port side was a gigantic hole – the remains of the blast made when one of *Rodney*'s shells ignited the ready-use magazine for the 15cm guns.

The hangar structure was still standing, but the mainmast which had once surmounted it was gone, apart from a stump. Ballard ripped another piece off his plastic model. The searchlights had been blasted away, their location marked only by their bases. Between them only the base of the searchlight director still remained. At the after end of the after superstructure was the after main gun director, which had been knocked out early on in *Bismarck*'s final battle. The structure was intact, although the director itself had been blown away by that important hit from *King George V*. On either side of the after superstructure there was another 15cm gun turret, and two twin 10.5cm anti-aircraft mounts. The ones on the port side were still there, and trained outboard, their barrels pointing towards the port bow.

Beyond this the deck stepped down to 'Caesar' turret. Like the other superimposed turret forward all that remained was the large circular barbette. The remnants of a crane now lay across the empty circular opening. 'Dora' turret astern of it was also missing. On the starboard side of this after turret was another large shell hole. Accounts by survivors tell of men falling into this chasm in the upper deck as they ran aft, in an attempt to abandon ship. *Argo* now moved over the quarterdeck. Here another large swastika could be seen on the teak deck. Although both of these swastikas had been painted over while *Bismarck* lay in Norwegian waters, the paint had lifted away, revealing the faded Nazi emblems that lay beneath the thin layer of deck paint. The video revealed that the bottom of the swastika was missing, as the aftermost portion of the stern had been sliced off. Ballard suspected this had occurred as the battleship sank. This initial survey took 6 hours to complete. Now that Ballard had a good idea of how intact *Bismarck* was, *Argo* was winched back to the surface.

The decision was made to lower *Argo* again the following day – 9 June. Unfortunately the video link failed as she was being lowered and had to be recovered and repaired. So it was later that evening before the submersible returned to the wreck site. This time she had been rigged to carry colour video cameras, and the exploration began again, this time supplying video footage that the National Geographic team could use. At one stage *Argo* was lowered into one of the empty main turret barbettes, but nothing could be seen – it was just a large black void. The superstructure was scarred by multiple hits from smaller-calibre guns – either the main 8in guns of the British cruisers, or the secondary armament of the British battleships. While there was no indication that any of these hits caused any major damage, some had penetrated the superstructure's armoured belt.

By this point the weather had deteriorated, so *Argo* was raised again. At this depth it took 2 hours to lower or raise the submersible, and throughout the operation the conditions grew steadily worse. However, the storm passed the following afternoon – 10 June – and Ballard's son Todd guided *Argo* as it moved (or 'flew') around the shipwreck. Some excellent images were recorded, but then the video link went down – the result of a collision with the barbette of 'Dora' turret. Ballard had hoped to conduct a close examination of the lower hull of the battleship, but this was no longer possible. *Argo* was recovered, as were the transponders.

Then, after conducting a dignified memorial service and dropping a wreath over the side, Captain Latter of *Star Hercules* headed back to port. The world was told the news of the discovery on 10 June. However, the exact location of the wreck was kept secret to prevent commercial salvors from pillaging the site, as had happened with *Titanic*. Another expedition would return to *Bismarck* 12 years later, led by David Mearns, followed by a third expedition in 2003, this time led by filmmaker James Cameron. The aim of these two expeditions was to answer the question which Ballard's expedition had been unable to answer – was *Bismarck* sunk by British torpedoes, or had she been scuttled?

BELOW HMS *Rodney* and her sister ship HMS *Nelson* were the two most powerful battleships in the Royal Navy. They were built during the early 1920s, and conformed to the terms of the Washington Naval Treaty by carrying their nine 16in guns in three triple turrets, which reduced the space taken up by protective armour. This explained their somewhat ugly design. Her appearance notwithstanding, *Rodney* was one of the few battleships in the world capable of meeting *Bismarck* on equal terms.

The sinking process reconstructed

When *Bismarck* sank, she rolled over on to her port side before capsizing. Then she slipped under the water, reportedly going down stern first. When Dr Robert Ballard found her remains in 1989, she was lying upright on the seabed, although at some stage during her descent her four main turrets had dropped out of their mountings. Using all of the available evidence, Ballard was able to work out what happened as *Bismarck* sank. He studied where the landslide had been on the underwater mud slope on the seabed, where the turret he discovered had detached and where the debris field had been. The other key piece of evidence was the hull of the ship itself, which despite its substantial battle damage was largely intact. In fact Ballard was surprised that the hull of the ship looked virtually intact.

The exception was the very tip of the stern, which looked as if it had been sliced off. The question remained whether this happened during the battle – and therefore had a part to play in the sinking process – or whether the aftermost part of the stern detached as the ship fell towards the seabed. Ballard compared the intact hull to that of the *Titanic*, the stern portion of which had been badly buckled by water pressure as the ship plunged towards the seabed. Much like a submarine reaching its collapse (or crush) depth, the hull could no longer resist the water pressure, and parts of it imploded so that water flooded in. This did not happen in *Bismarck* – apart from her stern the hull was relatively undamaged during the long descent. This suggests that the battleship's watertight compartments had flooded before the sinking ship reached its collapse depth.

The fact that the four main turrets had dropped out of their barbettes suggests *Bismarck* rolled upside down as she sank, and for some of her descent the keel was uppermost. She was found sitting upright on the slope of the seabed, which means that at some stage she righted herself, and completed her descent with the keel downwards. This

LEFT **This painting, *The Sinking of the Bismarck*, by Charles E. Turner, captures the final moments of the great German battleship. Blazing fiercely from stem to stern, she begins to list heavily to port. In the distance is the British heavy cruiser HMS *Dorsetshire*, whose torpedoes may well have administered the final *coup de grâce*.**

would have been her aspect when she struck the mud on the ocean floor. To work out the sequence of events, we need to look at the testimony of *Bismarck*'s survivors. None of them mention seeing the stern break away from the rest of the hull before she sank, but they do claim the battleship rolled over on to her port side and then capsized. While the underside of her hull was still above the surface *Bismarck* began settling by the stern, and she slid under the water gently, with her bow being the last part of the battleship to remain visible. Unlike *Hood* there was no wild rearing in the air – the result of the battlecruiser having broken in two. *Bismarck*'s sinking was less dramatic – the upturned battleship simply sank from sight.

While she was capsized, and most probably during these first few minutes of her sinking, her turrets would have dropped out of their barbettes, and plunged towards the seabed 3 miles below. They were only held in place by gravity, and so if the ship capsized it was inevitable they would become detached. Their descent would have been faster than that of the battleship, and they would have fallen relatively vertically. One of these turrets was discovered by Ballard's team, in an area within the underwater landslide caused by the hull when it struck the seabed, and close to a field of smaller pieces of debris. The supposition is that these pieces all fell from the capsized warship during this early stage of her descent.

LEFT **This blurred photograph was taken from HMS *Dorsetshire* fairly early on during *Bismarck*'s final battle. Shells from *Rodney* and *King George V* can be seen falling astern of *Bismarck*, while the splashes in the distance are probably *Bismarck*'s shells being fired at her two main adversaries.**

RIGHT Survivors from *Bismarck* pictured being rescued by the crew of HMS *Dorsetshire*. Many of these men were burned or wounded and found it difficult to clamber up the scrambling net. This being the case, British sailors used ropes fitted with bowlines to haul some of the more badly wounded men to safety.

Without the turrets in place the battleship would have righted herself underwater and continued her descent keel first. This was due to the low centre of gravity of the battleship, as without the turrets in place the heaviest elements of the *Bismarck* were her armoured lower hull and propulsion systems, rather than anything on or above her upper deck. In terms of hydrodynamics this also made good sense – the motion of the ship as it plunged through the water would have encouraged it to right itself, so that the relatively clean lines of the lower hull descended before the jagged and splintered upper hull, which would have acted rather like the centreboard on a capsized dinghy – the resistance it offered playing a major part in the righting of the vessel.

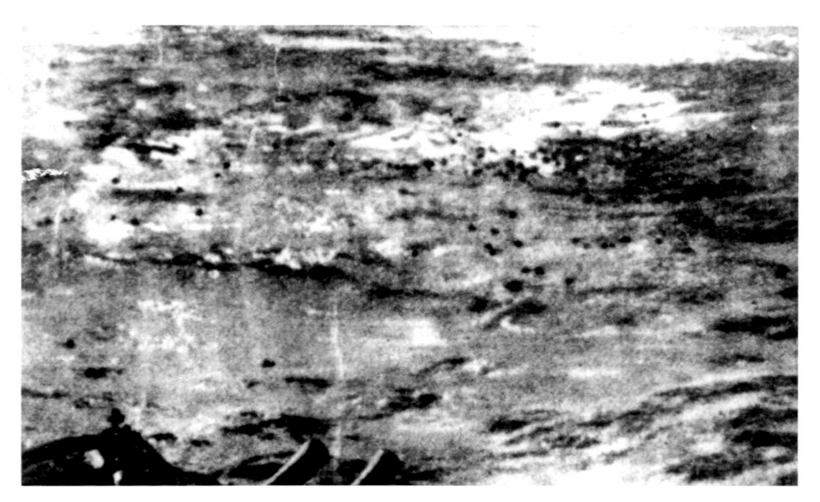

BELOW Regrettably, *Dorsetshire* was forced to abandon her rescue of *Bismarck*'s survivors, due to a report that a U-boat had been sighted. This blurred photograph shows hundreds of men still in the water as the cruiser began to pull away from them.

It was probably at this stage or earlier that the aftermost portion of the *Bismarck*'s stern detached itself from the rest of the hull. The bow and the stern were weak points in the ship, as they were unprotected by the thick armoured belt that ran along the length of the hull between the barbettes of 'Anton' and 'Dora' turrets. Behind hull section III and in front of section XIX the armoured belt was just 80mm thick in the stern, and 60mm in the bow. While this belt extended as far forward as *Bismarck*'s stem, in the stern it ended immediately above the rudder, halfway along hull section I. There the belt ended in a watertight bulkhead. Behind it the aftermost portion of the stern was unprotected. The hull was also pierced by scuttles – portholes – serving the officers' cabins and NCOs' cabins below them. This is the section of the hull that broke away from the rest of the ship.

According to both British and German eyewitnesses this area had been hit several times during *Bismarck*'s last battle, and without armoured protection it would have been structurally weakened by all this damage. The 18in torpedo launched by the Swordfish torpedo bomber the evening before *Bismarck*'s final battle might have added to the structural weakening of this aftermost part of the ship. When the battleship capsized on the surface this section might well have begun to detach itself. This helps to explain why the battleship began settling stern first. Either while she remained capsized or as she righted herself this heavily damaged stern section detached itself from the rest of the ship and made its own way towards the seabed. This explains why its remains were found some distance away from the battered but otherwise intact hull of the battleship.

Bismarck would have sunk rapidly, keel first, until she struck the seabed. The detached stern fell a little to the right of this point of impact, while the main turret discovered by Ballard's team landed ahead of it, 200m further down the mud slope of the seabed. At the point where the battleship struck the bottom, the ocean floor sloped upwards towards the foothills of the underwater mountain identified by Ballard's topographical survey of the area. The impact of the ship on the seabed produced a crater, which created the landslide identified during Ballard's survey. The momentum generated by her descent then caused *Bismarck* to slide down the slope, following the path of the underwater avalanche. She finally came to rest about three-fifths of the way down the landslide, and approximately 300m from her likely point of impact.

The stern of the battleship was more deeply embedded than her bow – another indication that she landed stern first. As she slid down the muddy slope of the seabed *Bismarck* turned to starboard, so she ended up lying almost at right angles to the direction of the landslide and to the direction of the slope. Afterwards, lighter pieces of debris would continue to fall around the shipwreck, creating the debris field discovered by Ballard. This way the smaller pieces of debris were not buried by the landslide – the fate Ballard thinks may have befallen the battleship's three remaining large turrets. This is one of several questions that remained unanswered after the operation was completed. Others surround the location of other missing pieces of her superstructure, or the source of secondary debris trails. For the moment, though, the sea retains the answer to her secrets.

LEFT ***Korvettenkapitän*** **(Lieutenant Commander) Müllenheim-Rechberg, pictured here in 1934 when he was a** ***Leutnant zur See*** **(lieutenant), was the most senior officer to survive the sinking of the** ***Bismarck*****. He was rescued by the crew of the** ***Dorsetshire*****.**

Controversial questions – scuttled or sunk?

One of the questions that remained unanswered after the discovery and survey of the *Bismarck* in 1989 was whether she had been sunk by the shells of *Rodney* and *King George V*, by the torpedoes fired by the heavy cruiser *Dorsetshire,* or whether she finally succumbed as a result of the scuttling of the battleship by her own crew.

In June 2001, a Seattle-based company called Deep Ocean Expeditions returned to the *Bismarck*'s wreck site to conduct another survey of her remains. This commercial company operates and charters deep-sea submersibles, largely for scientific or film-making purposes. In 2000 they approached the Woods Hole Oceanographic Institution which, with Dr Ballard's approval, agreed to work in partnership with the company. This American team used a Russian-built mini submarine to reach the *Bismarck*, and after surveying the vessel they concentrated on an examination of her hull. They found no sign of shell or torpedo holes in her main armoured belt on either side of the battleship, but they did identify long, largely horizontal gashes or rents in the hull. These were attributed to damage caused after *Bismarck*'s hull struck the seabed, during her slide down the underwater slope. Their conclusion was that the hull had been largely undamaged when the battleship sank.

William Lange, a research specialist from Woods Hole went so far as to deny that the

BELOW In this view of HMS ***Rodney*** **all three of her 16in turrets are trained to port as is the battleship's secondary armament of 6in guns. The main fire-control position was sited at the top of the mainmast. It was from there that** ***Rodney*****'s salvos at** ***Bismarck*** **were directed.**

ABOVE The British County class heavy cruiser HMS *Dorsetshire* was similar to *Norfolk* and *Suffolk*, although she belonged to a slightly different batch of cruisers based on the same general design. The survivors she rescued later spoke of the compassion shown by *Dorsetshire*'s sailors to their prisoners.

battleship was sunk by the British. He said that the lack of any shell holes below the waterline, and relatively few in her hull, compared to the numerous examples of shell damage above the upper deck indicated that her armoured belt had protected the *Bismarck* from British shells and torpedoes. The inference is, of course, that she was scuttled by her own crew. Later that summer another Anglo-American expedition arrived over the wreck site to film the remains of the battleship. Again, this expedition was conducted with the approval of Woods Hole.

It was led by British-based but American-born marine scientist David Mearns, who had made a study of locating and surveying important wrecks dating from the Second World War. He was accompanied by a TV documentary team who were keen to film the evidence. Like Ballard this team used remotely operated vehicles (ROVs) to explore the wreck. They concentrated on those gashes in the hull identified by the Seattle-based team. These lay on the underside of the hull, below the waterline – exactly the place where a torpedo might have struck the battleship.

While Woods Hole identified these as being caused by 'mechanical damage', occurring after *Bismarck*'s hull struck the seabed, Mearns and his team considered this an unlikely explanation. In a press statement, Mearns later declared: 'My feeling is that those holes were probably lengthened by the slide, but initiated by torpedoes.' While admitting he found no direct evidence of torpedo damage, Mearns argued convincingly that the torpedoes fired by *Dorsetshire* were unlikely to have merely 'bounced off' the hull, as had been claimed by William Lange. He declared that while scuttling might have hastened the inevitable, the process of sinking had already begun.

Dr Eric Grove from Hull University accompanied the expedition and confirmed that *Bismarck* was 'heavily holed' below the waterline. The inference was that the gashes were first

LEFT The quadruple 21in torpedo tubes of a British heavy cruiser, pictured as the torpedo men prepare to launch a salvo. There is still some considerable controversy over what actually sank the *Bismarck* – German scuttling charges or British torpedoes. The real answer might well be a combination of the two.

caused by torpedoes, not a collision with the seabed. The argument was still raging when another expedition visited the wreck site. This time the object was to film a documentary about *Bismarck*, directed by James Cameron, the Canadian director behind the films *Terminator*, *Aliens*, *The Abyss*, *Titanic* and *Avatar*. This time the expedition used small Mir manned deep water submersibles, capable of carrying a crew of three people. The film company then used these submersibles as launching platforms for miniature ROVs, which were able to enter inside the hull and superstructure of *Bismarck*.

The submersibles explored the lower hull, including the gashes, and they examined the landslide where *Bismarck* slid down the underwater slope before coming to rest. If these gashes were made there, then some evidence might be found to explain what caused them. While no visible reason for the gashes was found, Cameron and his team of expert advisers concluded that these were made when *Bismarck* struck the seabed, the result of a 'hydraulic outburst' of internal pressure from within the hull.

However, he then produced evidence to suggest that the gashes may have developed due to man-made damage. When he sent his miniature ROVs inside the gashes he found evidence of torpedo damage – hits which had penetrated the outer hull of *Bismarck*, but had failed to breach the inner hull. In between was a sacrificial layer within the two layers. In other words, the torpedoes had damaged the hull, but this damage was only skin deep. This seemed to contradict Deep Ocean Expeditions' evidence, which claimed there was no sign of torpedo damage. Clearly there had been, but just how effective the torpedoes had been was still open to debate.

The controversy still rages and appears to be waged along largely national lines. American experts tend to favour the theory that scuttling alone caused the *Bismarck* to sink, while British experts argue that this merely sped up the process, which had already begun owing to damage inflicted by British shells and torpedoes. What is clear from the evidence collected during these expeditions is that to a large extent *Bismarck*'s armoured belt protected the battleship from British shellfire, but by the time she sank her superstructure had been heavily battered. Torpedoes fired from *Dorsetshire* may well have penetrated her hull below the waterline, but the question of whether these actually caused her to sink remains unanswered. What most experts can agree on is that *Bismarck* would have foundered eventually, thanks to the damage she suffered during her last battle. The loss of her stern is a clear indication that she had been structurally compromised before she sank. Scuttling merely hastened *Bismarck*'s sinking, and put an end to her suffering, and that of her crew.

Above all, they remain the reason why further expeditions to *Bismarck*'s wreck site are discouraged, and why her exact resting place continues to be a closely guarded secret. Otherwise salvors might pick over her remains in search of trophies. She is a war grave, where more than 2,000 German sailors are still entombed. Many survivors from both sides viewed her discovery and subsequent exploration with misgivings. The late Ted Briggs, one of the three survivors of the sinking of *Hood*, summed up this feeling: 'She put up a bloody good fight, took on half the ruddy Navy, and went down with honours. She should have been left alone, and revered as a war grave.' Let us hope this wish is kept, and *Bismarck* and her crew are allowed to rest undisturbed, 3 miles below the site of their last great battle.

LEFT The mainmast of *Bismarck* was located above the ship's [illegible]ble hangar. It was dominated by a strange-looking box, which functioned both as a lookout position and as a list indicator. A [illegible] each of its sides served to indicate the degree by which the battleship was listing or was down by the bow or stern.

Index